DRIVEN BY RAGE FUELED BY DIESEL

The Forgotten Victims of the Tennessee Highway Hunters

Elizabethton High School
Tennessee Student Investigators

Driven by Rage
Fueled by Diesel
The Forgotten Victims of the Tennessee Highway Hunters
Elizabethton High School Tennessee Student Investigators
Edited by Alex Campbell
Published May 2026
Little Creek Books
Imprint of Jan-Carol Publishing, Inc.

Graphic Design: Tara Sizemore

ISBN: 978-1-970471-32-8 (Paperback)
ISBN: 978-1-970471-33-5 (Hardcover)
Library of Congress Control Number: On file
Printed in the United States of America

You may contact the publisher:
Jan-Carol Publishing, Inc.
PO Box 701
Johnson City, TN 37605
publisher@jancarolpublishing.com
www.jancarolpublishing.com

Dedicated to the victims, known and unknown,
and to Tina, Lorie, and Linda.

The Victims

From the very beginning, we knew this work had to center on the victims. Not the headlines, not the offenders, and not the way tragedy is so often turned into something to watch or consume. The work had to focus on the people who lost their lives, their futures, and their voices. They had to remain at the heart of everything we did. We have seen how easily stories like these can glorify those who caused harm while reducing victims to a name or a moment. That is something we reject.

We began this year with the victims, and we hope this work continues to honor them while offering some measure of remembrance and support to the families who still carry that loss. Because for them, this is not history. It is still present. Although this book is filled with hundreds of victims, there are three representative people who came to shape and center our work in a deeper way.

Tina

Through Tina, we came to understand the kind of pain that can exist behind closed doors. We asked ourselves what would drive someone so young to leave home and take to the road, leaving all that she loved behind. In searching for that answer, we realized she was not just leaving, but she was trying to escape. She was running from one kind of danger and unfortunately found another even more sinister type.

That forced us to confront something uncomfortable. Not everyone has a safe home. Not everyone is given good choices. Some people are forced to choose between several options, but all of them are bad. From the outside, those options look like choices, but when the situation has already cast the die, they don't really seem like choices at all.

Tina changed the way we see that. She taught us not to label people, especially young women, whose decisions felt more like a last desperate attempt at escape. She was the first victim connected to the Redhead Murders to be identified, to have her name returned to her. But even with answers, the pain does not stop. Her loved ones are still devastated. Loss does not fade just because time passes. Through Tina, we learned that even when questions are answered, the hurt remains.

Lorie

Through Lorie, we learned what it means to truly know someone beyond what happened to them. After more than 40 years, her brother chose to speak with us, to share her story, and to trust us with her memory. Because of him, we did not just study a case. We got to know Lorie.

Her story helped us understand how much of life can be shaped long before someone ever has control over it. Genetics, illness, family circumstances, and decisions made by others, even generations before, can all play a role. And yet, despite everything she faced, she worked to turn her life around. She was building the life she always dreamed of. She was getting there.

From Lorie, we learned that people are not defined only by what happens to them. They can fight to change their path. But we also learned how fragile that progress can be. Just when it seems like someone has found their way forward, it can be taken from them.

Through her brother's words, we heard the love that still exists, even after decades. We saw the patience, the strength, and the pain of still not having all the answers. Lorie reminds us why this work matters. It reminds us to keep going, not just for the past, but for the people still living with that loss.

Linda

Linda showed us what it truly means to fight and to survive. She came face to face with evil in a way most people cannot imagine, and she refused to let that be the end of her story. She fought first just to live. Then she fought just to crawl from the side of the road and find help, press charges, and stand in court and face the person who tried to take everything from her, even while still carrying the physical and emotional scars from the attack. She fought to raise her voice above a whisper so the truth could be heard. And after that fight for justice was over, she found out that the real fight had only begun.

She fought to rebuild her life and be the mother her children deserved. She battled to be a sister, daughter, partner, a grandmother, and someone who shows up for her family with love and consistency. Now, she spends time with her grandchildren, with sleepovers and tea parties, creating the kind of moments that once seemed impossible. Her volunteer work helps children all over the world, turning what she went through into something that gives back.

Linda taught us that survival is not just about living through something. It is about what comes after. She showed us that even in the worst circumstances, it is possible to take what was meant to destroy you and turn it into something that can build something beautiful.

We see her now as the person she fought to become. But we do not forget that she was once a young woman, terrified, fighting for her last breath. And with that breath, she chose to speak, to seek justice, and in doing so, she helped us find our own voice.

Conclusion

This book is for the victims. The known and the unknown. The named and the unnamed. Those who have been found, and those who are still waiting.

What you are reading is student work. It is built from their effort, their questions, and their determination to understand and to speak for those who no longer can. But work like this does not happen on its own. It is only possible because of the lives of these victims and the people who continue to carry their stories forward. The victims are not just part of this book. They are the reason it exists.

They have taught us how to look deeper, how to question what we think we know, and how to approach others with more empathy and understanding. Their stories have shaped us in ways that will last far beyond this classroom. And it is for them, always, that this work is done. It is our own feeble attempt to learn from the past and speak for those who can no longer speak for themselves. It is to correct the mistakes of those who came before us, so the memories of these women can live on after us.

TABLE OF CONTENTS

FOREWORD

By Scott Barker

In 2022, after 32 years of service, I retired from the Federal Bureau of Investigation (FBI) as a Special Agent. Assigned to the Chattanooga Resident Agency within the Knoxville Division, I investigated criminal matters within the FBI's jurisdiction. I also served as the Knoxville Division coordinator for the FBI's Behavioral Analysis Unit (BAU). In this role, I assisted both agents within the Knoxville Division and local and state investigators in presenting cases to the BAU in Quantico, Virginia, for consultation. I also helped state and local agencies with joining the FBI's Violent Criminal Apprehension Program (ViCAP). This database houses data from various violent criminal cases and assists investigators with identifying and matching different aspects of a crime to a particular offender.

As part of this work, I gave presentations to local organizations and schools about the BAU and its work. In 2018, a supervisor in the FBI's Johnson City Resident Agency (located in Johnson City, Tennessee), contacted me about presenting on the BAU to a sociology class taught by Alex Campbell at Elizabethton High School (EHS) in Elizabethton, Tennessee. When I contacted Mr. Campbell, he explained his students were developing a criminal profile for a series of unsolved murders that occurred in the 1980s along major interstates in Tennessee and surrounding states, including Arkansas and Kentucky.

This set of unsolved murders was named the "Redhead Murders" because all the women had red or reddish-blonde hair. Despite investigative efforts spanning multiple years and law enforcement agencies, the murders remained unsolved, and all but one of the victims still remained unidentified. Intrigued by Mr. Campbell's class project, I traveled to EHS and spoke to his students about the BAU.

During my presentation, his students remained attentive and asked numerous questions about the BAU. They were very interested in how BAU develops offender profiles. At the conclusion of the presentation, the class came to a consensus that the offender was possibly a truck driver who traveled the interstate system in Tennessee, and that he was a white male.

A few weeks after my presentation, Mr. Campbell forwarded me his class's complete profile of the offender they believed responsible for some of the Redhead Murders. I told Mr. Campbell that the profile was well done, particularly their overall conclusions about the offender. It was obvious they had spent a lot of time developing it. He asked me what grade I would give them if I were their teacher. I said, of course, an A.

The students' profile matched Jerry Johns, a long-haul trucker from Cleveland, Tennessee, who had been incarcerated for the attempted murder of a woman in Knoxville in the 1980s. In 2016, a year after Johns died in prison, DNA in the Combined DNA Index System (CODIS) linked Johns to the murder of Tina Farmer, one of the confirmed Redhead Murder victims, whose body was found in 1985 off Interstate 75 near Jellico, Tennessee.

Since my retirement, I have given numerous presentations to Mr. Campbell's classes on victimology and other BAU-related matters. Even though the students differ from year to year, their desire to identify victims, help victims' families, and develop information that may help solve unsolved murders has never changed.

Mr. Campbell and his students are passionate about each project they undertake. They are the ones doing the hard work on these cases, and this book is the result of this hard work. It has truly been my pleasure to work with Mr. Campbell and his students these past several years.

By Darrell E. Mealer

My sister, Lorie Mealer Pennell was a missing person for 40 years. To be honest, I had given up hope of ever finding out what happened to her. Then a couple years ago, out of the blue, I got a call from a woman about my DNA, asking if I had a missing sister.

To be honest, it had been so long that I thought I was the only one that cared about Lorie anymore. But last year when I journeyed to Tennessee to meet Mr. Campbell's sociology class at Elizabethton High School and saw the passion in the faces of Mr. Campbell and his students, I knew I had been wrong for so many years.

The power of knowing people still care means more to the family members of victims than anyone else could ever know, but I could tell that it meant so much to the students as well. Because of my own life experiences as a little boy in school, I know that many students struggle with their own traumatic experiences in their own lives. This book will help them realize that they are not on their own to face the trauma.

It is vitally important for young people to learn to see others as human beings instead of labels, numbers, or statistics. The relationships I have developed with the students of this class are life changing. A book like this will get the story out about these victims, many forgotten and some still not even identified, just like my sister was. It can give hope to family members like me, who have had a loved one missing for 40 years, that as technology advances, there can be answers in cold cases like my sister's.

The closure that I have from the help of the students has changed my own PTSD, as it gives me closure over my sister and, as a 100% disabled

American veteran, it has given me hope that other trauma in my life can find the same closure as well.

I cannot say enough about the dedication of all the students that have worked on this. It has changed the life of so many people, including myself. My hope is that through this book, more people like me, people waiting around for decades for that one phone call that will change their lives, can have that day too. Although my sister Lorie now has her name back, we still await the phone call which tells us which monster is responsible for taking her from us. I hope this book can deliver such phone calls to families just like mine.

I pray God will bless each one of the students for reminding me that there are people who care. They have learned to see people for who they are as human beings, they have learned to take responsibility for people they have never even met, and they are trying to help victims and family members despite sometimes not even knowing their names. Because of them, I no longer feel alone in this journey, and I carry renewed hope that justice and healing are still possible.

INTRODUCTION

What is a serial killer? You can find the simple definition in any textbook: a serial killer is an individual who commits two or more separate murders, occurring in distinct events, with a cooling-off period between them, and typically driven by psychological motives rather than immediate practical gain. That seems simple enough, until it isn't.

We were in the middle of a video call with a highly esteemed retired FBI profiler when he brought up the idea that serial killing should be looked at as more than just a number of victims. He argued that it should be considered not only quantitatively, but also qualitatively.

If I have a pair of tennis shoes, but I never play tennis, are they still tennis shoes? Most people would say yes, as long as they have the characteristics of tennis shoes. As long as the shoes have lateral support, are designed for quick and multidirectional movement, have a durable outsole, provide cushioning, and offer low-to-the-ground stability, their owners will consider them tennis shoes whether they ever see a tennis court or not.

When this class began to research the highway killers and their victims in our home state of Tennessee, we realized we had a problem with relying only on the simple definition of a serial killer often used, which has the requirement of multiple confirmed kills. If many of these cases did not receive the attention they deserved, did not have the resources required, did not benefit from modern DNA technology and forensic techniques, and involved killers who were highly mobile and able to escape jurisdictional oversight, we knew we were dealing with offenders whose actual number of victims would be difficult to quantify. Several of them, such as Jerry Johns and Harry Edward Greenwell, were not even discovered to be serial killers until after they were dead. Some only revealed the number of murders they committed on their way to the gas chamber, such as Tracy Lee Housel.

One offender, Sedley Alley, was only ever convicted for one murder, but later his wife revealed that he had killed before. Some members of law enforcement have published their beliefs that he may be tied to additional murders on the other side of the country. But after he was executed, the work stopped, the witnesses passed away, and the cases were set aside. If you were to examine the disturbing specifics of Alley and his one confirmed murder case, there would be little doubt that Alley fit the psychological hallmarks of a serial killer: unstable childhood, family dysfunction, superficial charm, manipulative behavior, lack of empathy, instability in work life, substance abuse, compulsion, and vivid fantasy life. The only thing missing is the one quantitative characteristic—proof that he killed more than one victim. And realistically, that proof may never come, given that he is dead, many witnesses are gone, most of the investigators have passed on, and the case itself has grown cold.

What are we to do with killers like Sean Patrick Goble and John Allen Chapman, who we know were killing in Tennessee and are confirmed serial killers? They killed in the early 1990s. Law enforcement believed Goble may have been responsible for as many as 46 additional murders, and Chapman likely began killing near his home before transitioning into a highway killer. Can we say with certainty that they did not offend or even kill in Tennessee in the 1980s? Goble grew up watching his father commit horrible crimes and was most likely criminally active quite early. The fact that Chapman began with fire starting and smaller crimes around his home then traveled as part of the National Guard could mean there are other victims that don't match his highway murder. Is it possible that they, too, have victims from that decade who have not yet been identified?

And what are we to do with Tracy Lee Housel and Warren Luther Alexander? Housel had a long history of violent crime and confirmed victims from California to Georgia. In 1985, he went on a rampage, killing and assaulting at least four people across at least four states while traveling through many more. He later admitted to killing as many as 17 people before his execution. He traveled through Tennessee and many other states during his six-week crime spree, admitted to additional unidentified victims, and there was a trail of unsolved murders across the region during that time.

Alexander is equally difficult to define. Law enforcement has DNA evidence linking him to three murders in California from the 1970s, where he is still awaiting trial. There is at least one additional case from that time for which he is a prime suspect. He later became a truck driver and was arrested in 2024 for the 1992 murder of a woman in North Carolina, again based on DNA evidence. He was also a suspect in a murder very close to the Tennessee border. Given his decades on the road, it is reasonable to assume he traveled through Tennessee many times while continuing his pattern of violence for those 20 quiet years. The man once known as the Ventura Strangler appears to have evolved into a highway killer. How many more victims does he have out on those highways? Could some of them be in Tennessee?

What you will find in this book is a mixture of offenders. Some are confirmed serial killers in Tennessee during the 1980s. Others are confirmed serial killers from that era who are suspected to have killed in Tennessee. Some are confirmed killers in Tennessee who may one day be shown to be serial killers as more evidence comes to light. Finally, there are confirmed serial killers from the early 1990s who likely began killing in the late 1980s.

We have included them all. We did not feel it was right to exclude potential serial killers simply because forensic science had not yet advanced far enough to fully connect their crimes, or because case files were lost and witnesses are no longer alive. If these people are known killers with all of the psychological qualitative hallmarks of serial killers, we decided to include them as potential serial killers, because possibly the quantitative results just haven't caught up with them yet.

Another reason that some of these killers may not have been confirmed as serial killers with victims in Tennessee in the 1980s is because of who they targeted. Many of these offenders targeted the most vulnerable: women who were poor, struggling with addiction, exploited by the sex trade, or living with mental illness. These killers knew that these victims would not be missed, would receive few resources, and the media would quickly move on from their stories. To exclude these cases would feel like rewarding the very strategy these killers relied on, choosing victims they believed no one would miss.

This book presents both confirmed and potential serial killers connected to Tennessee in the 1980s who hunted along highways and interstates. Perhaps the most unsettling truth is that there were about as many more serial killers in this state during that decade who did not operate along the highways. It is difficult to comprehend how such a beautiful place could be home to so many, and even more difficult to accept that not even a group of more than 20 dedicated students, working for an entire school year, could uncover them all.

We do not present this work as the final word or a complete account. It is only a glimpse, a snapshot in time of where we are now. Our hope is that this book helps move the work forward, that it encourages others to keep searching for the killers and identifying the victims. We see this book as not the conclusion of more than 40 years of research, but just the beginning of a still unsolved investigation. Above all, we hope their families know that their loved ones have not been forgotten.

If you are reading this, you are part of the answer. You are refusing to forget about these victims no matter their struggles in life. You will not let these killers continue to silence their victims because they were wicked enough to choose the most vulnerable in society. You are keeping the attention on these cases. May we continue to advocate so that every victim—known and unknown, identified and nameless, suspected or confirmed—may have their measure of justice and their families a modicum of closure. So, here is to the beginning.

PROLOGUE

Tennessee in the 1980s was booming. The cities like Memphis and Nashville were in their primes as people flocked to the urban centers that still felt like small towns compared to the sprawling metropolises of New York, Chicago, and LA. Property taxes were cheap, there was no state income tax, and it was affordable to raise a family. What Tennessee lacked in the way of operas, Broadway plays, and the movie industry it made up for with pristine forests, meandering waterways, and the Grand Ole Opry. The Great Smoky Mountains, not Yellowstone or the Grand Canyon, was America's most visited National Park. People were moving to the Bible Belt, of which Nashville is the buckle, and it was bulging at the waistline.

However, something darker was lurking along those scenic byways and picturesque downtowns. Troubadours thought they were leaving the mean streets of Philadelphia and the cold strands of Chicago for a more temperate climate and warmer people, but in some ways, they were dead wrong. Away from the bright lights of Broadway in Nashville and secluded from the strains of blues and rock and roll on Beale Street, there was something sinister happening in Tennessee.

After the hint people received about serial killers in the 1960s, things exploded in the 1970s before reaching their peak in the 1980s. Hundreds of serial killers stalked the United States in numbers the average citizens just couldn't fathom. Moving to Tennessee and away from the Killing Fields of Texas or the drug infused violence of Southern California seemed the safe and responsible thing to do. But what these unsuspecting innocents didn't know is that they were moving into the birthplace of the highway serial killer.

America's first documented serial killers were actually a pair of brothers that killed throughout Tennessee and Kentucky and possibly other states in the late 1700s and early 1800s. Micajah and Wiley Harpe killed at least 39 and possibly over 50 victims as they traveled interstate routes between the frontier towns of Tennessee and surrounding states (including the famous Natchez Trace). When the land that would go on to make up Tennessee was purchased from the Cherokee by Richard Henderson and the Transylvania Company in 1775, one Cherokee chief, Dragging Canoe, who opposed the sale, predicted the land would always be "dark and bloody ground." In little more than 20 years, the Harpe Brothers were doing their best to make that prediction a reality.

The Harpe Brothers were not just the first serial killers in America, but they could also be called highways hunters—the type of serial killers that would reach their peak in the 1980s. Just as Tennessee was at the intersection of frontier travel from the overmountain trails from the east, the Cumberland Gap from Kentucky, and the Natchez Trace that led to Mississippi, the state again found itself at the center of overland travel. Interstate 40, 65, 24, and 81 crisscrossed the state, bringing a new generation of Highway Hunters to the Volunteer State.

Tennessee's geography puts it at many modern crossroads. Just as it was the state with the second most battles during the Civil War, its strategic location put it at the center of interstate violence. It is one of the gatekeeper states to the deep south. If you want to move goods from the industrial heartland to the ports along the Gulf of Mexico, you have to pass through the nearly 450-mile-long state. It has the major hubs of Nashville, Chattanooga, and Memphis where goods come in and go out on the rivers, railroads, and highways like spokes on a wheel. And the major rivers of the Cumberland, Tennessee, and Nashville have powerful ports and cities. The trade and travel routes of the eastern United States spread out like a spiderweb from Tennessee, but no one ever thought about the spiders.

When my students first began to research the possibility of just a single serial killer active in Tennessee in the 1980s, they were met with a lot of skepticisms. There had been a Redhead Murders Task Force that convened in 1985 from various local law enforcement agencies from 5 states, the Tennessee Bureau of Investigation, and FBI. They met once, stated they could not determine if an actual serial killer was at work, and then never met again. But my students followed the advice of an FBI behavioral analyst, put in the work, and released their findings in May of 2018. You should have seen the response.

Not only did many doubt that the high school students could do work that required so much investigative research, but many even doubted their conclusions. Over and over again, we read comments from authorities saying things such as there were no links, no confirmation, no conclusion, no announcements from official agencies were to come, etc. The most crushing blow came from the quote printed in a Tennessee newspaper from a state official saying, "At this time, agents have no evidence to indicate the... homicides are connected."

Every one of those comments came from agencies that never even bothered to look at the information the students accumulated. They never cared that it was vetted by a seasoned, highly-experienced law enforcement agent with years of training in behavioral analysis by the largest law enforcement agency in America. What stands out now is not that the students chose to say there was obviously a serial killer at work along Tennessee's interstates, which they termed the Bible Belt Strangler. The most impressive observation looking back is that the students didn't even know how right they were.

Eight years later, we now know that it wasn't just one serial killer active in Tennessee in the 1980s, but so many more. Currently, my new class of students have documented that 8 serial killers (Clark Perry Baldwin, Samuel Little, Aaron Ronald Williams, James Antonio Barnes, Cecil Johnson, Henry Eugene Hodges, Michael Wayne Howell, and Paul David Johnson) were active in this state in the 1980s. This is not speculation; this is irrefutable fact. The students predicted this 8 years ago when many doubted them. Many times, leaders aren't wrong; it is just that their ideas are too far in front of the evidence needed to back up the claims. In this case, exactly 8 years too far in front, but that is not where it ends.

These new students have found even more groundbreaking evidence to show that, most likely, many more serial killers were stalking Tennessee as well. There are three more killers who are confirmed to have serial victims that are thought to also have victims in the state (Harry Edward Greenwell, Tracey Lee Housel, and Warren Luther Alexander). Add in three more killers who have killed one officially, but law enforcement believes they have killed many more, also making them serial killers (Sedley Alley, Jerry Johns, and Nicholas Todd Sutton). Finally add in two more confirmed serial killers who killed in the very early 1990s but are often believed to have killed in the late 1980s as well, and the number now stands at 16.

By looking at census records and the work of the Radford/FGCU Serial Killer Database, managed by Radford University and Florida Gulf Coast University, which is a primary academic source tracking over 4,000 US serial killers since 1900, we find some very telling statistics. In the 1980s, there were roughly 173 serial killers active in the 1980s in a total US population of 248,709,873 (using the 1990 US Census). If you look at the population of Tennessee at the end of the 1980s (again by using the 1990 US Census), it was 4,877,185 people (or 3.395 of the total US population). This should equate to 3.40 serial killers. Yes, Tennessee had 8 confirmed serial killers and likely 8 more (for a total of 16), which means the state had more than double (2.36) the amount of confirmed killers that would be expected from population estimates and possibly as many as almost five times more (4.72) than the statistics indicate should have been present.

The supposition that Tennessee had one serial killer active in the 1980s, which seemed heresy by many just 8 years ago, is now confirmed to have been not just right but almost laughable at how that prediction was just scratching the surface of the buried truth. With more information now pointing to the existence of several more Tennessee serial killers that could put the number to twice that, the real question becomes, why has this gone unnoticed?

Bundy, Gacy, the Zodiac, and Manson; names that live in infamy across America as the high priesthood of serial killers. California and Texas, as well as the major population centers of Chicago, New York, and Phoenix, are seen as the hotbed of serial killing. But the statistical evidence is quite the contrary. Yes, those areas may be unrivaled by sheer volume of killers or victims, but they also have huge populations. We need to dive deeper into the statistics to see what was happening in the 1980s in these perceived serial killer hotbeds.

We would be led to believe that the undisputed capital of serial murder in the 1980s was California. Confirmed numbers show as many as 20 confirmed serial killers active in the state in that decade, including Randy Kraft, Leonard Lake, and Richard Ramirez. Just as in Tennessee, there are many offenders who are proven to be murderers and suspected of more crimes which would make them serial killers. These estimates are another 5 to 15. This combines to a total of possibly 35 serial killers active in the state of California in the 1980s. However, if we compare the same population statistics as above, we would expect California to have 21.69 serial killers. Although this is higher than the expected, it is not even double the rate expected (1.61), which shows that although there was definitely something contributing to more serial killers being active and possibly active in the state, it doesn't even begin to approach the nearly 5 times more killers active and possibly active in Tennessee. Statistically, California turns from the home of serial homicide in the 1980s to a sleepy little one-horse town of horrors.

And what about Texas, with the massive Killing Fields and an outrageous number of unsolved homicides in places in its sprawling metropolitan areas of cities like Houston and Dallas? How does it compare to Tennessee in the 1980s? It appears there were only 6 identified serial killers in Texas in the 1980s and possibly another 4 who are suspected. These include offenders like David Wood, Curtis Brown, and Henry Lee Lucas. So, a total of 10, and with their population, they should have expected nearly 7 (6.83). Although larger than expected, showing that state, too, was experiencing more serial killer activity than expected, they were again far outpaced by Tennessee.

Although other areas of the country are often considered hotbeds of serial killers based on total numbers, when you actually look at them statistically, they fall short of percentages of serial killers active in Tennessee—which makes it even more interesting that a quiet little state like Tennessee has more than double and as many as 4 or 5 times the numbers of serial killers active in the decade of the 1980s. Just exactly what is going on here? My students and I noticed this pattern, and we wanted the truth. Just exactly how many killers were operating in our home state, how many have gone undetected, who were these monsters, how many victims of these killers are there, and what exactly was going on in our state those decades ago to allow this to happen?

This is how we have spent our time this school year. We researched these killers and their victims, but it wasn't easy. It is amazing how popular true crime has become. There are so many documentaries, YouTube channels, podcasts, books, and many more forms of media that focus on these people and their crimes. Yet some of these Tennessee predators don't even have a mention on Wikipedia, only one single website about them, no podcasts, no books, and their case files had been destroyed. How could so many cause so much damage across our state, and many of them go unnoticed and their victims erased? Why do evil people like John Wayne Gacy get books, movies, documentaries, and even comic books made about them, yet John Allen Chapman, Sedley Alley, and Tracy Lee Housel do something so heinous they were executed, yet people have forgotten?

They say there are two major philosophies of law enforcement. One is that law enforcement works for the community. Indeed, the taxes from the shared community are used to fund those agencies. When they are sworn in, it is into a government agency. They try to protect the people. If that is your philosophy, then I assume you have done your job when the crime is solved. After all, John Allen Chapman is in jail for life, and Tracy Lee Housel and Sedley Alley could be executed. They can't hurt anyone in the public ever again. Hands dusted, backs patted, and jobs complete. The community is safe.

However, there is another philosophy. It is that law enforcement doesn't work for the community at all. Instead, they work for the victims and their families. In these cases, law enforcement again works hard and puts bad guys away by solving crimes, however, once that offender is locked away or even executed, that does not mean their duty is over. There are still victims and their families that deserve justice. Are there victims undiscovered, crimes unsolved, and families still left waiting? The community may be safe from further molestation, but the victims and their families have not received closure or justice.

In this second philosophy is where my students and I decided to live. Every single killer we focused on was either dead or in jail. They can't hurt anyone in society anymore, but we felt the job was still undone. When Housel admitted to more than a dozen more unsolved murders and law enforcement sincerely believes that Sean Patrick Goble had as many as 46 unknown victims (based on evidence from his home), what are we to say? That justice has been done because they were given their day in court, were found guilty, or are serving a life sentence? But how about the dozens and potentially hundreds of victims and families who still don't know who is responsible for hurting and killing their loved ones? Are we to forget about them? Or are they still awaiting, and righteously deserve, justice?

In this book, my students will introduce you to why they wanted to look at these cases, how they investigated, what research they uncovered, and what the broader impacts of these cases are. They will walk you through the five different factors that turned Tennessee in the 1980s into a cesspool of serial murder. And finally, they will present their research on just some of these killers, the "Highway Hunters": their lives, their timelines, their victims, how they killed, and how many other potential victims there are out there that are still waiting on justice.

The sad part is that we didn't even have time to research the rest. Too much crime, too much evil, and too many victims. The students decided to focus on only the killers that preyed upon mostly vulnerable people along the highways, which we will call the "Highway Hunters." We have not forgotten the other half of these killers and their victims, but there was so much evil that in one year we only had time to properly investigate this category.

We hope that the work of our students will open up an entirely new discussion about crime in our state of Tennessee and possibly the entire nation. What causes some states to be so above the statistical expectations for serial murder? What went wrong in Tennessee to allow this to happen? What can others learn from the issues that were plaguing this state to allow it to turn into a virtual playground for the most evil, highly mobile serial killers in America, and has our state (and others) addressed these issues, making things safer today?

We also hope that by including the timelines, MOs, signatures, and suspected and potential victims of each killer that we spark a renewed interest in bringing justice to the many unknown victims of these killers. It seems that law enforcement did their job in many cases of investigating, capturing, and punishing these killers for some of their crimes, but once they were put away, the rest of the victims were forgotten. Exactly where are the other 46 victims of Sean Patrick Goble? Who were these other 20 to 30 victims of

Samuel Little that he just couldn't remember, and who were the other 14 victims that Tracey Lee Housel admitted to killing? There is still so much work to be done, evil to uncover, and justice to be delivered.

The fact that you are reading this book means you are part of the solution that my students long for. You want to understand the factors that allowed this to happen so they won't be replicated. You want to know how they target vulnerable people so we can educate and protect those in our society who are still vulnerable. And you want to learn about the victims that still don't have justice so it can be rectified. You are the ones my students had in mind when they were filling out hundreds of records requests, doing interviews, and scouring records. As law enforcement officials, both active and retired, were pouring into the students and vetting their work, it was you they were thinking about. Now, this work is in your hands, because once you understand how much work is left to be done, you can never go back to the time when you could plead blissful ignorance. Now you know, and now is the time for the rest of the work to be completed.

SECTION I:

Introduction to This Project

1.

THE PURPOSE OF THIS BOOK

Our class first became interested in writing this book because we wanted to answer a question that had been on our minds since the beginning of the school year: why were there so many serial killers active in Tennessee during the 1980s? We spent months researching, discussing, and collaborating in groups to understand the issue and gather the information needed to explore it fully.

This topic is deeply important to us because it touches on real people whose lives were tragically changed, and families who continue to live with grief and unanswered questions. Many of the victims were women around our own age, facing dangers they should never have had to face alone. Thinking about their lives is a sobering reminder that people our age today may still face challenges they cannot face alone. Through this project, we hope to honor the victims of the past and raise awareness for those in the present: our peers, fellow citizens of Tennessee, law enforcement, and members of the media.

We also wanted to show that teenagers are capable of serious, thoughtful work. Our goal was not just to collect facts, but to gain a deep understanding of these cases, communicate it clearly, and highlight ways society can improve. By creating a book rather than a report or essay, we could reach a wider audience and reflect the seriousness and sensitivity of these stories.

We wanted our work to stand alongside adult research in its depth and care.

Sociology helped us understand these crimes from a broader perspective. It allowed us to see the lives of victims and offenders through the lens of society and social conditions. We considered how someone with a difficult upbringing, abusive past, or struggles with addiction might feel, think, or make decisions. Sociology taught us to look beyond the surface, to consider context, and to approach each story without judgment.

We also studied how social systems (like family, friendship networks, and community status) can influence choices and vulnerabilities. People are often shaped by their environments, and sometimes loyalty, pressure, or lack of resources can lead someone down a harmful path. Poverty, isolation, and lack of opportunity can increase the risk of crime for both victims and offenders. Understanding these patterns helped us see why these tragedies happened and how society may prevent them in the future.

Even though these cases happened decades ago, they remain relevant today. Studying them helps us recognize patterns, stay aware of risks, and protect ourselves and those we care about. Many social issues (like judgment based on wealth, background, or job, and the neglect of mental health) still exist in modern society. By examining the past, we can see where systems failed and where improvements are needed, from law enforcement resources to community support.

This book reflects the dedication of a group of students who care deeply about justice for victims. We understand that work does not end when a killer is caught or sentenced. Families still struggle with unanswered questions about their loved ones, and we wanted to honor their experiences by approaching each case with empathy, respect, and careful research.

Our class comes from different backgrounds and life experiences, which allowed us to see these cases from multiple perspectives. We also had guidance from professionals like Scott Barker, Mike Little, Jim Clemente, and JD Anderson. These experiences strengthened our understanding and helped us approach the material thoughtfully and responsibly.

Our goal was not only to understand the victims and their lives, but also to explore the investigative process that uncovered these cases. How do detectives piece together clues? How do social systems, research, and careful observation reveal truths hidden for years? Understanding these questions is the next step in our journey. In the following chapter, we will show how our class approached this investigation, using research methods, analysis, and critical thinking to uncover patterns, provide new insights, and honor the victims' stories.

2.

THE INVESTIGATION

Our investigation began when we received a comprehensive file of cold case information on several victims found in and close to our state in the 1980s. We carefully reviewed each case, analyzing the victims' lives and histories before presenting our findings to the rest of the class to identify possible connections. Using a process of elimination, we narrowed our focus to cases we believed were likely related, which required extensive research into suspects. Even so, we concluded that not all cases were linked to a single perpetrator and instead turned our attention to other serial offenders known as the Tennessee "Highway Hunters."

To determine which cases were relevant, we compared multiple factors: methods of killing, geographical locations, how bodies were disposed of, the victims' characteristics and occupations, and many more. We found that serial offenders sometimes targeted individuals in certain vulnerable professions, such as sex workers, and those working along highways and interstates. This careful analysis helped us focus on patterns that might otherwise have gone unnoticed.

These cases were especially meaningful because we empathized with the victims and their families. Many occurred near our own communities, and most of us had chosen this elective out of an interest in criminal justice. Understanding that these victims lacked justice motivated us to demonstrate that their cases deserved attention and resolution. Through class discussions, we learned the importance of approaching these cases with care and empathy.

During our research, several groups made significant discoveries. One team identified the Tuscaloosa Jane Doe as a potential victim of Samuel Little. Another group found possible connections between victims and Sedley Alley, specifically Deborah Alley and Sherri Jarvis. Other groups uncovered additional leads, deepening our investigation. As we explored further, our process became increasingly complex. New evidence often pointed us toward additional cases, creating a cycle of discovery that expanded our understanding of how some cases might be interconnected in ways previously unrecognized by law enforcement.

A key part of our work involved victimology—the study of victims and their experiences. After we spoke with retired FBI agent Scott Barker, he encouraged us to always start with the victims first. We learned various theories of victimology, such as theories like victim facilitation, victim precipitation, and victim provocation, which helped us understand why some people become targets without blaming them for their circumstances. Victim facilitation examines behaviors that may make someone more vulnerable. Victim precipitation looks at situations where victims unintentionally contribute to a crime. Victim provocation considers instances where victims' actions directly trigger an incident. Understanding these concepts helped us reconstruct events and see the dynamics between victims and offenders more clearly.

One example of victim facilitation is Alice Rebecca Haynes, who was victimized by Sean Patrick Goble. Involvement in sex work and periods of disappearing made her more vulnerable, but these choices were often the result of limited options rather than personal fault. Learning about her life and others like her reminded us to approach victims with empathy, recognizing the systemic challenges they faced. Similarly, in the Redhead Murders, victims such as Michelle Inman, Lisa Nichols, and Lorie Pennell were taken from urban areas and left in rural locations. Tracy Sue Walker's case also taught us patience and attention to detail, as weeks of research sometimes led only to frustrating dead ends.

Applying these theories to real cases taught us crucial investigative skills. We learned to examine each victim's life, behaviors, and circumstances before drawing conclusions, which helped prevent premature judgment or bias. This victim-centered approach revealed patterns in offenders' decision-making and criminal behavior, allowing us to understand the reasons behind each crime.

Our research extended beyond the classroom. We used data analysis, mapping, interviews, FOIA requests, and other tools to uncover new leads. Many students worked late into the night, emailing law enforcement and advocating for renewed attention to these cases. We faced countless challenges, including sleep deprivation, dead-end leads, and contradictory sources, but these obstacles strengthened our resilience and determination to seek justice for the victims. Some FOIA requests returned little or no information, which was frustrating, but collaborating with peers allowed us to develop solutions and ensure our research was accurate.

Through our study, we learned that many victims did not come from stable homes or supportive environments. Some were involved in prostitution, not by choice but as a way to survive or cope with difficult circumstances. Initially, it was easy to fall into assumptions about why they were targeted. Researching their stories showed us that these individuals did not ask for harm to come to them. Many were simply trying to survive or improve their situations, and understanding that completely changed our perspective on their lives.

We also learned about the limitations of the justice system. In many cases, DNA evidence and other crucial materials were mishandled or discarded, leaving families without closure. Modern forensic technology could have helped identify suspects and reopen investigations, but opportunities were lost when evidence was not preserved. These realities made our work feel even more important, motivating us to be thorough, thoughtful, and persistent.

Through our research, interviews, and analysis of haunting cases like the Redhead Murders, we learned that effective investigations start with discipline: patiently developing theories grounded in facts rather than chasing every loose lead. Protecting access to essential files and evidence allowed us to connect scattered fragments into cohesive theories. Keeping detailed lists of investigative topics made it easier to retrieve critical details and strengthened the credibility of our findings. We saw firsthand that law enforcement faces persistent challenges, from incomplete evidence to pre-DNA era struggles in linking cases, and we learned the importance of clear, precise communication when presenting findings to others.

Finally, our study of these victims drove home a profound lesson: approach them with empathy and without judgment. Victims' childhoods, home lives, survival choices, or work in risky environments did not make them responsible for the crimes committed against them. Understanding that is essential in any investigative work, whether in a classroom, as a city cop, or in federal law enforcement. Our experience transformed us, giving us both purpose and practical skills that will stay with us for life.

But maybe the most impactful sociological premise we learned was about the bystander effect. The murder of Kitty Genovese in 1964 is one of the most well-known examples of the bystander effect (sometimes even referred to as Genovese Syndrome), where witnesses fail to act in an emergency because they assume someone else will. Reports at the time claimed that dozens of neighbors saw or heard parts of the attack but did not intervene, which highlighted how social pressure, fear, or uncertainty can stop people from helping others in critical moments. Learning about this case had a profound impact on our class. It made us realize that waiting for someone else to act can have deadly consequences, and that taking initiative, even in small ways, can make a difference. As students studying these Tennessee cases, we felt a responsibility to act, to investigate, and to shine a light on the victims' stories, rather than assume that others would do the work for us. Kitty Genovese's story reminded us that action matters, and that awareness, empathy, and courage are essential to preventing harm and honoring the lives of those affected by crime. Even if we are not members of law enforcement, don't have degrees in criminal justice, or are not even adults yet, we should not wait for someone else to act.

As we wrapped up our investigations into individual cases, it became clear that understanding a victim's story is only part of the picture. Many of the challenges we faced, such as scattered evidence, jurisdictional gaps, and overlooked leads, were connected to larger social patterns that shaped crime and vulnerability across Tennessee. To fully grasp why certain crimes went unnoticed or why some victims were especially at risk, we needed to step back and examine the bigger picture. This meant looking at the communities where crimes occurred, the highways that connected cities, the isolation of rural areas, and the social and economic pressures affecting everyday life. By combining what we learned from individual cases with this broader perspective, we could better understand not just how crimes were committed, but why some killers went undetected and victims went unidentified for so long. This approach allows us to see how individual stories are connected to larger patterns, and it sets the stage for exploring how various factors shaped crime in Tennessee during the 1980s.[1]

1 Dombrink, John. "The Touchables: Vice and Police Corruption in the 1980's." *Law and Contemporary Problems*, vol. 51, no. 1, Winter 1988, pp. 201–232. National Criminal Justice Reference Service (NCJRS).

Policing 30 Years Ago: A Detective Visits the 1980s." *Police1*, Lexipol.

"The Drug Enforcement Administration (DEA) 1980–1985." *DEA History*, US Drug Enforcement Administration.

3.

THE SOCIAL CONTEXT

When we began examining crime patterns in Tennessee, one of the first things we noticed was how easily crimes and offenders can slip out of public memory. Public attention moves quickly, and older cases often fade as new stories take over. Crimes that don't appear dramatic or unusual usually receive limited coverage, and victims from marginalized or vulnerable communities are even more likely to be overlooked. Without strong early attention, a case can almost disappear entirely from public conversation, leaving victims and their families without justice or recognition.

Mobility adds another layer to this problem. Highways, long-distance travel, and transient lifestyles allow offenders to move freely, leaving evidence scattered across multiple regions. When crimes occur in different locations, no single agency sees the full picture. This makes it difficult to connect victims, track an offender's movements, or recognize that one person may be responsible for multiple crimes. Offenders who travel frequently, such as truck drivers or people who move between states, can exploit this lack of continuity, committing crimes in one area and then disappearing into the next.

Jurisdictional boundaries complicate investigations even further. Each police department operates with its own rules, resources, and databases, and information sharing is not always consistent. When a case crosses county or state lines, it can easily become fragmented between agencies, making it harder to connect crucial details. Even today, gaps in communication can delay investigations or leave important evidence unnoticed.

Media coverage also plays a major role in which cases remain visible. Stories that fit familiar or emotionally compelling narratives tend to receive attention, while others are ignored. When the media does not highlight a case, both the public and investigators can overlook it, especially when the victims were already socially invisible. A clear example of this can be seen in victims connected to offenders like Clark Perry Baldwin and Jerry Johns. Many women linked to these men were never widely reported on when they disappeared or were found deceased. Several were travelers, hitchhikers, or women living in vulnerable circumstances, which made it easier for their cases to be dismissed or ignored. Because Baldwin and Johns operated across multiple states, their victims were scattered across different jurisdictions, and agencies often did not realize they were dealing with related crimes. Combined with limited media attention, these factors allowed many victims' stories to fade from public memory for years.

Another factor in vulnerability is involvement in the sex work industry. Many people enter sex work because they are financially struggling, abused, neglected, or coerced. They often have few supportive family members or friends and face societal judgment. In the 1980s, even when police attempted to investigate crimes against sex workers, they were limited by the technology and resources of the time. Few surveillance cameras, rural and forested crime scenes, and underfunded departments made thorough investigations nearly impossible. Police departments often lacked sufficient staff, time, or money to properly investigate these crimes, and evidence was sometimes discarded, including blood samples or clothing that could have helped convict offenders. Sadly, these issues still occur today, though to a lesser degree, and learning from past failures is essential to prevent future victims from being forgotten.

Tennessee's geography also shaped crime patterns. The state's major interstates, especially I-40, I-24, I-65, I-81, and I-75, acted as busy travel corridors, connecting cities like Memphis, Nashville, Knoxville, and Chattanooga. These urban centers sit at key crossroads of highways, rivers, and rail lines, concentrating population, nightlife, and drug markets, which led to higher murder rates than in rural areas. Meanwhile, the Appalachian and Cumberland Plateau regions were far more isolated in the 1980s, with limited police coverage and slower communication. Violent crimes in these areas sometimes went unreported or took longer to investigate. Tourism areas like the Smoky Mountains were growing quickly, bringing more visitors and occasional spikes in crime tied to crowded areas. Altogether, Tennessee's mix of mountains and major highways created patterns where murders clustered in transportation and population centers, while rural areas experienced more hidden crime dynamics.

Interstates made it easier for offenders to commit crimes and leave an area before police could respond. Busy highways allowed them to move between cities without drawing attention, blending in with normal traffic. Highways also offered exits, motels, gas stations, and rest areas where offenders could stop unnoticed, switch vehicles, or meet accomplices. In the 1980s and 1990s, limited communication and surveillance gave offenders even more freedom to move quickly and avoid detection.

Urban and rural areas also shaped law enforcement responses differently. In cities, departments usually had more officers, faster backup, and shorter distances to cover, along with specialized units for homicide, narcotics, or gangs. Rural areas covered vast territories with far fewer officers, slower response times, and reliance on state police for major crimes. Geography, staffing, and communication all affected how quickly cases moved forward and how crimes were handled.

Social and economic factors increased vulnerability for certain groups. Poverty pushed families into high-crime neighborhoods with limited job options, while poor education limited career opportunities. High unemployment and industrial losses in 1980s Tennessee led to increased drug activity and gang involvement. Social isolation, unstable housing, and limited community resources removed protective networks, making populations easier for offenders to target and harder for authorities to protect.

Our research showed that crime tended to appear where life was busiest and most pressured. Big cities like Memphis, Nashville, Knoxville, and Chattanooga experienced the most serious crimes because so many people, highways, and social pressures came together. Areas along major interstates also saw higher crime rates due to ease of travel. Rural and mountain communities had fewer reported crimes, but their isolation sometimes meant serious incidents went unnoticed for longer periods. Crime was most common where movement, stress, and crowded living intersected, while quieter areas faced their own challenges shaped by distance and limited support.

Poverty and instability increased risk because struggling individuals often had fewer people and resources to rely on. Limited services meant fewer places to go when help was needed. Some people were forced into unsafe environments just to survive, increasing their vulnerability. Communities did not just lose a person; the sense of safety and normalcy in towns was disrupted, and families and neighbors were left with grief and unanswered questions for years.

Studying the social context helped us understand why many victims were targeted and why some crimes went unnoticed for long periods. Victimology revealed that many victims were women involved in sex work, and societal attitudes at the time meant their disappearances were often not taken seriously. This also explains why similar types of victims appeared in multiple cases. Tennessee, often known for its music, natural beauty, and southern charm, also has a darker side. Research shows that the state's interstate system alone had three times the expected number of serial killers connected to it. This has changed how we think about Tennessee's history.

Growing up, we always thought Tennessee was quiet and uneventful, but these cases revealed a much more complicated and sometimes dangerous past that many people never realize exists.

By examining Tennessee's geography, highways, urban-rural differences, and social conditions, we can see how crime, vulnerability, and investigative challenges intersect. Recognizing these patterns is essential not only for understanding past cases but also for preventing future victims from being overlooked. Studying these conditions allows law enforcement, communities, and researchers to approach investigations more thoughtfully, ensuring that no case fades silently into memory.

However, recognizing patterns is only part of the story. Many of these cases were also shaped by systemic failures, limited resources, and delays in justice that allowed victims to remain unidentified or cases to go unsolved for years. To fully understand what happened in Tennessee during this time, we must also examine how investigative systems worked, and sometimes, failed. The next section explores these challenges and how they affected the pursuit of justice for victims and their families. [2]

2 Gibbs, J. J. *Crime Against Persons in Urban, Suburban, and Rural Areas: A Comparative Analysis of Victimization Rates.* NCJ Number 53551, 1979. NCJRS Virtual Library, https://www.ncjrs.gov/.

4.

THE SYSTEMS OF POWER AND JUSTICE

Many crimes and offenders quietly slip out of public memory, often because of how society chooses to pay attention. Public focus moves quickly, and as new stories dominate the news, older cases fade into the background. Crimes that do not appear dramatic or unusual often receive limited attention from the start, and when victims come from marginalized or vulnerable communities, their cases are even more likely to be overlooked. Without strong early coverage, a case can disappear from public conversation almost entirely, leaving victims and their families without justice for years.

With the serial offenders we studied, only a portion of their victims were identified and fully investigated. Some of the serial killers, such as Jerry Johns and Harry Edward Greenwell, were not even confirmed as serial killers until after their deaths. These individuals often lived long, full lives, while justice was delayed or never served for their victims. This lack of justice resulted from multiple barriers within the legal system during the 1980s and 1990s, including limited technology, poor documentation, and minimal empathy for vulnerable populations. Jurisdictional boundaries and poor communication between agencies also significantly hindered investigations. Different police departments operated under their own rules, often overlapping geographically, which led to fragmented case files and unresolved crimes.

Tennessee's location, with its numerous interstate highways and surrounding states, created advantages for mobile offenders. Criminals could travel freely, committing crimes in one location and leaving evidence in another. Coordinated efforts like the Redhead Murders Task Force, established in 1985, aimed to address this problem. Officials from multiple states met to discuss Tennessee cases, yet the task force ultimately produced inconclusive results. Despite these efforts, many cases remained unsolved for decades, highlighting a pattern of justice delayed or incomplete for victims, particularly those from vulnerable communities.

Many victims were also marginalized by societal biases and media portrayal. Women involved in sex work, for example, were often blamed for their circumstances and dismissed in reports and news coverage. Headlines such as "Prostitute Found Dead" reduced victims to stereotypes rather than acknowledging them as individuals with complex lives. Jeanne Gilbert and Margaret Gill, murdered on the same night but in different counties, were not connected by law enforcement due to poor interdepartmental communication. It was not until 2022 that genetic genealogy identified Harry Edward Greenwell as their killer, showing how delayed coordination can leave cases unresolved for decades.

Social services were limited in the 1980s, and few programs existed to assist women in crisis. Mental health care was underdeveloped, with outdated practices like shock therapy sometimes misused, causing additional harm. Bias in policing, particularly sexism and racism, often meant that victims who were poor, mentally ill, or involved in sex work were not prioritized. Some people at the time even suggested these victims "deserved" their fate, reflecting systemic prejudice that compounded the failure of justice.

Despite these challenges, persistence in investigations has produced results in recent years. Advances in DNA analysis and modern forensic techniques have identified victims decades later. Cold cases reopened through genetic genealogy, such as those linked to Warren Luther Alexander, demonstrate the importance of perseverance. Society must also address ongoing issues, including at-risk youth, addiction, and abuse, by providing support programs and ensuring accountability for offenders. Law enforcement agencies must maintain dedicated resources for missing persons and cold case investigations to prevent repeat patterns of neglect.

Communities themselves can play a role in protecting vulnerable populations. Local oversight, increased policing in high-risk areas, and enhanced security measures at truck stops and rest areas can help prevent crimes. Programs addressing homelessness, poverty, and substance abuse provide safer alternatives for people who might otherwise enter high-risk situations. Raising awareness about the experiences of vulnerable groups also reduces victim blaming, stereotyping, and bias, creating a culture in which justice can be more equitably served.

Institutions and correctional systems of the time also demonstrated major weaknesses. Some incarcerated individuals, like Samuel Little who was arrested dozens of times for violent offenses, were released prematurely, undermining containment, and rehabilitation efforts often failed, with offenders leaving institutions in worse condition than when they entered. Studying these patterns revealed how authority and responsibility were compromised. Decisions were frequently influenced by personal biases, rather than fairness or ethical standards, leaving victims and communities unprotected. Evidence and documentation were often inadequately maintained, further limiting the ability to achieve justice.

Through examining these failures, we recognized the importance of fairness, accountability, and impartiality. All people, regardless of background or circumstances, deserve equal protection under the law and a fair opportunity to receive justice. By studying these cases, we learned that systematic bias, institutional weaknesses, and social neglect can allow offenders to operate unchecked for years. Awareness, empathy, and persistent investigative efforts are crucial to preventing such injustices in the future.

Understanding these historical failures offers lessons for both society and law enforcement. It demonstrates that when vulnerable communities are overlooked and systemic gaps exist, crimes can remain unresolved for decades. Recognizing the importance of equitable treatment, robust social support, and diligent investigative practices ensures that victims are remembered and justice is not delayed. By reflecting on these patterns, we can work toward a safer society where offenders are held accountable, and the rights and dignity of all individuals are respected.

As we explored these historical failures, it became clear that understanding the past was not just an academic exercise; it was a call to action. Our research revealed the human stories behind the statistics, the victims whose lives were cut short, and the families who were left searching for answers. Investigating these cases challenged us as students to think critically, act responsibly, and approach each story with empathy and care. In the next section, we will share what our research uncovered, how it deepened our understanding of justice and social responsibility, and how this experience shaped us, not only as students but as people committed to making a difference in our communities.

5.

THE REFLECTION ON THE RESEARCH

We have always been fascinated by trying to understand the psychology behind why people commit serious crimes. What drives someone to hurt or kill another person, sometimes even someone they might care about, is something that is difficult to fully comprehend. It's a complex topic that can feel overwhelming, but it's also what drew us to this project in the first place.

What makes this work even more personal, and at times frightening, is realizing that some of these criminals lived in neighborhoods just like ours. It's terrifying to think that it could have been someone we know, or someone from our own families, who became a victim, and that their cases might never be solved. That sense of urgency and responsibility is what motivates us. There are so many unsolved cases where families are still searching for answers, and that drove us to take action rather than wait for someone else to step in.

Through this research, we also learned how important it is to learn from people with experience (seasoned detectives, forensic psychologists, and victims' families), because understanding the criminal mind requires insight beyond what we can learn from documents alone. Listening to experts and analyzing their perspectives has been crucial to developing our own understanding and will continue to guide us if we pursue this field in the future.

What surprised us most during our research was the patterns we began to see. Many victims were killed in similar ways and in similar places, and a large number of both victims and killers were connected to Tennessee. We were shocked to find that suspected victims were sometimes never fully investigated after a killer was arrested. For example, Sean Patrick Goble was convicted of four murders, but investigators suspected he may have killed up to 50 women based on items found in his home. After his imprisonment, many of these other potential victims were never fully investigated, and therefore many victims and their families were denied justice.

We also noticed recurring patterns among killers. Several were truck drivers who dumped bodies along highways or remote roads. Many victims were considered "high-risk," such as runaways or women involved in prostitution. This challenged a misconception that victims somehow bear responsibility for their circumstances. High-risk victims are still victims, and they deserve justice. Studying these cases helped us think more deeply about assumptions we often make about people based on limited information.

Researching these cases also changed how we view serial killers. We used to think of them as impulsive, uncontrollable, or easily recognizable. Now we understand that many appear normal, carefully plan their actions, and deliberately choose their victims. The case of Sean Patrick Goble, who reportedly gave items taken from his victims to family members for his own satisfaction, stood out to us as a chilling example of this calculated behavior.

Working as a class, we learned to dig deeper than the surface. Together, we analyzed thousands of documents, narrowed down essential information, and focused on facts that could be confirmed by reliable sources. This process strengthened our research and analytical skills, teaching us to form conclusions based on evidence rather than assumptions.

We also learned resilience. Plans to request public records were often denied or delayed, forcing us to seek alternative sources. These setbacks were frustrating, but they taught us persistence and creativity in problem-solving.

Speaking with a victim's family member was particularly powerful. Hearing firsthand the pain of losing a loved one and living without justice made the human cost of these crimes tangible. One statement that stayed with many of us was, *"I just wish she were here, so I could tell her I love her one last time."* Moments like that reminded us that our work represents real people and real families, and they inspired us to approach the project with seriousness and empathy.

This experience changed how we see others and how we understand human behavior. We began to put ourselves in the victims' shoes, imagining their experiences, fears, and struggles. Through their stories, we grew emotionally connected, caring deeply about what happened and feeling a strong responsibility to seek justice. We also realized that, as teenagers, we can accomplish meaningful work. This project helped us improve skills like public speaking, collaboration, and disciplined research, showing us that age does not define the impact we can have.

When people read our book, we hope they understand that teenagers can produce thoughtful, high-quality work for a meaningful cause. We want readers to recognize that victims are still waiting for justice decades later, not just in Tennessee but across the country. This book is a call to action: to inspire change, raise awareness, and encourage others (students, teachers, law enforcement, and communities) to continue searching for answers and supporting victims. Our work demonstrates that with dedication and care, even young people can make a lasting impact.

As we reflected on the victims, the killers, and the families affected, we began to see that these tragedies didn't happen in isolation. There were patterns, conditions, and social factors that made Tennessee particularly vulnerable to these crimes. Understanding these contributing elements became just as important as studying individual cases because they help explain why so many serial killers operated in the state and why some crimes went unnoticed for so long. In the next section, we will explore the five key factors that, together, created an environment where these tragedies could occur. By examining these influences, we hope to provide a clearer picture of the challenges investigators faced and the lessons that can help prevent similar patterns in the future.

SECTION II:

Why Were There So Many Serial Killers in Tennessee in the 1980s?

6.

THE GEOGRAPHY OF TENNESSEE

The geography of Tennessee appears to have played a significant role in the number of serial killers active in the state during the 1980s. During this time, Tennessee was undergoing major changes, shifting from predominantly rural areas to more urbanized cities across the state. Cities like Nashville and Memphis were growing at a rapid pace, which meant not only more residents but also more people involved in crime. This shift likely influenced serial activity by creating more industrial sites, factories, and job opportunities, while also increasing the number of potential victims. The growth of cities and the development of highways made it easier for mobile offenders to travel from city to city, targeting victims while remaining only a short drive away from rural areas and interstates.

One of the main factors in this topic is the dramatic transformation of Tennessee's landscape from rural to urban environments. For example, Nashville's population increased by over 300,000 people from 1970 to 1990, and Memphis grew by more than 150,000 residents during the same period. These numbers show how quickly the cities and surrounding areas expanded in size and population over just two decades. At the same time, truck stops in and around these large metropolitan areas became hubs for prostitution and other underground activities, bringing vulnerable people into concentrated urban areas. Nashville and Memphis also experienced extremely high rates of poverty and homelessness from the 1970s through the 1990s, which created additional risk for those living on the margins of society.

In the 1980s, people who were poor, transient, or socially marginalized (such as runaways, hitchhikers, sex workers, and low-income families) were especially at risk, not because of their personal choices, but because of systemic factors like the economy, highways, and social-service infrastructure. For example, cases like the Redhead Murders, including victims such as Michelle Inman and Lisa Nichols, show how vulnerable individuals were often left in isolated areas late at night, with few witnesses and little trust in law enforcement. Criminalization of sex work and drug use, combined with social stigma, created situations where predators could take advantage of these individuals with little fear of being caught.

During this time, the systems designed to protect people in Tennessee were often underfunded, poorly coordinated, and technologically limited. Police departments, social services, and communities struggled to share information, making it difficult to spot patterns across counties or even states. Many shelters and support programs for homeless or at-risk people were insufficient, leaving them exposed to danger. These conditions allowed serial killers easy access to both urban areas, where victims could be approached, and rural areas, where bodies could be disposed of with minimal chance of being seen. Tennessee's location also made it ideal for offenders to cross state lines; it borders eight other states, giving killers multiple escape routes, tied only with Missouri for number of states it borders with 8.

Research over the past few months highlights that most victims studied were taken from urban areas and murdered or abandoned in rural locations. For instance, Tina Farmer, killed by Jerry Johns, was abducted in Indianapolis, Indiana, and driven over 300 miles before being left in a remote part of Tennessee. Similarly, Lisa Nichols and Lorie Pennell, two suspected victims of Johns, were last seen at truck stops in West Memphis, Arkansas, yet both were later found a short distance into rural areas, one west and one south, demonstrating how killers used urban centers to access victims and rural areas to conceal their crimes.

Tennessee's geography, expanding cities, and growing interstate system in the 1980s created a landscape where social, economic, and infrastructural changes intersected with criminal opportunity. Vulnerable populations concentrated in urban centers and along highways, combined with gaps in law enforcement coordination and limited resources, allowed mobile offenders to exploit both urban interstates streets and rural highways. The patterns of travel, isolation, and access to victims shaped the behaviors of serial offenders in ways that were both unique to Tennessee and reflective of broader trends across the country. Understanding how geography and infrastructure influenced these crimes provides a foundation for examining the individuals themselves (the motivations, methods, and psychology of the offenders) which we will explore in the next chapter.[3]

---

3 Administration for Children and Families, US Department of Health and Human Services. "Runaway and Homeless Youth Act (RHYA) Legislative Timeline." *Administration for Children and Families*, accessed 4 Mar. 2026.

Burke, Minyvonne. "Teen Murder Victim Identified 41 Years Later." *NBC News*, 13 Oct. 2021.

"Distance Between Cities Places on Map, Distance Calculator." *DistanceFromTo*, www.distancefromto.net. Accessed 4 Mar. 2026.

McMahon, Becky. "The 'Redhead Murders' and the Quest to Find a Serial Killer Who Targeted Women Along the Highway." *A&E*, A&E Television Networks. Accessed 4 Mar. 2026.

"Nashville, Tennessee." *World Population Review*, worldpopulationreview.com/us-cities/tennessee/nashville. Accessed 4 Mar. 2026.

Watson, Nicole Elsasser. "Toward Implementation of a National Housing Insecurity Research Module." *Cityscape: A Journal of Policy Development and Research*, vol. 22, no. 1, US Department of Housing and Urban Development, Office of Policy Development and Research, 2019, pp. 277–96. Accessed 4 Mar. 2026.

7.

THE INTERSTATE HIGHWAY SYSTEM

The Interstate Highway System is one of the most important infrastructure networks in the United States, with more than 47,000 miles of interconnected highways that completely transformed how people and goods move across the country. Established in 1956, the system was designed to make travel and commerce faster and more efficient, but it also reshaped the patterns of where people lived, worked, and traveled. By connecting cities and rural areas alike, the highways allowed people to move more freely than ever, but they also unintentionally created opportunities for criminals who could exploit this mobility.

During the 1980s, Tennessee faced a turning point in how it managed its highways. Instead of focusing solely on expansion, the state prioritized repairing and updating older roadways that had fallen into serious disrepair. This effort came alongside growing concerns about traffic congestion and structurally deficient roads. Federal funding during this decade allowed Tennessee to modernize its highway system, while urban planners debated which routes should be prioritized to support new development. These changes affected not only traffic flow but also social patterns, including where people worked, lived, and traveled across the state.

The layout of Tennessee's highways during this period created conditions that could be exploited by mobile offenders. Interstate corridors like I-40, I-65, I-81, and I-75 became major transportation hubs, but they often lacked monitoring or oversight. The mix of heavy traffic, isolated stretches, and anonymous waypoints like truck stops and rest areas provided ideal locations for predators to select and approach victims. Because offenders could travel quickly across multiple counties or even states, law enforcement faced challenges in tracking criminal activity in a system that had no centralized databases or advanced forensic tools at the time.

Tennessee's geography made these risks even worse. The state's location at the crossroads of several major interstates meant thousands of transient travelers moved through relatively isolated areas every day. High traffic combined with geographic isolation created a "perfect storm" for criminal activity, especially in rest stops and roadside facilities, where law enforcement presence was limited and identifying offenders was difficult.

The 1980s also brought major construction projects and improvements to the interstate system, including the 1983 state route renumbering, completion of I-440 in Nashville in 1987, and the start of projects like I-840 and the Pellissippi Parkway to support suburban growth and events such as the 1982 Knoxville World's Fair. At the same time, Tennessee's economy was shifting, moving from a primarily rural, manufacturing-based state to a more industrial and technologically diverse economy. The population grew from 4.59 million in 1980 to 4.87 million by 1990, with high but slowly improving rates of poverty, the growth of the automobile industry, and new high-tech businesses moving into the state.

Truck stops along major routes became critical social and logistical hubs for long-haul drivers, and although hitchhiking declined due to safety fears, it remained a way for many travelers to get around. These locations also created opportunities for sex trafficking and other high-risk activities, particularly among vulnerable populations such as those experiencing homelessness, drug addiction, mental illness, or living with HIV/AIDS. The Motor

Carrier Act of 1980 increased trucking activity nationwide, raising the number of long-haul drivers from 1.368 million in 1980 to about 1.767 million by 1987 (a 29% increase in a decade). The combination of more highways, more truckers, and more people living on the margins meant offenders had access to a steady stream of potential victims along poorly supervised corridors.

Law enforcement in Tennessee during the 1980s was also working to catch up to these challenges. Police began using newer forensic technologies and community policing programs to improve investigations and build trust with neighborhoods. However, officers often struggled to connect with marginalized groups, like sex workers, who sometimes held critical information about crimes. Budget limitations and disorganized communication between different police departments made it even harder to track patterns across jurisdictions. Many cases were stalled or mishandled simply because investigative resources were limited, and key witnesses were reluctant to come forward.

Several factors combined to create the perfect environment for serial offenders. Expanding highways, vulnerable populations, and gaps in law enforcement all worked together in ways that made crime easier to commit and harder to solve. Long stretches of rural road allowed perpetrators to travel and hide criminal activity, while truck stops and rest areas became convenient locations to find victims. The increase in drug use and economic struggles in rural areas further exposed individuals to danger. These patterns show how infrastructure, social conditions, and crime can intersect, with highways serving both as a tool for economic growth and, unfortunately, as a network that predators could exploit.

The expansion of Tennessee's interstate system in the 1980s and 1990s, especially I-40, I-65, I-75, I-81, and I-24, reshaped not only economic activity but also patterns of serial criminal behavior. Truck stops and rest areas became loosely monitored spaces where strangers regularly interacted, giving mobile offenders opportunities to target victims. Vulnerable populations (including the homeless, those struggling with addiction or mental illness, and communities affected by HIV/AIDS) were often concentrated along these major highways, where social services were limited. Law enforcement faced challenges such as limited specialized resources, inconsistent coordination between agencies, and difficulty gaining trust from these communities. Altogether, these conditions allowed offenders to exploit Tennessee's highway system, reflecting broader patterns of serial crime during this era.[4]

4 Babor, Thomas F., et al. "Drug Policy and the Public Good: A Summary of the Evidence." *National Center for Biotechnology Information*, 2017.

Federal Highway Administration. "History of the Interstate Highway System." *US Department of Transportation*, Accessed 4 Mar. 2026.

Hardin Law, Matt. "Major Interstates in Tennessee." *Matt Hardin Law*. Accessed 4 Mar. 2026.

Kelling, George L., and James Q. Wilson. "Broken Windows Theory." *Encyclopaedia Britannica*. Accessed 4 Mar. 2026.

Nashville Metropolitan Planning Organization. *Regionalism: A Framework for the Future of Middle Tennessee.* Nashville.gov, 2025,

Tennessee Department of Mental Health and Substance Abuse Services. "Milestones – 1980s." *Tennessee Department of Mental Health and Substance Abuse Services*,

Tennessee Department of Transportation. *Tennessee Interstate System Booklet.* Tennessee Department of Transportation, 9 Mar. 2011,

US Government Accountability Office. "Drug Abuse: The Crack Cocaine Epidemic–Health Consequences and Treatment." GAO, 1989.

Werb, Dan, et al. "The Temporal Relationship Between Drug Supply Indicators: An Audit of International Government Surveillance Systems." *National Center for Biotechnology Information*, 2018.

8.

FRACTURES IN LAW ENFORCEMENT

During the late 1970s and 1980s, law enforcement in Tennessee faced many challenges when investigating violent crimes. Several serial offenders were active during this period, and many victims remained unidentified for years or even decades. Investigators had to work with limited technology, poor communication systems, and strict jurisdictional boundaries that separated police agencies from one another. These limitations often made it difficult to connect crimes or identify victims. While this section examines the broader challenges investigators faced across Tennessee and nearby states, the Redhead Murders will be used as one example that shows how these problems affected real cases.

Many murder investigations in Tennessee during this time, like the ones involving highly mobile long-haul serial killers, required cooperation between several law enforcement agencies. State police, local police departments, county sheriff's offices, and federal investigators often needed to work together when crimes crossed county or state lines. For example, a "Redhead Murders Task Force" meeting was held in early 1985, which brought together multiple investigative agencies connected to the Redhead Murders such as the Kentucky State Police, Arkansas State Police, West Virginia State Police, the Greene County Sheriff's Department, the Campbell County Sheriff's Department, the Tennessee Bureau of Investigation, the

Mississippi Bureau of Investigation, and the Federal Bureau of Investigation.

Despite the large number of agencies involved in cases like these, coordination was difficult. Departments often had different priorities, limited budgets, and different investigative strategies. As a result, multi-agency task forces were not always able to meet frequently or maintain long-term cooperation. The Redhead Murders Task Force, after most of the bodies stopped turning up beside the interstates in April 1985, never met again. For a group like this to be effective, it would have required many regularly scheduled meetings, follow up, communication, information sharing, etc. This never occurred in this case, and most other cases outside of Tennessee during this time period.

Funding was another major barrier to investigations during this period. Many police departments had limited budgets and could not dedicate large numbers of officers or resources to older or more complicated cases. In some cases, task forces were created but could not continue meeting because departments lacked the money to support ongoing investigations. The Redhead Murders Task Force could be an example. Travel from up to 10 hours away, hotel fees, and lost time at work, etc., were impossible to recoup on limited budgets of the time. Limited funding also meant fewer forensic tests (which were still very limited at the time), fewer investigators assigned to certain cases, and fewer opportunities for departments to share information with agencies in other states.

Another major challenge was jurisdiction. Law enforcement agencies generally only have authority within their own counties or states. When crimes crossed these boundaries, investigators had to rely on cooperation between departments. Before cell phones, the internet, and any help from the federal government and its policing programs (such as the Violent Criminal Apprehension Program), coordination was difficult, slow, and painstaking. Most agencies focused on their own cases and rarely even paid attention to other jurisdictions, even if they were only a few dozen miles away and separated by only an imaginary border.

This created confusion in many cases. Agencies sometimes disagreed about whether murders were connected, how many victims were involved, or which department should take the lead in the investigation. When victims were found in a different state from where they had lived or disappeared, identifying them became even more difficult. This is where the Highway Hunters of Tennessee were uniquely positioned. Because of their highly mobile travel patterns, they quickly acquired victims, drove to other jurisdictions, and dumped the bodies. The victims were often not identified for decades, giving law enforcement little investigative leads.

The Redhead Murders illustrate this problem clearly. Victims were discovered in several states including Tennessee, Kentucky, Arkansas, Mississippi, West Virginia, and Pennsylvania. Because each agency focused primarily on crimes within its own jurisdiction, important connections between cases were not always recognized immediately. Considering that the victims were often from a certain area, then became transient (because of addiction, hitchhiking, or the sex trade), were acquired by the killer, possibly killed in another location, and finally dumped in yet another, these cases were a knot of local, state, and even federal agencies, and law enforcement in the 1980s did not have the capacity to untangle the jurisdiction.

Another major barrier to solving crimes during the 1980s was limited forensic technology. Today investigators rely heavily on DNA testing, computerized databases, and digital communication. Many of these tools did not exist or were still developing during this time. For example, blood typing was one of the main forensic methods available. Blood typing could narrow down possible suspects but could not identify a specific individual. The other major forensic tool was finger printing. Some of the victims had minor run-ins with the law (usually over drug-related crimes or sex work), but most did not have criminal records, and therefore there were no fingerprints in the database. Considering that these women were left on the side of the road, there was a lack of items that usually yielded fingerprints of the offender, such as door handles, windows, and countertops (with one fantastic exception being when Sean Patrick Goble left a plastic grocery bag with a victim which yielded a finger print). The forensic technology just had not matured enough to allow highly mobile offenders and transient victims to be adequately tracked and identified. And with these needed technologies still developing, investigators often lacked the tools needed to link evidence between different crime scenes.

In 1985, the Federal Bureau of Investigation created the Violent Criminal Apprehension Program, known as ViCAP. This system collects information about violent crimes across the country and helps investigators identify patterns between cases. Before systems like ViCAP, detectives often had to compare cases manually. They relied on phone calls, mailed reports, or in-person meetings to share information with other departments. This made it much harder to identify connections between crimes that occurred in different counties or states. The development of centralized databases eventually improved how law enforcement agencies shared information and linked cases.

Many victims during this period came from vulnerable populations. Some were runaways, individuals experiencing homelessness, or women involved in prostitution. These individuals were often traveling or living in unstable situations, which made them easier targets for violent offenders. Unfortunately, victims from marginalized communities were sometimes given less attention by both law enforcement and the public. Police departments often had to prioritize cases based on available resources, and victims with strong community ties sometimes received more immediate attention. These biases meant that some victims remained unidentified for many years, and certain cases were not investigated as thoroughly as they might have been.

Highways also played a role in many cases during this time. Major interstate systems allowed offenders to travel quickly across long distances and between multiple states. This made it easier for perpetrators to avoid detection. Victims who were hitchhiking, traveling, or working near highways were especially vulnerable. In response to this pattern, the FBI later created the Highway Serial Killings Initiative as part of ViCAP. Since 2004, this program has connected more than 800 murders to long-haul truck drivers and other offenders who regularly travel long distances.

Despite these many obstacles, it would not be fair to say that law enforcement cooperation across many jurisdictions was not possible as we have clear examples from that era with other very complicated cases. The Green River Task Force in Washington State was a great example of how a case with many victims could be coordinated between multiple law enforcement agencies. The task force at its peak had over 50 full-time agents from five different agencies: King County, Kent County, Pierce County, the Washington State Police, and the FBI. The task force met daily with briefings every morning, and sometimes twice per day if information demanded it. The task force continued from 1984 to 2011 despite Gary Ridgeway's arrest in 2001. They showed that multiple counties could work with both state and federal law enforcement for over 25 years if needed. This is a small geographic area of crimes compared to the large expanse of states the Tennessee Highway Hunters were killing in; however, the sheer number of 49 confirmed victims and nearly 100 suspected is a tremendous number of crimes to be handled by one task force, which managed to keep track of over 40,000 leads all on paper.

When Leslie Mahaffy was abducted and murdered in June 1991, it was a tragedy. However, when Kristen French was abducted and murdered a few months later in April of 1992, the law enforcement of Ontario, Canada, quickly set up a task force to investigate the serial offenses against the girls of their province. Initially, the task force started with about 28 officers from the Niagara Regional Police Service and the Halton Regional Police Service, but as the investigation progressed, it expanded to include officers from up to 11 different police forces across Ontario. Even more agencies were brought on board to provide support resources and funding through the Criminal Intelligence Service of Ontario. More than a dozen agencies across two regions was impressive. They did only have a total of 5 cases that they investigated, eventually tying the original two together as being the victims of the same killers, Paul Bernardo and Karla Homolka.

The Green Ribbon Task Force lasted for three years and did many of the same things the Green River Killer Task Force did. They had daily strategy meetings at first and eventually tapered to several per week as leads trailed off. They also coordinated a bevy of experts including psychological profilers, geographic analysts, and behavioral scientists earlier than most US agencies did. They created a shared office space to streamline communications despite still using daily printed bulletin sheets, bulletin boards, and lead sheets. The victims were not nearly as numerous as the ones found in Tennessee in the 1980s and the region was not quite as large, but the task force handled very complicated multi-jurisdictional issues extremely effectively.

The other things that both of these task forces did was use the media effectively to disseminate information, solicit leads, and keep the cases in the public eye. Both groups had regular press conferences to release suspect sketches, urgent warnings, and request info all while being carefully controlled in their messaging and release of information to avoid helping the offenders. Although the Redhead Murders Task Force in Tennessee did take questions from reporters and several major news stories ran in the newspapers, they mostly said that the task force came to no conclusions on certain issues. Although controlling the narrative while also disseminating the proper information could be tricky, these other two task forces from that era show how it could be done effectively.

The Green Ribbon Task Force broke so much new ground that part of the subsequent public and legal response included the "Campbell Review." This was a formal review of investigative practices by Canadian authorities which examined how the task force and other agencies worked, communicated, and shared information. That review led to changes in how major investigations and serial cases are handled in Ontario, including better coordination and case management practices. There was a tremendous opportunity for Tennessee to take the lead in the US. However, due to certain decisions we will never know what could have been.

The Redhead Murders Task Force in Tennessee could have benefited greatly by implementing organizational strategies, communication practices, and media management techniques employed by the Green River and Green Ribbon Task Forces. Both of these task forces demonstrated the value of regular, structured meetings, dedicated multi-agency collaboration, and the inclusion of specialized experts, such as behavioral analysts and geographic profilers, to connect evidence and anticipate offender behavior. They also highlighted how a shared physical workspace and systematic documentation could streamline inter-agency coordination, even before the advent of modern digital databases. Moreover, these task forces effectively balanced public engagement with investigative security, using the media to solicit leads and maintain public awareness without compromising operational integrity. Had the Redhead Murders Task Force applied similar methods (establishing routine briefings, incorporating behavioral expertise, creating centralized communication hubs, and strategically managing media outreach), they might have been better equipped to track multi-state connections, prioritize leads, and prevent some of the critical gaps in their investigation that allowed offenders to remain at large for decades.

The investigations of violent crimes in Tennessee during the 1980s were shaped by many challenges. Limited forensic technology, poor communication between agencies, funding shortages, and jurisdictional boundaries all made it difficult to connect cases and identify victims. The Redhead Murders serve as one example of how these problems affected real investigations, but they were not the only cases impacted by these issues. Many victims across Tennessee and surrounding states experienced similar delays in identification and justice. Advances in forensic science, improved databases, and better cooperation between agencies have helped investigators reopen many cold cases in recent years. These improvements show how progress in technology and communication can eventually bring answers to cases that once seemed impossible to solve.

Although technology, funding, and jurisdictional barriers created serious obstacles for investigators, these were not the only factors that shaped how cases were handled. Social and economic conditions also influenced which victims received attention and which cases remained unsolved for years. Many victims during this time came from vulnerable backgrounds, including people experiencing poverty, homelessness, or unstable family situations. These circumstances often affected how quickly cases were investigated and how much public attention they received. Understanding these social and economic factors helps explain why some victims were overlooked and why justice was delayed in many cases. The next section examines how socioeconomic conditions influenced both victim vulnerability and the responses of law enforcement and society.

9.

DEPRESSED SOCIOECONOMIC FACTORS

This chapter examines the vulnerability of high-risk individuals in Tennessee during the 1980s, especially women involved in sex work, runaways, and those living in poverty, and the dangers they faced from predatory offenders. At the time, Tennessee was one of the poorest states in the United States, struggling with economic decline caused by widespread losses in manufacturing, high unemployment in urban centers like Nashville and Memphis, and persistent poverty in rural areas. Statewide poverty rates hovered around 18–20%, and housing and welfare options were extremely limited. Many people lacked family support, faced untreated addiction, or could not access shelters or outreach programs. Combined with the need to travel for work or survival, this left many vulnerable individuals mobile along highways, interstates, and truck stops, a situation that serial offenders could exploit repeatedly without being detected quickly.

Tennessee's unusually high number of serial offenders during this period can be explained by the intersection of socioeconomic instability, geographic mobility, and uneven law-enforcement resources. High poverty rates in both urban areas like Memphis and rural Appalachian counties created large populations vulnerable to predatory violence, particularly among unhoused individuals, sex workers, and low-wage service workers. These groups often lacked institutional protection, which meant missing-person reports were delayed and investigations were slower. Tennessee's position as a major transportation hub—where interstates like I-40, I-24, I-65, and I-75 converge—further increased risk by bringing transient workers, truck drivers, and travelers who could move anonymously across county and state lines. This mobility mirrored historical patterns, going back to the frontier era, when sparse settlements and limited policing allowed violent offenders to operate with minimal oversight. Modern law enforcement disparities, between under-resourced rural departments and larger urban forces, continued this pattern in the 1980s. Together, these socioeconomic pressures, mobility patterns, and structural gaps created conditions where serial offenders could target marginalized victims and avoid detection for long periods.

High-risk adults during the 1980s in Tennessee included runaways, sex workers, people struggling with addiction, and those without stable housing or family support. Many of these individuals worked alone at night or moved frequently from place to place, which left them more exposed to offenders traveling along the state's major highways. Poverty, limited healthcare, and weak social-service systems increased this vulnerability. Runaways and unhoused adults often relied on strangers for rides or shelter, while sex workers were often isolated in urban or semi-rural areas. Offenders could take advantage of these situations with little chance of being seen or caught.

The danger faced by these victims was the result of systemic failures rather than personal choices. Social-service agencies were underfunded and overwhelmed, and many families could not provide support, leaving individuals in crisis with no protection or early intervention. These gaps allowed serial offenders to operate with minimal risk of immediate detection. Female homicide victims in the United States between 1982 and 2000 were estimated to be around three times more likely to be involved in sex work (2.7% versus approximately 1%). In Tennessee, this percentage was likely higher due to the concentration of sex work along interstates and in urban centers. Many victims were older teens or young adults, with pimps often manipulating identification or paperwork to avoid legal consequences when young women were caught.

Many sex workers lived unstable lives, which made them even more vulnerable. Michelle Inman, for example had a difficult childhood; her mother probably struggled with mental health issues, sometimes leaving her in a difficult position, and her father served in the armed forces, often leaving Michelle and her sister unsupervised. She began using drugs and engaging in sex work at a young age. Pimps often exploited these vulnerabilities, placing women in high-risk areas along interstates and in urban centers. Tennessee's widespread poverty meant there were few safe spaces for sex workers, and many law enforcement officers treated victims harshly rather than protecting them. Victims were often blamed for their circumstances, which discouraged them from seeking help.

Cases such as Kelly Alsobrook's highlight this systemic failure. Alsobrook, who was gang-raped, avoided reporting the crime to police because officers often dismissed such complaints as "occupational hazards" and sometimes blamed victims. She is now an advocate for laws that protect victims of trafficking from being arrested for prostitution when reporting crimes. These experiences show how women in sex work were treated as criminals rather than victims, leaving them exposed to continued abuse.

Economic hardship, mental illness, and mobility further increased the risk for vulnerable populations. Poverty and unemployment pushed some individuals into sex work as a means of survival. Mental illness, poorly understood at the time, also left victims unstable and more susceptible to exploitation. Tennessee's location along major interstate corridors made it easier for offenders to travel between states, accessing victims along highways, rest stops, and truck stops. Victims such as Lorie Pennell, suspected in the Redhead Murders, were likely affected by mental health challenges that made them more vulnerable to predation.

The patterns of vulnerability among these populations explain why certain victims were repeatedly targeted. Unhoused women, those involved in sex work, and individuals living in poverty were less likely to be reported missing quickly, giving offenders more time to commit crimes undetected. Many offenders, including Samuel Little, Clark Perry Baldwin, Jerry Johns, and others, specifically targeted individuals without strong family connections or stable living situations. Crimes in low-income neighborhoods, rural communities, or military areas often went unnoticed for longer periods due to limited law-enforcement resources, staff, and technology.

Mobility played a key role in these crimes. Offenders frequently used Tennessee's interstate system, particularly I-40 and I-75, to travel across county and state lines. This made it difficult for law enforcement to connect related cases, especially when different agencies were involved. Cases spanning multiple states, like those of Harry Edward Greenwell, show how serial offenders could exploit gaps in coordination and evade detection.

Overall, the patterns seen in Tennessee show how larger social and economic conditions shaped serial homicide during the 1980s. Poverty, unstable housing, transient work, and gaps between urban and rural law enforcement created an environment where offenders could operate for long periods with minimal risk. These shared factors help explain why Tennessee experienced more serial offenders than might be expected for a state of its size and population.[5]

5 Alan, Charlotte. "The Happy Hooker?" *Publication Unknown*, 1 July 2004. Accessed 5 Mar. 2026.

Brewer, Devon D., Jonathan A. Dudek, John J. Potterat, Stephen Q. Muth, John M. Roberts Jr., and Donald E. Woodhouse. "Extent, Trends, and Perpetrators of Prostitution-Related Homicide in the United States." *Publication Unknown*, Sept. 2006. Accessed 5 Mar. 2026.

Catalo-Holmes, Anna. "Mental Health in Special Education: Comparing the 1970s to Today." *Publication Unknown*, 4 May 2018. Accessed 4 Mar. 2026.

Children of the Night. Website. Accessed 4 Mar. 2026.

Day, Sophie, and Helen Ward. "Violence Towards Female Prostitutes." *Publication Unknown*, 28 July 2001. Accessed 4 Mar. 2026.

Dudek, Jonathan Adam. "When Silenced Voices Speak: An Exploratory Study of Prostitute Homicide." *Publication Unknown*, Dec. 2002. Accessed 4 Mar. 2026.

EBSCO. *Drug and Alcohol Prevention Programs*.

Federal Bureau of Investigation. *Crime in the United States, 1980–1989*. Uniform Crime Reports, US Department of Justice.

National Center for Juvenile Justice. *Runaway Youth Trends in the 1980s*. NCJJ Research Bulletin, 1989.

National Institute of Justice. *Violent Crime and Vulnerable Populations*. NIJ Research Report, 1988.

Prostitute Homicides: A Descriptive Study. Publication Unknown, 2008. Accessed 4 Mar. 2026.

Southern Regional Council. *Poverty and Social Services in the Rural South*. Southern Regional Council Publications, 1984.

Stem, Scott W. "Rethinking Complicity in the Surveillance of Sex Workers: Policing and Prostitution in America's Model City." *Publication Unknown*, 2020. Accessed 4 Mar. 2026.

Tennessee Coalition to End Domestic & Sexual Violence. *Website*. Accessed 4 Mar. 2026.

Tennessee Department of Human Services. *Child Welfare Annual Report, 1982–1989*. State of Tennessee, Department of Human Services.

Tennessee Valley Authority. *Website*. Accessed 4 Mar. 2026.

US Children's Bureau. *National Study of Protective, Preventive, and Reunification Services*. US Department of Health and Human Services, 1987.

US Department of Justice. *Missing Children: Rhetoric and Reality*. Office of Juvenile Justice and Delinquency Prevention, 1985.

US Department of Justice, National Center for Juvenile Justice, FBI Behavioral Science Unit, and National Institute of Justice. *Reports on Juvenile Justice and Crime*.

University of Wisconsin-Madison Institute for Research on Poverty. *Publication Unknown*. Spring 1991. Accessed 5 Mar. 2026.

Wadhwani, Anita. "Tennessee Bill Would Protect Victims of Sex Trafficking from Arrest After Reporting Crimes." *Publication Unknown*, 23 Feb. 2023. Accessed 4 Mar. 2026.

10.

CHANGES IN THE TRUCKING INDUSTRY

Tennessee's highways in the 1980s were more than just roads connecting cities; they were lifelines for commerce, travel, and industry, but they also created unique risks for vulnerable populations. Highways like Interstates 40, 24, 65, and 75 carried thousands of transient workers, truckers, and travelers through the state every day, often passing through rural areas with little oversight or law enforcement presence. For people already at risk like runaways, sex workers, and the transient, these roads were not just paths to opportunity but also corridors of danger. The growth of trucking and trade hubs, combined with limited social services and under-resourced police departments, created the conditions that mobile offenders could exploit, making highways central to understanding Tennessee's unusually high rate of serial criminal activity during this period.

The passage of the Motor Carrier Act of 1980 transformed the trucking industry by reducing federal oversight and opening the field to a much larger number of drivers and smaller companies. Before the Act, trucking was dominated by large, union-run firms that required strict paperwork, schedules, and compliance with regulations (conditions that often discouraged individuals with antisocial or impulsive tendencies from entering the profession). By lowering these barriers, the industry allowed more independent operators and smaller companies to emerge, creating an environment with minimal oversight, fewer expectations, and limited accountability. For individuals with sociopathic or psychopathic traits, this deregulated system provided an unusual opportunity: the ability to move freely, manage their own schedules, and succeed in a profession where high-pressure rules and scrutiny were no longer a barrier.

As more drivers entered the industry, the sheer number of truckers increased the statistical likelihood that a small percentage might have violent tendencies. Long-haul routes, combined with minimal monitoring and self-managed records, meant offenders could travel hundreds of miles in a short period, exploiting the system's flexibility while avoiding detection. Deregulation not only expanded the number of trucking routes but also created a workforce with higher mobility, anonymity, and access to both urban centers and isolated rural areas; perfect conditions for mobile offenders to operate across Tennessee and beyond.

Truck stops along Tennessee's major interstates offered convenient but largely unsupervised locations for rest, refueling, and food. Many of these stops had only a few employees and limited or no camera surveillance, allowing drivers to remain anonymous while moving across state lines. Although only a small fraction of truckers engaged in violent crime, the growing number of drivers increased the likelihood that offenders could exploit their profession to commit murders without immediate detection. Trucking routes connected urban hubs with rural areas, creating opportunities to operate in places with few witnesses or law enforcement presence.

During the 1980s, Tennessee's busiest highways (Interstates 40, 24, 65, and 75) became vital corridors for freight and travel. Truck stops along these routes, such as those near Murfreesboro, Lebanon, and Knoxville, served as essential infrastructure for long-haul drivers moving goods across the Southeast. Pilot Corporation, founded in Knoxville, expanded multiple locations along I-40 and I-75, providing drivers with reliable stopping points for food, repairs, and rest. These interstates not only supported commerce but also enabled criminals to travel efficiently between urban centers and rural regions, giving offenders easy access to potential victims.

The state's economic and geographic contrasts also shaped these dynamics. Cities like Nashville, Memphis, and Knoxville experienced rapid growth, fueled by manufacturing, shipping, and distribution industries, while rural counties faced declining agricultural and industrial jobs. This urban-rural divide created vulnerable populations in both settings: transient workers, runaways, and individuals involved in the sex trade often relied on highways and truck stops to move, seek work, or find shelter. The mobility of both drivers and victims combined with sparse monitoring made Tennessee's highways ideal hunting grounds for offenders.

Financial pressures and broader social conditions further contributed to risk. Trucking became highly competitive after deregulation, lowering wages and increasing stress on drivers. Rising fuel costs and the growth of the War on Drugs shifted law enforcement priorities, leaving limited attention for safety at truck stops or protection for high-risk individuals. Vulnerable populations (especially women involved in sex work, runaways, and the transient) often faced systemic neglect, making them accessible targets.

Another factor potentially contributing to aggressive behavior among long-haul drivers was exposure to leaded gasoline, which was widely used from the 1920s through the 1980s. Leaded fuel can cause neurological damage over time, including mood disorders, aggression, and cognitive deficits, particularly in individuals exposed as children and then again as adults. Given the hours truckers spent on the road inhaling exhaust from leaded fuel, prolonged exposure could have contributed to hostility and violent tendencies. The phase-out of leaded gasoline began in 1973, and most vehicles switched to unleaded fuel by the mid-1980s, with a complete ban in 1996.

Overall, the combination of deregulated trucking, high-traffic trade hubs, minimally monitored truck stops, economic pressures, and long-term environmental exposures created a uniquely dangerous environment. These factors allowed mobile offenders to exploit both infrastructure and vulnerable populations with minimal risk of detection. Tennessee's highways, while crucial for commerce, also facilitated the movement of offenders and made the state a hotspot for serial criminal activity during this period.

With these conditions in mind, it becomes easier to understand how individual offenders were able to operate undetected for so long. Each of the killers we studied exploited the same highways, truck stops, and patterns of movement, but their methods and motivations varied. By examining their specific actions, we can see how the broader environment intersected with personal choices and psychological factors to produce tragic outcomes. In the following sections, we will explore the stories of these offenders, the victims they targeted, and the patterns that connect them, providing insight into both the human and systemic aspects of these crimes.[6]

---

6 "Community Policing in the 21st Century: A Framework for Measuring Performance." *Manhattan Institute*.

"Decades of Leaded Gasoline Tied to US Mental Health Crisis." *Psychiatrist.com*.

Ellig, Jerry. *The Regulatory Review: 40 Years After Surface Freight Deregulation*. The Regulatory Review.

"Final Use of Leaded Gasoline in the World." *NPR: All Things Considered*, Camila Domonoske, 30 Aug. 2021.

"Lead Exposure: Symptoms and Complications." *Centers for Disease Control and Prevention*.

Makuto, Nyasha, et al. "Factors Associated with Depressive Symptoms in Long-Haul Truck Drivers." *ScienceDirect*, September 2023.

"Why Do We Have a Truck Driver Shortage?" *RelayPayments.com*.

SECTION III:

The Highway Hunters of Tennessee

11:

WARREN LUTHER ALEXANDER: CONFIRMED SERIAL KILLER

SUMMARY

Warren Luther Alexander was born on November 12, 1951, to Hazel Inez Alexander and Luther D. Alexander. His mother, Hazel, was born on September 27, 1930, in Mackeys, North Carolina, and later built a career as a civil servant for the US Navy. His father remained a more distant and less clearly understood figure in Warren's life. Warren was the second eldest child and the oldest son among six siblings. During his childhood, the family eventually relocated to Oxnard, California, where Warren spent much of his formative years during the 1950s and 1960s. A photograph used in research materials typically depicts him later in life, reflecting the period when he became associated with the crimes under investigation.

The most serious allegations against Warren Alexander stem from crimes that occurred in California during the late 1970s. Investigators have connected him to three confirmed murders that took place in 1977 in the Ventura County area. The victims were Kimberly Fritz, who was 18 years old, Velvet Sanchez, who was 31, and Lorraine Rodriguez, who was 21. All three women died by strangulation. Authorities have also considered Alexander a suspect in at least one additional homicide, that of Nona Cobbs in North Carolina. The crimes attributed to Alexander involve murder and sexual assault, and law enforcement has described the California cases as part of an enhanced multiple-murder investigation. Although the murders occurred decades earlier, charges were formally brought many years later as investigators revisited cold cases using modern forensic methods.

Investigators believe that Alexander's crimes followed a consistent behavioral pattern centered around the targeting of women. The confirmed victims were adult women ranging from their late teens to early 30s, suggesting a victim profile focused on young women who may have been vulnerable in public settings. The murders occurred in California, particularly around Ventura County, which served as the geographic area where Alexander was known to live and work during the 1970s. While detailed behavioral signatures remain under investigation, the known cases involve strangulation and sexual assault, indicating a violent and personal method of killing. His career as a long-haul truck driver may also have allowed him to move frequently and travel long distances, potentially providing opportunities to encounter victims in different locations.

Alexander's early life appeared outwardly stable and typical. After growing up in Oxnard, California, he attended local schools before his family relocated to Long Beach following his sophomore year of high school. He graduated from Long Beach High School in 1969. During his youth he enjoyed playing baseball and showed no outward signs of violent or antisocial behavior that people around him could identify. Following graduation, Alexander joined the US Marine Corps, serving as an electrician from 1969 to 1970. After completing his military service, he worked briefly as a taxi driver before becoming a long-haul truck driver in the 1970s or early 1980s, a profession that required him to travel extensively across the United States.

Over time, Alexander appeared to establish what many observers considered a normal adult life. He married Marca Lyda Boyer and fathered at least one child. While trucking remained his primary profession, he may have explored other business ventures, including possible work related to real estate photography. Later in life he relocated to Diamondhead, Mississippi, in 2005, where he lived quietly and accumulated several property investments, including residential land and other real estate holdings. Despite appearing outwardly stable, his earlier criminal record included minor legal incidents, such as traffic violations and a juvenile offense involving the theft and crash of a car at age 15.

Alexander's legal troubles resurfaced decades after the murders when authorities began reexamining older homicide cases. In March 2022, he was arrested in St. Tammany Parish, Louisiana, on an unrelated charge, and the following day another incident involving him was recorded in Hancock County, Mississippi. The situation escalated in April 2024 when he was charged with a felony related to extradition as a fugitive from another state in connection with crimes that allegedly occurred many years earlier. On August 6, 2024, Alexander was arrested again and brought to court to face charges connected to the 1977 murders of Kimberly Fritz, Velvet Sanchez, and Lorraine Rodriguez in California.

Today, Warren Luther Alexander, now in his 70s, faces three counts of murder linked to those strangulation deaths. He has entered a plea of not guilty. Investigators also continue examining whether he may be responsible for additional killings, including the death of Nona Cobbs in North Carolina. The legal proceedings related to the California murders and any potential additional cases remain ongoing as the justice system continues to review evidence gathered from crimes that occurred nearly five decades earlier.

VICTIMS

CONFIRMED

Kimberly Carol Fritz

On the morning of May 29, 1977, a young woman's body was discovered in the small town of Port Hueneme, California. Kimberly Carol Fritz, 18, was found inside a room at Marv Inn, located at 645 E Port Hueneme Road, naked and strangled with panty hose. Fritz lived a nomadic lifestyle moving from state to state, a known runaway. Authorities later discovered she had up to 12 fake identities, one of which claimed she was 21 years of age. This could indicate she is not a recent runaway. One identity led her to Port Hueneme with the job of a sex worker at the Plaza Marina Shopping Center.

Lorraine Ann Rodriguez

On December 27, 1977, a grim discovery was made. Along a quiet sketch of Laguna Road in Ventura County, California, the body of a 21-year-old woman was discarded on a bridge. Lorraine Ann Rodriguez had been strangled by her panty hose and dumped from a vehicle to be left in the cold. Her case became one of the many women who were so wrongly mistreated. Her name faded from public view, but she was more than a girl in sex work leading to murder. She was a mother of two children. She turned to sex work as a means of survival. The choice was dictated by a desperate need to provide for her children. Lorraine lived in a Villa Motor court motel prior to the tragedy, where another woman with a similar fate to hers had lived previously.

Velvet Ann Sanchez

On September 8, 1977, Velvet Ann Sanchez was found in Oxnard California in a Villa Motor hotel room strangled by her own bra. She lived in the Villa Motor court motel for about a month leading up to her death. She created a life for herself during the 1950s-1960s with a home in Ventura County. She was a wife and mother until life took a different turn, and for unknown reasons, she and her husband were separated by 1977. She had previously worked as a clerk typist for Port Hueneme Construction Battalion Center before she turned to sex work.

Nona Kay Stamey Cobb

Nona Kay Stamey Cobb was born on November 16, 1962, in Lincoln County, North Carolina. Her life was marked by both personal struggles and love for her family. At 29 years old, Cobb's life was tragically cut short. On July 7, 1992, her body was discovered by a truck driver at approximately 6:15 a.m. on the northbound side of Interstate 77, near Elkin, in Surry County, North Carolina. Prior to her death, Cobb had been seen at a rest area on Interstate 85 in Cleveland County, where she was reportedly seen getting into a tractor-trailer with a man. This man, identified as 41-year-old Alexander, became a key figure in the investigation into her death. Despite the circumstances, Cobb's tragic end remains surrounded by mystery, with her death being classified as a homicide.

In the months leading up to her death, Cobb had faced significant personal difficulties. She had struggled with substance abuse, which had led to the loss of custody of her 3-year-old son, Josh, about 7 months before her untimely passing. This loss weighed heavily on her, and despite her challenges, Cobb's love for her son and her family was undeniable. Her sister, Vickie S. Gregory, shared that Cobb had a deep love for her family, especially her son. Although Cobb had made mistakes and struggled with addiction, her family remained close and held onto the positive memories of their relationship.

Cobb's tragic passing led to a criminal investigation, which included the collection of semen from her body for DNA testing. Her case remained an open mystery for years, as investigators worked to piece together the circumstances surrounding her death. In the years following her passing, Cobb was buried in Mountain Rest Cemetery in Kings Mountain, Cleveland County, North Carolina.

SUSPECTED

Cassandra Lee Miller

Cassandra Lee Miller, who was found dead Oct. 1, 1975, at the Surfside Motel in Port Hueneme, was a known sex worker. She was strangled with her pantyhose and was found dead on her bed in the hotel. Not many details have been released about this murder, but many in law enforcement believe this crime was committed by Alexander as well.

TIMELINE

9/29/1922	Luther Dallas Alexander, Warren Luther's father, is born to James Dallas and Ethel Harrison Alexander Cockerel (location unknown).
9/27/1930	Hazel Inez Hardison (later Hazel Inez Alexander), Warren Luther's mother, is born to Lucy Isolind Twiddy Hardison and Church Warren Hardison in Mackeys, N.C.
1/12/1951	Warren Luther Alexander is born to Luther Dallas Alexander and Hazel Inez Hardison-Alexander, most likely in or near Oxnard, Calif.
6/12/1958	Kimberly Carol Fritz is born on June 12, 1958, in Ann Arbor, Michigan, to Dean Reuben Fritz and Carolyn Marie Fritz.

8/??/1958 Marca Lyda Boyer, Alexander's wife, is born.

??/??/1959 Warren is known to be in Oxnard, Calif.

11/16/1962 Nona Kay Stamey Cobb is born to parents James Stamey and Allie Lee Dellinger Stamey in Lincoln County, N.C.

??/??/1967 Warren leaves Oxnard, Calif.

??/??/1967 Warren arrives in Long Beach, Mississippi.

??/??/1968 Warren is in Gulfport, Mississippi (went back and forth between Gulfport and Long Beach for the next year).

5/??/1969 Warren Luther Alexander graduates high school from Long Beach High School in Long Beach, Mississippi.

??/??/1969 Sometime after his high school graduation, it is known that Warren left Mississippi.

??/??/1969 Warren is seen in Parris Island, Jacksonville, and Camp Lejeune, North Carolina, during this time period.

??/??/1970 Warren still remains in N.C., going between Parris Island, Jacksonville, and Camp Lejeune.

1969–1970 Warren Luther Alexander serves as an electrician for the US Marine Corps.

??/??/1970	Warren Luther Alexander works as a taxi driver (most likely in Oxnard, Calif.).
??/??/1970	Warren travels over to Iwakuni, Japan.
??/??/1971	Warren travels to Las Vegas, Nevada.
??/??/1973	Warren goes to Anaheim, Calif.
??/??/1973	Warren is in Oxnard, Calif.
??/??/1974	Warren is in Pendleton, Calif.
??/??/1975	Warren goes back to Oxnard Calif.
10/01/1975	Cassandra Lee Miller's body is found at Surfside Motel, Port Hueneme, Calif.
5/28/1977	Kimberly Carol Fritz's body is found completely nude, strangled with her own stockings in Port Hueneme, Calif.
9/08/1977	Velvet Ann Sanchez is found dead at the Villa Motor court motel in Oxnard, Calif.
12/27/1977	Lorraine Rodriguez's body is discovered on a bridge on Laguna Road in unincorporated Ventura County. She was strangled with her bra.
??/??/1978	Warren is in Oxnard, Calif.

??/??/1980 Warren Luther Alexander starts truck driving.

??/??/1981 Warren leaves Oxnard, Calif.

??/??/1982 Warren goes to Long Beach, Mississippi.

??/??/1983 Warren leaves Long Beach, Mississippi.

??/??/1984 Warren goes to Pensacola, Florida.

7/03/1986 Luther Dallas Alexander, Warren Luther Alexander's father, dies (location unknown).

??/??/1988 Warren is in Long Beach, Mississippi.

??/??1990 Warren and his wife divorce.

??/??/1990 Warren is in Medina, Ohio.

??/??/1991 Warren goes to Saint Tammany, Louisiana.

??/??/1992 Warren goes to Pershing County, Nevada.

1/02/1992 Crystal Sedam is found deceased on the northbound entrance ramp off I-69 in Muncie, Indiana. Sedam, a known sex worker, was partially dressed in one pink sock, and her bra had been pushed up above her breasts. She had been strangled with a small rope or cord. She was last seen two days prior at a truck stop in Indianapolis, Indiana, which is approximately 70 miles from where her body was recovered. Alexander is considered a strong suspect in this case.

??/??/1992 Warren is in Long Beach, Mississippi.

??/??/1992 Warren is in Pontiac, Illinois.

7/07/1992 Nona Kay Stamey Cobb is found dead by a truck driver at approximately 6:15 a.m. in Surry County, N.C.

??/??/1992 Nona Kay Stamey Cobb's sister, Vickie S. Gregory, reportedly told the *Journal* that Cobb had been struggling with a drug problem at the time of her death, but loved her family, especially her 3-year-old son, Josh.

??/??1992 Warren stops truck driving around this time.

??/??/1992 Warren is in Indianapolis, Indiana.

??/??/1994 Warren is in Suitland, Maryland.

??/??/1995 Theories about connections between Sean Goble and Warren Luther Alexander begin after Sean Goble confesses to the murders of Brenda Kay Hagy, 45; Sherry Tew Mansur, 34; and Alice Rebecca Hanes, 36. According to a 1995 article from the *Virginian-Pilot*. Goble, of Asheboro, N.C., targeted sex workers and transported them over state lines before dumping their bodies on varying interstates.

??/??/1995 Warren returns to Gulfport/Long Beach, Mississippi.

??/??/2002 Warren leaves Long Beach, Mississippi.

10/15/2007 Hazel Inez Hardison Alexander, Warren's mother, dies in Long Beach, Calif.

??/??/2007 Warren is in Lucas, Ohio.

??/??/2010 Warren is in Harrison County, Mississippi.

??/??/2011 Warren Luther Alexander writes a letter to the editor published in the *Sun Herald* under his name. In this letter, Alexander railed against what he called the "political correctness" of the NBC television network and worried that liberal forces would threaten Christianity.

??/??/2015 Warren is in Hancock County, Mississippi.

??/??/2016 Warren is in Diamondhead, Mississippi.

4/??/2021 "Special agents from the SBI's (State Bureau of Investigation in North Carolina) Cold Case Investigation Unit and investigators from the Surry County Sheriff's Office returned to the physical evidence in the case, which was reexamined to include DNA." (According to the State Bureau) "While working with Dr. Colleen Fitzpatrick, founder of Identifiers International LLC, agents were able to identify Warren Luther Alexander as a possible suspect in Cobb's murder using DNA." (According to the State Bureau)

??/??/2022 Warren leaves Diamondhead, Mississippi.

2/??/2023 The Ventura County Sheriff's Department's cold case unit revisits the 1977 murders of Fritz, Sanchez, and Rodriguez after Warren is arrested. DNA evidence from the crime scenes is reprocessed and matched to Alexander's profile in CODIS, linking him to these California murders.

3/15/2022 Advancements in DNA technology leads to the arrest of Warren Luther Alexander, then 73, in Diamondhead, Mississippi, for the 1992 murder of Nona Cobb. His DNA is subsequently entered into the Combined DNA Index System (CODIS).

1/21/2024 Alexander appears in Courtroom 12 behind bars on Tues day, Jan. 21, for his information arraignment, where he again enters a plea of not guilty, denies all priors and special allegations related to the case, and where the Public Defender's Office is reappointed.

8/06/2024 Alexander is extradited from Surry County, N.C., to Ventura County, Calif.

10/08/2024 Warren Luther Alexander is charged with three first-degree murders of Kimberly Carol Fritz, Velvet Ann Sanchez, and Lorraine Ann Rodriguez. Authorities announce the possibility of additional victims due to his extensive travel history as a truck driver.

10/18/2024 Suspected Ventura County serial killer Warren Luther Alexander, 73, is scheduled to stand trial for three cold-case murders from 1977, following a ruling by Judge Paul Feldman during a preliminary hearing on Friday, Oct. 18.

11/01/2024 Alexander is scheduled for an information arraignment in Ventura County, Calif, which was supposed to provide a trial date within 60 days of the arraignment.

2/18/2025 Alexander has a jury trial date set for Feb. 18 at 8:30 a.m. in Courtroom 14 at the Ventura County Government Center.

3/17/2025 Warren Luther Alexander's trial is moved from February to March 17.

3/26/2025 Despite a jury trial date set for March 17, 2025, Alexander must wait until May due to a motion filed by the District Attorney's Office requesting to add a criminal protective order, which is intended to protect a victim or witness from harm, threats, or harassment by the defendant.

MODUS OPERANDI (MO)

(Latin for "way of operating")

The confirmed murders attributed to Warren Luther Alexander occurred in 1977 within Ventura County, Calif. Known incidents took place on May 29, Sept. 8, and Dec. 27 of that year, indicating that the offender was active over several months rather than in a short, concentrated spree. The spacing between attacks suggests intermittent offending, consistent with someone maintaining conventional routines while acting opportunistically.

While the exact time of day for each murder is not fully documented, contextual evidence indicates that at least two of the crimes occurred in motel rooms, environments typically associated with nighttime activity and reduced observation. The third victim was discovered outdoors after being transported from the original scene, suggesting that Alexander may have chosen low-visibility periods for both the offense and disposal. The timing appears driven by victim isolation and opportunity rather than strict scheduling.

Overall, the temporal pattern reflects an offender capable of patience, willing to wait for favorable conditions and acting when the likelihood of detection is minimized. The spacing between attacks and variation in environments demonstrates situational awareness rather than impulsivity.

Alexander's known crimes occurred within Ventura County, particularly in Oxnard and Port Hueneme, Calif. The offender targeted locations that combined accessibility with relative privacy, including motels and isolated roadways. These environments offered transient populations and limited surveillance, allowing him to operate without attracting attention.

Two victims were discovered inside motel rooms, which provided immediate privacy and minimal oversight from staff or the public. Another victim was discarded along Laguna Road after being transported from the original scene, demonstrating the offender's comfort with both indoor and outdoor environments. This pattern indicates familiarity with the geographic area and the ability to exploit spaces where victims could be isolated quickly.

The geographic clustering of crimes suggests that Alexander operated within areas he knew well, selecting locations that balanced accessibility and control. Vehicle access and proximity to roadways likely influenced site selection, enabling both rapid approach and efficient escape.

Alexander appears to have accessed victims through direct personal contact rather than deception or forced entry. Many victims were transient, involved in sex work, or otherwise vulnerable, which allowed him to gain proximity without raising immediate suspicion. Motels and other transitional spaces provided a context in which strangers could enter private areas without attracting attention.

Control over victims was achieved primarily through close physical dominance, consistent with the use of ligature strangulation. Once contact was established, Alexander appears to have restrained victims efficiently, reducing resistance and maintaining authority without relying on firearms or other weapons at the initial approach.

Exit strategies involved leaving the scene quickly and deliberately, often using a vehicle. Transporting victims or disposing of bodies in remote areas allowed him to distance himself from the crime scene before discovery. These departures reflect careful planning and situational awareness rather than chaotic flight.

The primary method of killing in Alexander's early California murders was ligature strangulation using items belonging to the victims, such as pantyhose or a bra. This indicates opportunistic use of available materials, allowing him to maintain control without carrying a weapon that could connect him to the crime. The consistency of this method across multiple incidents demonstrates both familiarity and confidence with physical domination as a killing technique.

Across all cases, the use of ligatures demonstrates both adaptability and a preference for personal, hands-on methods of killing. The evolution from opportunistic improvisation to deliberate preparation highlights an offender learning from experience while retaining his primary technique.

Victim interaction in Alexander's crimes involved initial social engagement, often facilitated by the victims' transient lifestyles or involvement in sex work. This allowed him to gain proximity without alarming them immediately. Victims were typically adult women in their late teens to early 30s, many of whom faced economic or personal vulnerability, making them more accessible targets.

Once contact was established, Alexander exerted physical control efficiently, using strangulation to incapacitate victims quickly. Interaction was brief and focused, with minimal conversation or hesitation once the assault began. The consistency of his method indicates a practiced approach to controlling victims and managing compliance during the attack.

The interaction patterns reflect calculated, task-focused behavior rather than emotional engagement, emphasizing domination and the offender's ability to maintain authority without unnecessary escalation.

Alexander's escape methods relied heavily on vehicular mobility and knowledge of local roads. In some cases, he transported victims or bodies to secondary locations, allowing for disposal in areas with minimal likelihood of immediate discovery. This strategy demonstrates planning and familiarity with both the environment and transportation routes.

There is no evidence that the offender remained at crime scenes longer than necessary. Quick departures and calculated use of vehicles suggest confidence and situational awareness, enabling him to avoid detection by bystanders or authorities. The escape pattern remained consistent across incidents, highlighting an offender experienced in leaving scenes efficiently.

Across his known offenses, Warren Luther Alexander demonstrates a combination of patience, situational awareness, and adaptability. His method evolved over time, shifting from opportunistic use of victim-provided ligatures to carrying prepared tools, reflecting increased premeditation and efficiency. Victims were selected based on accessibility and vulnerability, with crimes occurring in locations that balanced isolation and mobility. Interaction was brief and focused on control, while exits were deliberate and facilitated by vehicular access. Collectively, these patterns suggest an offender capable of maintaining a conventional life while exploiting opportunity, demonstrating both calculated planning and experiential learning in the execution of his crimes.

SIGNATURE

Signature Statement

The unsub demonstrates a repeated need for control, both physical and psychological, often exercised through manipulation of vulnerable women and careful orchestration of his offenses over time. His signature reflects an emphasis on domination, exploitation of situational opportunity, and the ritualized use of ligature strangulation, which evolved from improvised items to prepared tools. Emotional reinforcement appears to derive from exerting authority over victims, orchestrating undetected crimes, and maintaining anonymity while exercising premeditated influence, rather than from the acts themselves alone.

Narrative

Warren Luther Alexander demonstrates a consistent behavioral pattern that extends beyond the immediate requirements of committing murder. Across multiple decades, his offenses exhibit repeated use of strangulation with ligatures—initially improvised from victim garments, later brought intentionally—highlighting the ritualized nature of the killing process. The repeated selection of vulnerable women, often involved in sex work or transient lifestyles, and the consistent targeting of motel or roadside environments, reflects an offender who seeks control over both victims and the situational context of the crime.

These rituals fulfill specific psychological and emotional needs. By choosing victims whose circumstances allowed him to dominate easily, Alexander appears motivated by the maintenance of physical authority and the anticipation of compliance. The evolution of his method, from opportunistic use of clothing to prepared ligatures, demonstrates adaptive learning and a desire to increase efficacy while reducing risk, suggesting an organized and deliberate offender. Emotional reinforcement likely arises from the sense of mastery, the control over life and death decisions, and the ability to evade detection for extended periods.

From these patterns, probabilistic personality traits can be inferred. Alexander exhibits characteristics of an organized offender, shown through premeditation, spatial awareness, and the capacity to travel extensively while remaining undetected. His behavioral consistency over decades indicates patience and planning, while the occasional long intervals between known offenses suggest calculated restraint rather than impulsive aggression. The repeated selection of vulnerable targets and ritualized killing methods point to manipulative tendencies and a focus on exercising power over those less capable of resistance.

Environmental context further shapes his signature. Motels, transient housing, and isolated roadways provided anonymity, opportunities for prolonged control, and environments where victims could be isolated without attracting attention. His experience as a long-haul truck driver offered both mobility and familiarity with highways, allowing him to navigate across state lines while preserving secrecy. These environmental factors, coupled with the victim selection and ritualized methods, reinforce the offender's sense of control and mastery over both the physical and social contexts of his crimes.[7]

---

7 Gillies, Andrew. *Mississippi Man to Face Trial for Three 1977 Cold Case Murders in Ventura County. KEYT Hancock County Jail*, 21 Oct. 2024.

KCLU. *Prosecutors Say He Killed at Least Three Women in Ventura County, and There May Be More Victims. KCLU Local News*, 9 Aug. 2024.

Orozco, Lance. *Man Charged With Trio of 1970s Murders in Ventura County Pleads Not Guilty to Killings. KCLU*, 21 Aug. 2024.

Suspected Serial Killer Charged With 1977 Murders. Forensic Magazine, 12 Aug. 2024, www.forensicmag.com/3594-All-News/614479-Suspected-Serial-Killer-Charged-with-1977-Murders/.

Suspected Serial Killer Charged With 1977 Murders – Ventura County District Attorney. Ventura County DA, 7 Aug. 2024, da.venturacounty.gov.

Three Women Were Found Strangled in California. Four Decades Later Police Arrest Suspected Serial Killer. The Independent, 8 Aug. 2024.

12:

SEDLEY ALLEY: CONFIRMED KILLER, POSSIBLE SERIAL KILLER

SUMMARY

Sedley Alley (August 13, 1955 – June 28, 2006) was an American convicted murderer active primarily during the early to mid-1980s. He is confirmed to have killed one victim, US Marine Lance Corporal Suzanne Marie Collins, near the Millington Naval Base (Naval Air Station Memphis) in Tennessee in July 1985. Within our research group, and among a small number of officials, there is a belief that he may also be responsible for the death of his first wife, Deborah Skeans-Alley, and the murder of Sherri Ann Jarvis, based on shared patterns of violence and behavior rather than court findings. Over the course of his adult life, Alley's movements took him from his birthplace in Ashland, Kentucky, through Michigan, where he lived intermittently with his brother and "wandered" to the point that he later could not recall his own whereabouts for stretches of time. Ultimately, he moved to Tennessee, where he lived near and on the naval base. His case is historically significant for its extreme sexual violence involving foreign-object penetration, the possibility of additional victims connected by a distinctive pattern of assault and biting, and prolonged capital litigation that ended with his execution by lethal injection in 2006.

Alley's early life was rooted in Ashland, Kentucky, where he was born and raised and where his two children from his first marriage later lived with relatives. He began abusing substances in late adolescence, around age 16 to 18, a pattern that would continue throughout his adult life. As a young adult, he married 15-year-old Deborah L. Skeans on May 23, 1975, when he was 19, beginning a marriage marked by conflict and instability. The couple had a daughter, April, around 1976. Alley joined the military sometime in the 1970s, before the breakdown of this marriage, but his ongoing alcohol use and possible involvement with other substances contributed to long-term instability and his eventual discharge on substance-abuse grounds rather than a stable completion of service. By around 1980, the relationship with Deborah had deteriorated into serious arguments, her decision to leave him, and the filing of divorce paperwork, placing her later death squarely in the context of a collapsing and volatile marriage. Psychological evaluations in the mid-1980s, including testing by Dr. Sam Craddock at Middle Tennessee Mental Health Institute, documented hallucinations, dissociative or sleepwalking episodes (such as attempting to open his mother's robe while calling her by another name at age 16), anger problems, and sexual difficulties including impotence. These long-standing issues, combined with chronic substance abuse and contentious intimate relationships, form the backdrop to his later violent behavior.

Alley's known and suspected criminal activity spans from about 1980 into the mid-1980s and involves both domestic and stranger-victim contexts across several states. On February 28, 1980, his first wife, Deborah Skeans-Alley, was found dead in the bathtub of her home shortly before their divorce was finalized. The medical examiner ruled the death an accident, citing food regurgitation lodged in her throat, but our group and some officials consider the possibility that the scene was staged and that this may have been a concealed homicide rather than a true accidental drowning. After Deborah's death, their children went to live with family members in Ashland, while Alley moved to Ypsilanti, Michigan, to stay with his brother. During roughly 1980–1984, he reportedly moved in and out and often wandered, leaving large gaps in his own recollection of where he was during this period. In the broader time frame, the November 1, 1980 murder of Sherri Ann Jarvis near Huntsville, Texas, where she was beaten and sexually assaulted, shares significant similarities with the later Collins case in terms of object penetration and biting, and is regarded within our group, and by at least a few officials, as a possible Alley victim, though no court has made that determination. By the early 1980s, Alley had remarried, wedding Lynne Baker on July 2, 1983, and later lived with her in on-base housing at the Millington Naval Base in Tennessee while working for a local heating and air-conditioning company in Millington.

The crime for which Alley was convicted occurred on the night of July 11, 1985. Around 10:00 p.m., 19-year-old Marine Suzanne Collins left her barracks at Millington Naval Base to jog along Navy Road. At approximately 10:30 p.m., Alley abducted her, driving her in his dark green 1970 Ford station wagon with wooden side panels toward Edmund Orgill Park, a nearby city park. Witnesses saw his car traveling in the same direction Collins had been running and, minutes later, heard screaming from that area. As they moved toward the sound, they saw the same vehicle returning at high speed, forcing them to dodge it to avoid being struck. Collins was later found in Edmund Orgill Park, where she had been beaten and sexually assaulted. Alley used a tree branch pulled from the environment as an improvised weapon and instrument of penetration, consistent with the disorganized, highly violent pattern associated with him. After returning home that night, he was interviewed by Naval Investigative Service personnel about Collins' disappearance and death. On July 12, 1985, at approximately 10:40 a.m., military police at the Millington Naval Base arrested him for her murder, based on witness observations, his vehicle, and his movements between the base and the park.

Alley's prosecution and sentencing unfolded in the Tennessee courts over the next several years. In the Criminal Court of Shelby County in Memphis, a jury convicted him of the murder of Suzanne Collins on March 17, 1987. The following day, March 18, 1987, the same court, presided over by Judge Joseph B. Dailey, sentenced him to death. During the lead-up to trial and sentencing, Dr. Sam Craddock, a clinical psychologist at Middle Tennessee Mental Health Institute, testified on May 15, 1986, about psychological tests administered to Alley, putting his mental health history and cognitive functioning into the official record. Over nearly two decades, Alley pursued appellate and post-conviction relief. On January 16, 2004, the Tennessee Supreme Court granted the State's motion to set an execution date, and on March 29, 2006, the Court formally set and finalized that date. As the execution approached, Alley filed an action under 42 U.S.C. § 1983 on April 11, 2006, challenging Tennessee's lethal-injection protocol, and on May 4, 2006, he sought a stay of execution pending the outcome of Hill v. McDonough, a US Supreme Court case concerning whether death-row prisoners may use such civil-rights actions to challenge their method of execution. These efforts ultimately failed, and Alley was executed by lethal injection at Riverbend Maximum Security Institution in West Nashville, Tennessee, on June 28, 2006. He was pronounced dead shortly after 2:00 a.m., bringing his formal legal case to a close.

The impact and legacy of the Alley case lie in its combination of extreme sexual violence, potential serial offending, and significant capital-punishment litigation. Behaviorally, our group and some officials have highlighted repeated elements across the confirmed Collins homicide and the suspected cases of Deborah Skeans and Sherri Jarvis: late-night or early-morning offenses clustered around weekdays and weekend transitions; attacks in environments he knew well, such as his own home, the roads and wooded areas near Millington, and remote highway or park settings; use of improvised weapons, especially tree branches, for sexual assault and killing; the presence of bite marks as a means of marking and dominating victims; and chaotic escape behavior, including reckless driving in a distinctive vehicle and committing crimes close to where he lived or worked. Taken together, these patterns suggest a recognizable signature centered on compensating for sexual impotence through object penetration and biting, expressing anger and a need for dominance over women rather than seeking conventional sexual gratification.

At the same time, because Deborah's death was officially ruled accidental and no court has found Alley responsible for Jarvis's murder, debate continues over the true scope of his offending and the degree to which these additional cases can be reliably attributed to him. Legally, his attempts to challenge Tennessee's lethal-injection protocol through civil-rights litigation, in parallel with national developments such as Hill v. McDonough, have made his case part of broader discussions about the rights of death-row prisoners and the scrutiny of execution methods. For these reasons, his case remains significant as an example of how severe sexual violence, unresolved questions about additional victims, long-term mental health and substance-abuse issues, and the mechanics of capital punishment intersect in a single offender's history.

VICTIMS

CONFIRMED

Suzanne Collins

Born June 8, 1966, in Fairfax County, Virginia, Suzanne played on her high school softball team and graduated from Robert E. Lee High School before enlisting in the military from 1984–1985. At the time of her death, she was stationed at Naval Support Activity (NSA) Mid-South in Millington, Tennessee, undergoing avionics training and scheduled to graduate the next day. On the evening of July 11, 1985, while running laps on base, Sedley Alley severely beat her, fracturing her skull before repeatedly shoving a 31-inch tree limb up her vagina with enough force to penetrate her abdomen and tear one of her lungs. He then dragged her body to Edmund Orgill Park. The autopsy determined she died from blunt force trauma to the head and internal hemorrhaging from the tree limb, with bite marks on her left and right breasts. Two Marines jogging nearby heard her scream, saw a car leaving the area, and later identified Sedley Alley's vehicle.

SUSPECTED

Deborah Lynn Skeans

On February 20, 1980, Deborah Lynn Skeans was found dead in the bathtub of the home she shared with Sedley Alley in Ashland, Kentucky. Married with two children, their relationship was rocky, and it appears Deborah had filed for divorce 5 days previously. Her death was officially ruled an accident, but there was suspicion that Sedley may have killed her in a fit of anger.

POSSIBLE

Sherri Jarvis

Born March 9, 1966, in Stillwater, Minnesota, Sherri was a known truant removed from home and placed in a Stillwater Juvenile Center before running away with two others to Green Bay, Wisconsin, then continuing alone. In August 1980, she wrote to her mother from Colorado, stating she wouldn't contact them until age 18 or 21 due to anger over incarceration.

On October 3, 1980, witnesses at the South End Gulf Station and Hitch n' Post Truck Stop near Huntsville, Texas, reported seeing a teenage girl claiming to be a runaway from Aransas Pass/Rockport, Texas, who wanted to visit Ellis Prison to see a "friend" (denied by staff). Her body was discovered on November 1, 1980, along the roadside. She was beaten (blunt force trauma to right skull), strangled with pantyhose (used to stop bleeding), and raped with a tree branch inserted vaginally and anally, tearing her lungs and penetrating her abdomen, with a deep bite mark on her right shoulder.

Famed FBI profiler, John Douglas, who assisted on the case, also mentioned two other murders that Alley was considered for in California in his book, *Journey into the Darkness*. No names or specifics have been made public. However, by looking at case files and police records, it appears that Douglas and other agencies felt he had all of the hallmarks of a serial killer and other victims that were unknown.

TIMELINE

08/13/55	Sedley Alley (SA) was born to George and Jainie Alley.
02/20/60	Deborah Skeans was born to Rose Marie Brislin and John C. Skeans.
??/??/71-72	SA's substance abuse issues began.
05/23/75	SA married Deborah L. Skeans (she was 15 and he was 19).
??/??/76	April was born to Deborah and SA.
??/??/??	David was born to Deborah and SA.

??/??/80	Deborah and SA had a fight. Deborah left. Deborah was found dead 5 days later after filing for divorce.
02/28/80	Deborah Skeans-Alley was found dead in her home in the bathtub. It was ruled an accident after the medical examiner found food (possibly regurgitated) lodged in her throat. There are some indications that the death might have been staged.
??/??/??	After Deborah's death, SA attempted suicide twice.
??/??/80	SA moved to Ypsilanti, Michigan, to live with his brother, J.M.
07/02/83	SA married second wife, Lynne Baker (she was 19 and he was 27).
??/??/80–85	SA was later discharged from the military due to the same substance abuse issues.
??/??/??	SA moved with his wife to the Naval Air Station Memphis (also known as Millington Naval Base) in Millington, Tennessee, where she worked.
07/11/85	Suzanne Collins left her barracks at Millington Naval Base to go on a jog along Navy Rd. at 10:00 p.m.
07/11/85	SA abducted Suzanne Collins and drove to Edmund Orgill Park, where he 10:30 p.m. assaulted, sexually assaulted, and killed her using a tree branch. Witnesses observed SA's vehicle traveling in the direction that Collins had been

running. After several minutes elapsed, they began to hear screaming from that area. The witnesses then proceeded toward the sound to check on Collins' condition. They subsequently observed Sedley's car driving erratically as it passed them, requiring them to dodge the vehicle to avoid collision.

07/11/85	SA returned home and was interviewed by officers of the Naval Investigative Service (NIS) regarding the murder of Suzanne Collins.
07/12/85	SA was arrested for the murder of Suzanne Collins by military police on the Millington Naval Base in Millington, Tennessee. (10:40 a.m.)
05/15/86	Dr. Sam Craddock, a clinical psychologist at MTMHI, testified that he administered psychological tests to the defendant.
03/17/87	SA was convicted of the murder of Suzanne Collins by a jury in the Criminal Court of Shelby County, in Memphis, Tennessee.
03/18/87	SA was sentenced to death by a jury in the Criminal Court of Shelby County presided over by Judge Joseph B. Dailey in Memphis, Tennessee.
01/16/04	The Tennessee Supreme Court granted the State's motion to set an execution date.

03/29/06	The Tennessee Supreme Court set and finalized SA's execution date.
04/11/06	SA filed what he denominated as an action pursuant to 42 U.S.C. § 1983, challenging Tennessee's lethal injection protocol.
05/04/06	SA filed a motion for a stay of execution pending the outcome of Hill. "Hill" refers to the US Supreme Court case Hill v. McDonough, which addressed whether death-row prisoners may use a civil rights action under 42 U.S.C. § 1983 to challenge the method of execution.
06/28/06	SA was executed by lethal injection on June 28, 2006, at Riverbend Maximum Security Institution in Nashville, Tennessee, while on death row.

MO

Based on the documented evidence, Sedley Alley demonstrates limited situational awareness and inadequate escape planning across both criminal incidents. His approach to post-crime behavior reveals several concerning patterns that suggest both impulsiveness and poor risk assessment capabilities.

Alley's planning depth appears superficial at best. While he demonstrated some rudimentary forethought (such as staging Deborah's death to appear accidental), his overall escape strategies lacked sophistication and thoroughness. In the Collins case, his decision to continue driving the same vehicle that witnesses observed at the crime scene indicates a fundamental failure to anticipate investigative procedures. This suggests either overconfidence in his ability to avoid detection or a significant underestimation of law enforcement capabilities.

His approach to avoiding detection reveals critical tactical errors. The retention of the same vehicle used in Collins' abduction represents a significant oversight that demonstrates poor operational security. Additionally, his willingness to commit crimes in close proximity to his residence shows limited geographical awareness of risk factors. These behaviors suggest someone operating without sophisticated planning protocols or risk mitigation strategies.

Regarding adaptation over time, Alley's criminal progression shows both evolution and persistent weaknesses. Initially targeting someone within his intimate circle (Deborah), he later expanded to a random target at the military base he lived in (Suzanne). This progression indicates adaptive learning in victim selection strategies, moving from familiar targets where his presence wouldn't arouse suspicion to stranger victims who offered different opportunities. However, his fundamental escape methodology remained consistently flawed, suggesting limited improvement in operational security despite potential lessons from previous incidents.

The risky nature of his escapes, particularly continuing to operate the witnessed vehicle and committing crimes near his home base, indicates either dangerous overconfidence or inadequate risk assessment capabilities. His escape methods suggest someone who acts on impulse within his comfort zone rather than someone who carefully calculates risk-to-benefit ratios or employs systematic approaches to avoid detection. This pattern demonstrates a concerning combination of adaptive victim selection with persistently poor escape planning.

SIGNATURE

Signature Statement

Sedley Alley demonstrates a repeated need for sexual dominance and psychological control, shown through ritualized penetration with foreign objects and marking behaviors through biting. This suggests an individual who values control over vulnerable victims, exhibits disorganized and impulsive tendencies, and is comfortable operating within familiar outdoor environments. Emotional reinforcement appears to come from compensating for sexual inadequacy and asserting dominance over female victims rather than achieving conventional sexual gratification.

Narrative

The offender demonstrates a consistent pattern of behaviors that extend beyond what is required to commit the crimes themselves. Across multiple incidents, the offender repeatedly penetrates victims with tree branches and leaves distinctive bite marks on their bodies. The persistence of these specific actions suggests that fulfilling particular psychological needs is central to the offender's behavior pattern.

These repeated rituals appear to fulfill specific psychological and emotional needs. The offender's consistent use of tree branches for penetration directly compensates for documented sexual impotence, providing an alternative means of sexual expression when conventional methods are physiologically impossible. The ritualistic biting behavior indicates a need for marking and claiming total power over victims, demonstrating a desire for control and possession. The targeting of female victims exclusively suggests that emotional reinforcement is derived from exercising power over women, likely compensating for feelings of inadequacy and frustration throughout his life.

From these patterns, several probabilistic personality traits can be inferred. The offender appears disorganized, as evidenced by impulsive behavior and lack of comprehensive planning during these attacks. The continued escalation and risk-taking despite potential consequences suggests thrill-seeking tendencies rather than careful risk assessment. The documented sexual impotence and resulting relationship difficulties imply social isolation paired with deep-seated anger toward women. The need to substitute objects for sexual contact reflects the direct impact of his physiological limitations on criminal behavior.

Environmental context further supports the development of this signature. The offender's preference for nighttime attacks suggests either an attempt to avoid detection or the influence of work or family obligations during daylight hours. The selection of locations within his familiar geographic area indicates a comfort level with known terrain and escape routes. [8]

---

8 "After Minnesota Girl Identified as 1980 Texas Homicide Victim, Hunt for Her Killer Continues." *Pioneer Press*, reproduced in *The Doe Network*.

"Case File 91UFTX – Walker County Jane Doe." *The Doe Network: International Center for Unidentified & Missing Persons*.

Liptak, Adam. "Her Father Was Executed for Murder. She Still Wants to Know if He Did It." *The New York Times*.

"1980 Jane Doe Murder Case in Walker County." *K-Star News*, Huntsville, TX.

Sedley Alley v. William R. Key, Clerk, Criminal Court. United States Court of Appeals for the Sixth Circuit. Court opinion.

"Sherri Ann Jarvis." *National Missing and Unidentified Persons System (NamUs)*, US Department of Justice.

"Sherri Ann 'Tati' Jarvis (1966–1980)." *Find a Grave*, memorial page.

Tennessee Attorney General. "Answer in Opposition to Appeal, Sedley Alley, No. 22." *Supreme Court of Tennessee*, 26 June 2006.

"Unidentified Decedent Notice. Medical Examiner File. NamUs UP #4630." *National Missing and Unidentified Persons System (NamUs)*, US Department of Justice.

"Walker County Cold Case." *Montgomery Police Department*, report on the homicide of Sherri Ann Jarvis.

"Walker County Sheriff's Office and Othram Team to Identify Walker County Jane Doe." *Othram*, DNASolves.com.

13:
CLARK PERRY BALDWIN: CONFIRMED SERIAL KILLER

SUMMARY

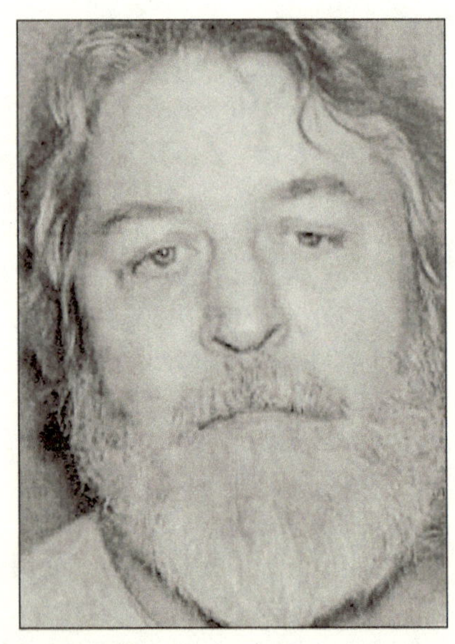

Clark Perry Baldwin (born 1962) was an American serial killer active during 1991–1992. He is confirmed to have murdered at least three women in the Wyoming area and committed an additional murder in Tennessee, though investigators suspect he may have been responsible for other unsolved cases. Baldwin's crimes remained unsolved for nearly three decades until advances in DNA technology led to his identification and arrest in 2020, making his case significant for demonstrating the power of modern forensic science in solving cold cases.

Baldwin grew up in the Midwest and had a history of transient employment, often working in construction and manual labor jobs. Little is publicly documented about his early childhood or family background, as much of his personal history remains sealed in court records. Law enforcement officials noted that Baldwin had previous encounters with the criminal justice system for minor offenses, but no clear pattern of escalating violence was documented until his first murder attempt in 1991. His ability to blend into communities and maintain employment allowed him to avoid suspicion for years.

Baldwin's confirmed crimes occurred between 1991 and 1992 across multiple states, including Wyoming and Tennessee. His victims were adult women who were found in remote locations outside populated areas. The murders followed a consistent pattern of abduction and disposal in isolated areas, suggesting familiarity with local geography in both states. The cases went cold for decades due to limited forensic technology available at the time and the lack of eyewitness testimony. The breakthrough came when investigators used genetic genealogy and advanced DNA analysis to connect Baldwin to biological evidence preserved from the crime scenes across state lines.

Baldwin was arrested in 2020 at his residence in Wyoming after DNA evidence definitively linked him to the murders in both Wyoming and Tennessee. He was charged with multiple counts of first-degree murder across jurisdictions. In 2021, Baldwin pleaded guilty to the murders and was sentenced to life in prison without the possibility of parole. The resolution of these cases brought closure to the victims' families after nearly 30 years of uncertainty.

Baldwin's case represents a significant victory for cold case investigations and demonstrates how genetic genealogy has revolutionized forensic science. The successful identification and prosecution highlighted the importance of preserving evidence from unsolved cases and the potential for new technologies to solve decades-old crimes across state lines. The case also brought attention to the challenges faced by families of victims in long-term unsolved cases and the persistence required by law enforcement to achieve justice. Baldwin's conviction serves as an example of how patience, technological advancement, and dedicated investigation can ultimately bring accountability even decades after crimes are committed.

VICTIMS

CONFIRMED

Mary Ann Newton

On February 1991, Baldwin was arrested for raping a 21-year-old hitchhiker named Mary Ann Newton in Wheeler County, Texas. After putting her in his truck, Baldwin threatened her with a gun, tied her mouth and legs, then beat, raped, and tried to strangle her. However, Newton fought back fiercely, culminating in Baldwin releasing her of the restraints and offering to let her go. According to Newton, her assailant then gave her a handgun and offered her to shoot him, but she instead demanded that he let her go at the next possible opportunity. Baldwin then drove along until Newton stopped him at a gas station, threw the handgun back into the truck, and called the police. Baldwin was interviewed concerning the incident, but the charges were eventually dismissed.

Pamela Rose McCall

On March 10, 1991, McCall's body was found on the side of the I-65 near Spring Hill, Tennessee, about 30 kilometers south of Nashville. She had been raped and strangled. During the investigation of her murder, investigators found traces of semen on her pantyhose while examining the crime scene. At the time of her death, McCall was five months pregnant.

Irene Vasquez

On March 1, 1992, the body of "Bitter Creek Betty" was found lying face down in the eponymous Bitter Creek rest stop on the west side of the I-80, approximately 40 kilometers east of Rock Springs, Wyoming. She was completely naked, but investigators found the victim's underwear and sweatpants nearby. She was wearing a gold wedding ring on one the ring finger of her left hand and a solid gold necklace around her neck. During the postmortem examination, the coroner noted signs of strangulation, injuries to the face and jaw, as well as signs of sexual assault. He found it difficult to determine the time of death, stating that the woman could have been killed elsewhere and that the body could have been dumped at the crime scene between October 1991 and February 1992.

Cindi Estrada

In April 1992, the body of the "Sheridan County Jane Doe" was found on the side of the I-90, approximately 5 kilometers south of the Wyoming-Montana border. She was found fully clothed, except for her socks and shoes. At the time of her death, she was approximately three months pregnant.

SUSPECTED

Rhonda Annette Knutson

A 22-year-old clerk was killed while working the overnight shift at the Phillips 66 convenience store along US Highway 63 in Williamstown, Iowa, on September 7, 1992. Her workplace sat directly on a major trucking corridor, and investigators later confirmed that long-haul truck driver Clark Perry Baldwin was living in Nashua, Iowa, less than 30 miles from the store during the early 1990s, placing him in the immediate region at the time of her murder. After Baldwin was arrested in 2020, Iowa authorities publicly stated that Knutson's case was one of the unsolved homicides being re-examined for a possible connection.

POSSIBLE

At this time, we have seen no other victims who match his timeline, MO, and signature. However, we feel that with his age and expansive distance between his crimes that there are possibly other victims.

TIMELINE

08/22/1961	Clark Perry Baldwin (CPB) was born in Charles City, Iowa.
??/??/1970	CPB moved with his family to Nashua, Iowa.
05/26/1979	CPB graduated high school.
??/??/1980	CPB worked as a long-haul truck driver for Marten Transport.
??/??/1987	CPB got married to Rochelle Bobenmoyer.
??/??/1988	CPB divorced Rochelle Bobenmoyer.
??/??/1988	CPB's daughter was born to Rochelle Bobenmoyer, but he was not aware that she was his daughter.
??/??/1990	CPB's early crimes started.
02/??/1991	CPB was arrested for raping a 21-year-old hitchhiker named Mary Ann Newton in Wheeler County, Texas. He tied her mouth and legs, then beat, raped, and tried to strangle her.
03/10/1991	CPB committed his first confirmed murder: Pamela Rose Aldridge McCall. Her body was found along I-65 near Spring Hill, Tenn. She had been raped and strangled. McCall was 24 weeks pregnant.

03/10/1991 McCall's body was found on the side of the road in Spring Hill, Tenn.

03/01/1992 CPB committed a second murder: Bitter Creek Betty, who was found naked at Bitter Creek rest stop (I-80) in Wyoming. There were signs of sexual assault and strangulation.

04/13/1992 CPB's third murder: Sheridan County Jane Doe. She was found near I-90 in Wyoming. She was 21 years old and 3 months pregnant.

10/28/1997 Baldwin and two accomplices were arrested in Springfield, Missouri, for creating counterfeit money. He served 18 months in prison.

08/??/1999 CPB was released from prison and returned to Nashua, Iowa, to live with his parents.

??/??/2005 CPB quit his job as a trucker.

??/??/2008 CPB started a candle business, which later burned in a fire; the cause was unclear.

??/??/2012 DNA testing of the semen confirmed 2 Jane Does were killed by the same person.

??/??/2018 Baldwin's daughter's DNA test helped confirm his connection to the cold case DNA years later.

04/??/2019 The same DNA linked CPB to the murder of Pamela McCall.

??/??/2019 CPB became a suspect.

05/06/2020 CPB was arrested at home in Waterloo, Iowa, and charged in connection with three murders from 1991–1992.

05/17/2022 Bitter Creek Betty was identified to be Irene Vasquez.

05/02/2025 CPB was convicted of the 1991 murder of Pamela McCall in Tennessee and sentenced to life in prison.

07/17/2025 County Jane Doe was identified as Cindi Arleen Estrada, 21, from California.

07/18/2025 CPB died in a Tennessee hospital due to a heart attack before he could be extradited to Wyoming for trial.

MO

Clark Perry Baldwin's MO demonstrates the behavioral profile of an experienced, methodical offender who combined occupational advantages with systematic criminal planning. His consistent patterns across timing, location selection, access methods, tool use, victim interaction, and escape strategies indicate procedural learning and operational refinement over time.

Baldwin's criminal methodology reflects sophisticated risk management, environmental awareness, and adaptive learning capability. His ability to maintain operational consistency while operating across multiple jurisdictions demonstrates advanced planning skills and confidence in proven methods. The evolution of his techniques shows experience-based refinement rather than impulsive or experimental behavior.

The integration of his legitimate trucking profession with criminal activity provided natural operational advantages including geographic mobility, victim access, occupational credibility, and escape facilitation. This systematic approach to criminal activity indicates a mature, experienced offender capable of long-term operational planning and execution.

Clark Perry Baldwin's confirmed murders occurred between March 1991 and April 1992, spanning just over one year. His attacks demonstrated opportunistic timing rather than strict scheduling, with crimes occurring when victims were most vulnerable and isolated. The rape of Mary Ann Newton in February 1991 established his pattern of targeting lone travelers during periods of reduced surveillance.

Baldwin's criminal timeline shows escalation from his early crimes beginning in 1990 to his first confirmed murder in March 1991. The relatively short intervals between the murders of Pamela McCall, Bitter Creek Betty (Irene Vasquez), and Sheridan County Jane Doe (Cindi Arleen Estrada) suggest an offender capable of acting repeatedly within compressed timeframes while maintaining operational security.

His timing decisions were driven by opportunity assessment and victim availability rather than ritualistic scheduling. The consistency in targeting isolated individuals during travel periods indicates deliberate selection of low-guardianship situations when victims were most accessible and least likely to receive immediate assistance.

Baldwin's crimes occurred along major interstate highways, particularly I-65, I-80, and I-90, spanning multiple states including Tennessee, Wyoming, Texas, and potentially others. These locations provided him with mobile victim pools and jurisdictional complications that hindered law enforcement coordination.

His selection of highway corridors and rest stops demonstrated strategic geographic awareness. These transitional spaces offered access to vulnerable travelers while providing multiple escape routes and reducing the likelihood of witnesses. The interstate system allowed Baldwin to operate across vast distances, making crime linkage difficult for investigators.

The progression from Texas (Newton assault) to Tennessee (McCall murder) to Wyoming (Vasquez and Estrada murders) shows a pattern of geographic mobility that served both operational and investigative avoidance purposes. His familiarity with trucking routes, gained through his employment with Marten Transport, provided intimate knowledge of these corridor systems and their associated vulnerabilities.

Baldwin accessed victims through deception and assumed authority rather than forced entry. His approach method involved gaining situational trust from travelers who perceived him as a legitimate trucker or helpful stranger. This eliminated the need for violent initial contact and reduced victim resistance.

As a long-haul truck driver, Baldwin possessed inherent credibility in highway environments. Victims likely viewed him as part of the legitimate transportation infrastructure rather than a threat. This occupational camouflage allowed him to approach potential victims without triggering defensive responses.

His exit strategies involved immediate departure from crime scenes using established transportation routes. The mobility afforded by his trucking profession provided natural cover for rapid relocation across state lines. Baldwin's ability to blend back into legitimate trucking traffic made pursuit and identification extremely difficult for law enforcement.

Baldwin relied primarily on ligatures, ropes, and cords for victim restraint and killing. His method of manual and ligature strangulation emphasized close-contact control rather than distance weapons. This approach required physical dominance but left minimal ballistic or blade evidence that could be traced.

His restraint methods were practical and reusable, suggesting cost-consciousness and evidence avoidance rather than ritualistic behavior. The absence of firearms or knives reflects a deliberate strategy to avoid weapons that could be linked across jurisdictions or traced through registration systems.

Baldwin's tool selection demonstrated awareness of forensic detection methods. By avoiding conventional weapons and relying on common materials available in trucking environments, he minimized the creation of unique evidence signatures that could connect his crimes.

Baldwin's victim interactions were characterized by initial deception followed by rapid control establishment. His approach involved gaining trust through his legitimate trucker appearance before transitioning to restraint and assault. This method minimized victim resistance and reduced the likelihood of escape attempts.

The evidence suggests brief, task-focused interactions once control was established. Baldwin demonstrated efficiency in managing victim compliance without prolonged psychological manipulation or conversation. His focus remained on completing the assault and murder while minimizing time exposure and witness risk.

His interaction patterns reflect practiced control methods and an understanding of victim psychology. The minimal defensive injuries found on victims indicate his ability to establish dominance quickly and maintain it throughout the criminal process.

Baldwin's escape methodology involved transporting victims to remote disposal sites, creating distance between abduction and discovery locations. This transportation phase served multiple purposes: reducing immediate crime scene evidence, complicating jurisdictional responses, and providing time for his departure from the area.

His return to routine trucking activities immediately after crimes provided perfect operational cover. Baldwin could legitimately be hundreds of miles away from crime scenes within hours, making him nearly impossible to connect to specific incidents without physical evidence.

The geographic distribution of his crimes across multiple states created investigative fragmentation that served as a natural defense against detection. His mobility, combined with the delayed discovery of victims in remote locations, provided substantial time advantages for avoiding capture. This systematic approach to escape and evidence avoidance demonstrates sophisticated criminal planning and execution.

SIGNATURE

Signature Statement

Clark Perry Baldwin's offender signature reflects a ritualized pattern closely tied to his long-haul trucking career. He consistently used ligature strangulation and transported victims before abandoning them along isolated interstate corridors, behaviors that went beyond what was necessary to commit the murders. The repeated mobility and deliberate body placement demonstrate a structured method rooted in control and occupational access.

Narrative

Clark Perry Baldwin is an American serial offender whose criminal activity reflects a sustained pattern closely intertwined with his long-haul trucking career. He has been linked to the murders of multiple women across different states, with offenses spanning decades. Several victims were left unidentified for years before advances in forensic genealogy restored their identities. The geographic distribution of the bodies, found along or near interstate corridors, demonstrates consistent mobility and deliberate use of occupational access.

Beyond the act of homicide itself, Baldwin's crime scenes reveal repeated behavioral elements that suggest signature rather than necessity. He consistently used ligature strangulation as the method of killing, despite the availability of other means, indicating a ritualized preference. The victims were transported and abandoned in rural or semi-rural roadside areas, a step not required to complete the crime but one that reflects a patterned post-offense behavior. This repeated disposal strategy suggests psychological reinforcement derived from control over both the victim and the final placement of the body.

The act of transporting victims across distances before disposal further reflects behavioral consistency. Moving bodies away from initial contact points increased investigative complexity, but it also required time, effort, and risk, indicating this step held significance beyond simple concealment. The repeated selection of isolated highway-adjacent locations implies comfort operating within a familiar geographic framework. The disposal sites were not random; they aligned with routes consistent with long-haul trucking patterns, reinforcing the occupational fusion present throughout the offenses.

Another notable element of his signature is the sustained separation between the crime and victim identification. Several victims remained unnamed for decades, partly due to the cross-jurisdictional nature of the offenses and the selection of vulnerable individuals encountered along travel routes. Targeting individuals encountered within transient environments reduced immediate detection risk but also reflects a consistent victim selection pattern. This repetition suggests structured decision-making rather than situational impulse.

Environmental context reinforces these signature elements. The trucking profession provided both mobility and isolation, allowing Baldwin to integrate victim contact, homicide, and body disposal within the same occupational setting. The repeated use of ligature strangulation, transportation of victims, and abandonment along interstate corridors formed a coherent behavioral pattern extending beyond what was strictly required to commit the murders. Together, these elements demonstrate a sustained and ritualized method in which occupation, movement, and post-offense control combined to define his identifiable criminal signature.[9]

---

9 "Accused Killer Was 'Gentle Giant.'" Des Moines Register, p. A8. Newspapers.com.

"I-90 Jane Doe Identified after 33 Years; Alleged Killer to Be Extradited to Wyoming." Oil City News, 17 July 2025. Archived 1 Sept. 2025.

"'I-90' Jane Doe, Suspected Victim of Serial Killer, Identified After 33 Years." Cowboy State Daily, by Clair McFarland, 17 July 2025.

"Maury County Grand Jury Finds Serial Killer Guilty of Murder for Killing a Woman in Spring Hill in 1991." Spring Hill Tennessee Police News, archived 1 Sept. 2025.

"Serial Killer Suspect Dies 1 Day after Third Victim Identification." ForensicMag, archived 1 Sept. 2025.

"Suspect in Serial Killings Arrested in 29-Year-Old Cold Case." CNN, archived 1 Sept. 2025.

"3 Indicted on Possession of Counterfeit Currency." Springfield News-Leader, 14 Nov. 1997. Newspapers.com.

"Trucker from Iowa Charged in 1990s Slayings of 3 Women, Including One from Gloucester." Daily Press, 7 May 2020.

"Who Are Tammy Zywicki Murder Suspects? Are Lonnie Bierbrodt and Clark Perry Baldwin Dead or Alive?" TheCinemaholic, archived 1 Sept. 2025.

14:

JOHN ALLEN CHAPMAN: CONFIRMED SERIAL KILLER

SUMMARY

John Allen Chapman (October 6, 1967 – present) is an American serial killer active during the early 1990s. He is confirmed to have murdered two women and assaulted a third in Tennessee. Chapman became notable for his geographic consistency, operating exclusively within Grundy County and along Interstate 24 corridors, demonstrating how local familiarity can both facilitate criminal activity and ultimately lead to capture.

Chapman's early life was marked by family instability and educational failure. Born to Sandra Jean Bess with an unknown father, he dropped out of high school in the 10th grade around 1982 and subsequently joined the Tennessee National Guard. After his military service, Chapman worked various jobs in the nursery business and briefly as a rest area attendant, positions that would later provide him access to his crime locations. His early criminal record included arson in 1987 and driving under the influence in 1988, establishing a pattern of impulsive behavior and poor decision-making.

Chapman's confirmed crimes occurred within a concentrated geographic area of Tennessee between 1990 and 1992. His victims were Michelle Darlene Blake, a 26-year-old woman abducted from a pit stop and found stabbed to death in Philadelphia Cemetery, and Vickie Metzger, a former nun traveling to a conference who was strangled near a Monteagle rest stop. Chapman's method involved deceptive approaches, often requesting help to lure victims away from safety. Witnesses described him as "timid" and "awkward," requiring extended interaction to gain victim compliance rather than immediate psychological dominance.

Chapman was apprehended on November 5, 1992, when he assaulted Pamela Sue Back at an I-24 rest stop where he worked. His arrest at the scene marked the end of his criminal activities. Through DNA evidence collected during the investigation, authorities linked him to the murders of Blake and Metzger. Chapman was convicted following two trials in 1993, receiving life imprisonment for the murders plus an additional 12 years for kidnapping, rape, assault, and robbery. He began serving his sentence on April 2, 1994, and will be eligible for parole in January 2054.

The human cost of Chapman's crimes affected multiple families and communities across Tennessee and Indiana. Two women lost their lives, and a third survived a violent assault. The geographic clustering of his crimes within familiar territory ultimately aided law enforcement in establishing connections between cases. Chapman's case contributed to understanding how workplace connections and environmental familiarity can both facilitate criminal behavior and create investigative vulnerabilities that lead to identification and capture.

Chapman's case remains a study in disorganized criminal behavior, demonstrating how inconsistent methodology and overreliance on familiar territory can limit an offender's operational longevity. His crimes are documented in criminal justice studies as an example of how geographic profiling and DNA evidence can effectively link cases and secure convictions. At 57 years old, Chapman remains incarcerated and continues to serve his life sentence.

VICTIMS

CONFIRMED

Michelle Darlene Blake

In April of 1990, the body of Michelle Darlene Blake was found at the Philadelphia Cemetery in Grundy County, Tennessee. At the time, she was identified as a missing person but later was identified as Michelle Blake, a 26-year-old white female. Investigators determined she was stabbed and raped and had been killed the night before her body was found. In 1993, DNA samples connected John Allen Chapman to her murder.

Vickie Metzger

In June of 1992, an ex-nun named Vickie Metzger left her home (Jeffersonville, Indiana) to go to a conference in Atlanta, Georgia. Vickie never did arrive at her destination, and police later found her car in the Eastbound I-24 rest area of Monteagle. A few hours later, an investigator named Roy Sain found her body covered in leaves approximately 1,100 feet away from her parked car. It was determined that she was raped and then manually strangled to death. Police found her body 2–4 days after she was killed. In 1993, DNA samples connected John Allen Chapman to her murder.

Pamela Sue Back

In November of 1992, Pamela Sue Beck was robbed and assaulted by John Allen Chapman at a I-24 Eastbound rest stop in Grundy County, Tennessee.

Agent Davis from the Monteagle Police Department was called to investigate a knife-point assault on Pamela Sue Back. John Chapman was arrested on the scene and admitted that he decided to assault her because he was smoking and drinking.

SUSPECTED

Although various investigators, such as Tennessee investigator Lt. Jerry Mayes, listed as many as a dozen murders as similar to those of Metzger and Back, he also said, "There's no way to say if all of these are related or, for sure, if any of them are related."

Various police sources have listed Lisa Maria Atwell, whose body was found in Cambridge City, Indiana, and Espy Regina Black Pilgrim, whose body was found near Corbin, Kentucky, as possible victims. Based on geographical circumstances and little to no information about Chapman's time in the National Guard, there is no way to verify Chapman's connection to these murders.

POSSIBLE

No possible victims that match Chapman's MO and signature were found in or near Grundy County, Tennessee, between the late 1980s and 1995.

TIMELINE

10/06/1967	John Allen Chapman (JAC) was born. His mother is Sandra Jean Bess, and he has an unknown father.
Circa. 1982	JAC dropped out of 10th grade. After dropping out of school, he joined the Tennessee National Guard.

??/??/1987 Since 1987, JAC has worked for various employers in the nursery business and, briefly, as a rest area attendant.

11/01/1987 JAC was arrested at 20 years old for starting a fire on Halloween in Altamont, Tennessee.

11/15/1987 JAC was released from police custody on a $2,500 bond.

??/??/1988 JAC was convicted of driving under the influence in Grundy County.

4/19/1990 At 8:55 p.m., Michelle Darlene Blake, an employee at the pit stop in McMinnville, Tenn., was taken into a truck and not seen alive again.

4/20/1990 Friday morning, Stacy Smart spots a pair of shoes lying in the Philadelphia Cemetery. Looking closer, she discovers Michelle Blake's body dumped in the cemetery. She quickly left, returning to her parents' home and calling the police. The TBI arrived at the cemetery to find the body of a woman. Though mostly clothed, her blouse was partially undone, and her bra was missing.

4/21/1990 The discovered body was identified as the missing Michelle Blake.

??/??/1992 JAC was honorably discharged from the National Guard, receiving the rank E-4.

6/07/1992 An ex-nun named Vickie Metzger left home (Jeffersonville,

Indiana) to go to a conference in Atlanta, Georgia.

6/08/1992 When Vickie Metzger did not arrive, a call was made to her mother asking about her whereabouts, and a search for her began.

6/11/1992 Police located Vickie Metzger's car at the Eastbound I-24 rest area of Monteagle. Hours later, investigator Roy Sain discovered Metzger's body 1,100 feet away from her parked car. He would later testify that she was covered in leaves and branches, and clothed in a bra, pants, and panties. A hunter finds various credit cards and a compact pill container belonging to Vickie, behind a fence, in the wooded area near the I-24 Eastbound rest area. After fur ther searches in the area, they located the victim's traveler's checks, change, business card holder, business cards, pocketknife, car keys, and makeup.

11/05/1992 JAC assaulted and robbed a woman named Pamela Sue Back at the I-24 Eastbound rest stop in Monteagle, Tenn.

11/05/1992 Agent Davis from the Monteagle Police Department was called to the Eastbound I-24 rest area to investigate a knife-point assault on Pamela Sue Back. JAC was taken into custody on scene.

11/??/1992 JAC confessed that he assaulted Pamela Back because he was smoking marijuana and drinking.

11/??/1992 JAC was interviewed by the TBI. He willingly provided hair

	and blood samples, which would later show a match, tying him to Vickie and Michelle.
??/??/1993	Following 2 trials, JAC was charged with life in prison for the murders of Vickie Metzger and Michelle Blake. An additional 12 years were added for kidnapping, rape, assault, and robbery.
04/02/1994	JAC's sentence began. He will be eligible for parole in January of 2054.
12/??/1996	Ricky Harrison, the hunter who found Vickie's belongings, testified that he was hunting in the area when he stumbled across her belongings in 1992.

MO

John Allen Chapman demonstrates a consistent operational pattern characterized by evening attacks in familiar rural locations, deceptive victim approach methods, and highway-based escape routes. His crimes reveal an unorganized offender who relied on environmental familiarity and workplace connections while exhibiting inconsistent weapon selection and evolving control methods. Chapman's MO indicates someone with moderate planning ability but limited criminal sophistication, ultimately leading to his capture through overconfidence in familiar territory.

John Allen Chapman's criminal methodology reveals a pattern of behaviors designed to accomplish his crimes while minimizing immediate detection risk. His operational approach remained remarkably consistent across three documented incidents spanning from April 1990 to November 1992, demonstrating both behavioral stability and critical limitations that ultimately led to his apprehension.

Chapman's temporal preferences established his most reliable pattern. His introduction to murder began on Thursday evening, April 19, 1990, at 8:55 p.m. when he targeted Michelle Blake. This initial crime established his signature timing preference—operating exclusively under darkness cover. Two years later, he struck again between June 7–8, 1992, targeting Vickie Metzger sometime after dark during the Sunday-Monday transition. His final documented crime occurred on Thursday evening, November 5, 1992, when he assaulted Pamela Back. This consistent preference for evening and nighttime operations, spanning different seasons and mixing weekdays with weekend periods, reveals an offender with scheduling flexibility but strong environmental preferences.

Geographic clustering represents Chapman's most distinctive operational characteristic. All three incidents occurred within Grundy County, Tennessee, specifically in areas adjacent to Interstate 24. Michelle Blake was abducted from a McMinnville pit stop and her body disposed of in Philadelphia Cemetery. Vickie Metzger was discovered 1,100 feet from her vehicle in a wooded area near a Monteagle rest stop, while Pamela Back was assaulted at an eastbound I-24 rest stop in Monteagle. These location choices reveal an offender who understood the strategic value of highway-adjacent rural areas, isolated enough to avoid immediate detection, yet accessible enough to allow rapid escape.

Chapman's victim approach methodology relied heavily on deception rather than force. In Michelle Blake's case, he employed a classic ruse, asking for help to lure her away from safety. Witnesses described Chapman as "timid" and "awkward" during initial contact, suggesting someone who relied on manipulation rather than natural confidence. This interaction required heavy engagement, indicating he needed prolonged contact to achieve victim compliance rather than quick, authoritative control. His access to Pamela Back through workplace familiarity shows adaptability in victim selection methods, though this ultimately proved his downfall.

Weapon selection reveals Chapman's most telling operational inconsistency. His first victim suffered seven stab wounds from a knife he brought to the scene, indicating premeditation. However, his second victim was manually strangled, representing a shift to improvised, hands-on violence. The alleged knife used in his final assault suggests a return to prepared weapons. This inconsistency demonstrates experimentation rather than habit formation, marking him as an unorganized offender still developing preferred methods.

Chapman's escape methodology showed both consistency and limitation. His documented escapes consistently involved immediate return to Interstate 24, utilizing his gray Chevrolet truck for rapid departure from crime scenes. This highway-focused escape pattern demonstrates situational awareness and basic planning, but his ultimate arrest at the scene of his final crime reveals overconfidence in familiar territory and declining operational security.

Environmental factors significantly influenced Chapman's operational development. Rural Tennessee rest stops along I-24 provided the isolation necessary for extended victim interaction while maintaining escape route accessibility. His workplace connections to these locations increased comfort levels and reduced perceived risk but also created investigative vulnerabilities. The consistent geographic clustering reveals an offender who prioritized environmental familiarity over strategic diversification, ultimately limiting his operational longevity and contributing to his identification and capture.

SIGNATURE

Signature Statement

The unsub demonstrates a repeated need for sexual control and environmental familiarity, shown through consistent geographic clustering in rural rest stops and ritualized removal of victim clothing. This suggests an individual who values predictable environments over victim variety, is likely comfortable in familiar work-adjacent locations, and gains emotional reinforcement from sexual dominance and trophy collection behaviors. The offender exhibits moderate organizational skills with inconsistent weapon methodology, indicating someone still developing criminal confidence while maintaining strong geographic and temporal preferences for evening attacks in rural Tennessee locations along the I-24 corridor.

Narrative

The offender John Allen Chapman demonstrates a consistent pattern of behaviors that extend beyond what is required to commit the crimes themselves. Across multiple incidents spanning from spring to autumn, Chapman repeatedly selected rural rest stops along the I-24 corridor during evening and nighttime hours, removed victims' undergarments and clothing items, and committed sexual assaults. These behaviors occur with such consistency that they indicate ritualistic rather than purely practical elements. The persistent choice of familiar work-adjacent locations and specific timing patterns suggests that environmental control is central to Chapman's criminal behavior. These repeated rituals appear to fulfill specific psychological and emotional needs. Chapman's consistent removal of undergarments and clothing items points to a need for symbolic possession and trophy collection, while the sexual assault components indicate a drive for dominance and control over victims. The geographic clustering within familiar territory suggests comfort-seeking behavior, while the progression from weapon use to manual strangulation indicates growing confidence in hands-on control methods. Emotional reinforcement appears to be derived from sexual dominance, physical control, and the collection of symbolic trophies from victims.

From these patterns, several probabilistic personality traits can be inferred. Chapman appears disorganized in his methodology, as evidenced by inconsistent weapon selection and varied killing methods that suggest experimentation rather than refined technique. His geographic stability within Grundy County indicates territorial comfort and likely local residence or employment connections. The opportunistic nature of victim selection through workplace connections suggests impulsive decision-making and limited ability to delay gratification. Witnesses' descriptions of "timid" and "awkward" behavior point to social inadequacy, requiring extended manipulation periods rather than immediate psychological dominance.

Environmental context strongly influences Chapman's signature development. Rural Tennessee rest stops along I-24 provided the isolation necessary for extended victim interaction while maintaining escape route accessibility. His workplace connections to these locations increased his comfort level and reduced perceived risk. The evening timing preference across different seasons demonstrates deliberate planning around darkness for concealment, while the consistent geographic clustering reveals an offender who prioritizes environmental familiarity and predictability over victim variety or strategic diversification.[10]

---

10 *Autopsy Report, Metropolitan Nashville Davidson County, Michelle DeNoyer Blake, Case No. OC90-77.*

Autopsy Report, Metropolitan Nashville Davidson County, Vickie Sue Metzger, Case No. OC92-153.

Bryan, Kim. "John Allen Chapman - Capture of a Budding Serial Killer." *HubPages.*

Huff, Steve. "The Forgotten Redhead Murders: Coincidence or Serial Killer?" *Inside Hook.*

"Laborer Indicted in Kidnappings, Slayings of Store Clerk, Former Nun." *The Tennessean*, Nashville, 16 Jan. 1993.

"Officer: 12 Murders Similar." *Lexington Herald*, Lexington, KY (AP).

"6 Charged with Arson." *Kingsport Times News*, 6 Nov. 1987.

State of Tennessee v. John Allen Chapman. In the Court of Criminal Appeals of Tennessee at Nashville, February Session 1997, 30 Sept. 1997, No. 01C01-9604-CC-00137.

State of Tennessee v. John A. Chapman. In the Court of Criminal Appeals of Tennessee at Nashville, January 1999 Session, 5 May 1999, C.C.A. No. 03C01-9802-CC-00080.

State of Tennessee v. John A. Chapman. In the Court of Criminal Appeals of Tennessee at Nashville, Assigned on Briefs, 15 Jan. 2020, 17 Apr. 2020, No. M2019-00429-CCA-R3-PC.

15:

SEAN PATRICK GOBLE: CONFIRMED SERIAL KILLER

SUMMARY

Sean Patrick Goble was a long-haul truck driver who was responsible for the murders of several women across multiple states during the mid-1990s. Investigators confirmed that Goble killed at least four women between 1994 and 1995, though authorities believe the true number of victims may be much higher. His crimes occurred along major highways and interstates, where he used his occupation as a truck driver to travel long distances without drawing suspicion. Goble became known for targeting women at truck stops who were involved in prostitution, allowing him to approach victims in a way that seemed routine and non-threatening.

Goble's early life showed several troubling influences that may have shaped his later behavior. He was born in 1966 in North Carolina and grew up in a family marked by instability and criminal behavior. His father was sentenced to prison for the rape of a 10-year-old girl when Goble was only six years old. As he grew older, Goble struggled to maintain stability in his own life. He dropped out of high school during his senior year to join the US Army and later worked a variety of jobs before becoming a commercial truck driver in the early 1990s. Prior to the murders, he had already faced legal trouble for writing false checks and for possession of cocaine.

Goble's confirmed murders took place in several states and often followed a similar pattern. He would pick up women from truck stops, usually those engaged in prostitution, and spend time with them before killing them. The victims were often strangled manually or smothered, indicating that Goble relied on his own physical strength rather than weapons. After killing the victims, he frequently disposed of their bodies along rural highways or exit ramps, locations that allowed him to quickly leave the scene and continue traveling without attracting attention.

Law enforcement eventually connected the crimes through forensic evidence and patterns in the locations of the bodies. Goble was arrested in April 1995 at a truck terminal in Winston-Salem, North Carolina, after investigators discovered evidence linking him to one of the victims. During the investigation, police found a victim's pocketbook in his truck, which helped confirm his involvement. After confessing to at least one of the murders, Goble was transferred between several jurisdictions as authorities built cases against him for multiple killings.

The impact of Goble's crimes was significant for the victims' families and the communities where the murders occurred. His case highlighted the challenges law enforcement faced when investigating crimes that crossed state lines and involved transient offenders such as long-haul truck drivers. The investigation also demonstrated the importance of forensic evidence and cooperation between different police agencies. Today, Goble remains imprisoned in Tennessee, where he continues to serve his sentence for the murders he committed.

VICTIMS

CONFIRMED

Lisa Susan O'Rourke

In January 1994, 29-year-old Lisa Susan O'Rourke of St. Louis, Missouri, was picked up by Goble along Interstate 10 in either Louisiana or Mississippi after leaving a travel point. After engaging in sexual activity, Goble strangled her to death and dumped her body under a bridge along Interstate 65 in Alabama. Her body was discovered on January 23, 1994, but was initially ruled a case of hypothermia. Months later, fingerprint analysis confirmed her identity and ruled her death a homicide linked to Goble's actions.

Brenda Kay Hagy

On January 22, 1995, 45-year-old Brenda Kay Hagy of Bloomington, Indiana, arrived at a service station in Tennessee after traveling from a shelter in Florida. Known for trespassing at truck stops and living a transient lifestyle, she was abducted by Goble, who raped and strangled her, breaking her neck. He then drove his truck to Bristol, Virginia, where he dumped her body along an access road off Interstate 81. Her body was found on January 23, 1995, by a newspaper carrier reporting along the roadside.

Sherry Tew Mansur

34-year-old Sherry Tew Mansur was last seen alive on January 31, 1995, when she left her sister's home in Bowie, Maryland, with her 2-year-old niece. Goble encountered her along the route and engaged in sexual activity before strangling her. He then transported and dumped her body along Interstate 40 in Guilford County, North Carolina, where it was discovered on February 19, 1995. Initially listed as a "Jane Doe," her identity was later confirmed by fingerprints.

Alice Rebecca Hanes

36-year-old Alice Rebecca Hanes, a native of Columbus, Ohio, was traveling when she was abducted by Goble. After leaving a truck stop in Salina, Kansas, she was picked up in Tennessee and then smothered to death by Goble. Her body was dumped along Interstate 81 in Virginia and was found on March 19, 1995. Her personal belongings, including her purse, were later discovered in Goble's truck, providing key evidence in linking him to her murder.

SUSPECTED

Tammy Zywicki

In August 1992, 21-year-old Tammy Zywicki (sometimes spelled Zywicik) disappeared after leaving college in Illinois, and her body was later found in Missouri. Her case remains unsolved and has been investigated in connection with several interstate killers. At one point, authorities briefly considered Sean Goble as a possible suspect due to similarities with other highway murders, but he was not officially charged or linked to her death. Zywicki's case continues to draw public interest as a cold case.

Marcia Matthews

Marcia K. "Pepper" Matthews, about 25 years old, was found dead along Interstate 71 in Ohio on June 12, 1985. Her killing bore the hallmarks of an unsolved series of highway murders. Authorities later looked into Sean Goble as a possible suspect in her death because he worked as a long-haul trucker with routes through the area, but no charges were ever filed. Matthews remains one of several cold case victims from the 1980s linked to interstate highway homicide investigations.

Shirley Dean Taylor

Shirley Dean Taylor, age 26, was found deceased on Route 224 in Medina

County, Ohio, on July 20, 1986. Her death was one of several unsolved roadside homicides involving women at that time. Goble was among the individuals law enforcement examined due to his trucking routes and similar victim profiles, but he was never charged in her killing. Taylor's murder remains part of a broader set of cold cases along Midwestern highways.

April Barnett

19-year-old April Barnett was discovered along Interstate 71 in Ashland County, Ohio, on December 4, 1986, after going missing. Her death is considered part of an unsolved string of highway homicides. Investigators at one time reviewed connections to Sean Goble because of the similarities in victim type and location, but there was no official link established. Barnett's case remains unsolved.

Anna Patterson

Anna Marie Patterson, also known by aliases such as Cindy Lawson or Jenny Morrison, was found near Interstate 71 in Warren County, Ohio, on March 23, 1987. She was about 27 years old when her body was discovered. Because her murder shared features with other roadside killings, law enforcement looked into possible suspects including truck drivers like Goble, but no charges were ever brought against him in her case. Patterson's killing remains a cold case.

Kathryn Hill (aka Wendy Turner)

Kathryn Hill, who was also known as Wendy Turner, was found deceased near Interstate 280 in Wood County, Ohio, on November 5, 1990. Her homicide was among several unsolved roadside deaths that investigators later reviewed for potential connections to itinerant truckers such as Sean Goble, but he was not formally tied to her murder. Hill's case continues to be unsolved.

Cheryl Mason

Cheryl Mason was a woman whose body was discovered in Guilford County, North Carolina, in 1991. Authorities at the time classified her death as an unsolved homicide found near a major highway. Due to the similarities in victim profile and location, law enforcement considered possible links to truck drivers like Goble, though no charges connected him to her murder. Mason's case remains one of many unsolved roadside killings from that period.

Margaret Goins

Margaret Sue Goins, 26, was found in Sullivan County, Tennessee, along Interstate 81 in 1995. Her cause of death was undetermined, but her body appeared to have been struck by a vehicle. While authorities reviewed her case along with other interstate deaths when Goble was arrested, he was never charged in connection with Goins' death. Her case is still listed among cold or unresolved highway homicide investigations.

Crystal Renee Forshee Sedam

Crystal Renee Forshee Sedam was born in October 1971 in Kentucky. Her life was marked by hardship, early motherhood, and a troubled past. At 20 years old, and 19 weeks pregnant, Sedam was found dead on January 4, 1992, at the base of an embankment near an I-69 ramp in Delaware County, Indiana. She had been strangled, and her unborn son, posthumously named Michael Paul Sedam, also died. Her death was ruled a homicide.

Sedam had worked as a sex worker at truck stops in Indianapolis. She was last seen on New Year's Eve after being dropped off by her husband, who was also her former stepfather. She radioed him early New Year's Day saying she'd be home soon, but she never returned.

Investigators believed her killer was a long-haul trucker. A strong suspect, Sean Patrick Goble later confessed to killing several women under similar circumstances, but stopped cooperating before Sedam's case could be resolved. Though her killer was never officially identified, Goble remains a prime suspect. Sedam and her unborn son were laid to rest in Indianapolis.

POSSIBLE

Police felt that Goble could be responsible for up to 50 murders based on the evidence (mostly victims' clothing and personal effects) found at his home at the time of his arrest. However, there have been no names made available to the public.

TIMELINE

11/01/1966 Sean Patrick Goble (SPG) was born to Kenneth and Emma Goble in Asheboro, N.C.

07/26/1972 SPG's father, Kenneth Goble, was sentenced to 4 years for the rape of a 10-year-old girl. 6-year-old SPG was in his father's car outside of the crime scene.

?/??/1976 SPG's father was released from prison.

?/??/1980 SPG started school at Auburn High School in Rockford, Illinois.

?/??/1984 SPG dropped out his senior year of high school at Auburn Hills and enlisted in the US Army. He was based some where in Columbus, Ohio, in the mid-1980s.

?/??/1988 SPG married an unknown woman and fathered a son before moving to N.C.

?/??/1989 SPG got in trouble with law enforcement for writing a false check. (exact location unknown)

06/03/1992 SPG received his commercial license for truck driving.

?/??/1992 SPG was charged once again for writing false checks. (exact location unknown)

?/??/1992 SPG began working as a truck driver. He worked for a company called Rocky Road Express that was originally based in Winston-Salem, N.C.

04/??/1991 SPG made up a story about being abducted to police to try and cover up the affair he was having behind his wife's back, leading to him and his wife divorcing.

?/??/1991 SPG was arrested on a misdemeanor for possession of cocaine in Cumberland County in N.C.

01/23/1994 Susan O'Rourke was picked up by SPG on I-81 in Lexington, Va. He murdered her and dumped her body under a bridge along Interstate 65 in Alabama. Her body was found on January 23.

01/23/1995 Brenda Kay Hagy was abducted by SPG at a service station in Baileyton, Tenn.

01/24/1995 Brenda Hagy's body was found on I-81 in Bristol, Va.

01/31/1995	Sherry Tew Mansur was last seen alive while seeing family in Bowie, Maryland. Sherry left with her 2-year-old niece.
02/01/1995	Sherry's niece was found abandoned in Washington, D.C.
02/19/1995	Sherry's body was found wrapped in a blanket on I-40 in Guilford County, N.C. (She was unrecognizable from de composition.)
03/18/1995	Alice Rebecca Haynes was kidnapped at a truck stop on I-70 in Salina, Kansas.
03/19/1995	Rebecca Haynes' body was discovered on I-81 in Kingsport, Tenn. DNA testing on a bag found at the scene led police to SPG.
04/13/1995	SPG was arrested at a truck terminal in Winston-Salem, N.C. While searching his truck, they found Rebecca Haynes' pocketbook, providing enough evidence for arrest.
04/13/1995	SPG was held in Winston-Salem, N.C., on a fugitive warrant with no bail.
04/17/1995	After confessing to the murder of Rebecca Haynes in N.C., SPG was transferred to Guildford County Jail.
06/??/1995	Records shows SPG was then transferred to Jefferson County, Tenn., where he awaited trial for the murder of Rebecca Haynes.

12/15/1995 SPG awaited his plea trial in Greene County, Tenn., where he was prosecuted for the murder of Hagy. Authorities believe she was murdered in Greene County, even though her body was dumped off of I-81 in Bristol, Va.

04/??/1996 After conviction and sentencing, SPG moved to the Northeast Correctional Complex in Mountain City, Tenn., where he still sits today. (Sean Goble is now 59 years old.)

09/05/1997 SPG filed a petition for post-conviction relief but was dismissed due to being filed past the statute of limitations.

11/05/2015 A petition was requested for DNA analysis, trying to state that the victim's vaginal swabs were not compared to SPG's DNA file.

MO

The four documented crimes attributed to Sean Patrick Goble occurred on 01/23/1994, 01/24/1995, 02/19/1995, and 03/19/1995. Each offense took place on a weekend, indicating a consistent temporal pattern rather than random timing. Seasonally, all incidents occurred during the winter months, with some nearing early spring but still falling within the winter classification.

This pattern suggests Goble's offenses were primarily opportunity-based rather than carefully preplanned. As a long-haul truck driver, Goble encountered victims while traveling for work, selecting women involved in prostitution at truck stops he happened to visit. The weekend timing aligns with his work schedule and extended periods on the road. The absence of concern for witnesses is notable, as women entering trucks at truck stops, particularly those engaged in prostitution, was a normalized behavior and did not draw attention.

All crime scenes associated with Sean Patrick Goble were linked to highway environments, including the sides of highways and an exit ramp. These locations were public and primarily rural or suburban. Victims were disposed of in Tennessee and Virginia, often near major roadways.

A clear geographic pattern emerges in Goble's repeated use of highways as disposal sites and escape routes. These locations provided immediate access to transportation corridors, allowing him to leave quickly after each offense. The clustering of body disposal sites near highways indicates familiarity with interstate travel and comfort operating in transient spaces where sustained observation was unlikely.

Sean Patrick Goble gained access to his victims through non-forced entry. He lured women involved in prostitution into his truck by presenting a sense of safety and routine rather than using overt physical force. This approach remained consistent across all incidents and relied on occupational norms common at truck stops.

Victims were disposed of along highways in nearly every case, with one deviation involving an exit ramp rather than the roadside. Goble used highways for escape following each offense. There is little evidence of advance planning; the murders occurred after prolonged interaction and sexual activity, followed by manual strangulation. Collectively, these behaviors demonstrate procedural familiarity, repetition of effective methods, and minimal adaptation over time.

In every documented case, Sean Patrick Goble used his body as the primary weapon, relying on manual strangulation or smothering. No weapons or tools were brought to the scenes, making each act improvised. In one instance, the victim's neck was broken during strangulation, reflecting extreme force rather than a change in method.

The consistency of Goble's weapon choice suggests habit formation and comfort with direct physical control. These methods were quiet, required no preparation, and eliminated the need to transport or dispose of tools. This reflects a focus on efficiency, control, and minimizing exposure rather than experimentation or escalation.

All victims experienced prolonged interaction with Sean Patrick Goble prior to their deaths. He engaged in non-demanding verbal behavior and later admitted to having sexual relations with the women before killing them. In most cases he would travel with the victims over state lines. However, we cannot say for certain whether or not they were dead or alive during that travel period.

This interaction pattern demonstrates Goble's confidence in maintaining control without overt threats or intimidation. Control was established through routine and familiarity rather than force at the point of entry. Escalation occurred gradually within each encounter, moving from interaction to homicide, suggesting experience managing resistance and maintaining dominance in a consistent manner.

Following each offense, Sean Patrick Goble escaped using highways, traveling in his long-haul truck. Bodies were disposed of in roadside locations, and concealment relied on geographic isolation rather than disguises or complex methods. Escapes were smooth and calm, even when disposal locations overlapped across incidents months apart.

Goble showed no clear concern about law enforcement detection and maintained consistent post-offense behavior throughout the series. The repeated use of the same escape strategy reflects situational awareness, confidence in routine methods, and demonstrated competence in avoiding detection rather than adaptive escalation or risk-taking behavior.

SIGNATURE

Signature Statement

Sean Patrick Goble demonstrates a repeated need for control, shown through strangulation and ritualized sequences by taking the women's jewelry. This suggests an individual who values sexual gratification is likely comfortable in low-risk situations and gains emotional reinforcement from regifting the jewelry and seeing it be worn by others.

Narrative

The investigation revealed a disturbing pattern in serial offender Sean Patrick Goble's behavior that painted a picture of calculated control and psychological manipulation. Across three documented crimes, Goble established a consistent ritual that would become his signature calling card.

In each case, the story unfolded in a similar manner. Goble would first engage in sexual interaction with his victims before ultimately strangling them with his bare hands, though one victim suffered such extreme violence that her neck was broken by the force of his legs rather than hands. After each murder, he would carefully select items from his victims—necklaces, rings, bracelets, and clothes/shoes, taking them as trophies that held deep psychological significance.

Goble's patient nature became evident through his willingness to travel great distances with his victims, sometimes even crossing state lines before committing his crimes. This revealed someone who was methodical and risk-averse, deliberately targeting women involved in prostitution rather than seeking higher-risk victims. His comfort with control allowed him to overpower his victims while maintaining the structured, repetitive behaviors that defined his criminal pattern.

The environmental context told its own story of Goble's careful planning. Weekend after weekend during the winter season, he would bring his victims to rural locations, deliberately positioning the bodies away from highway view to avoid detection by passersby. Two victims were discovered in Bristol during the month of January, suggesting seasonal patterns in his criminal activity. Police had reported after the murder of Brenda Kay

Hagy in Bristol, Va., that the crime scene was "the work of a serial killer."

Following events two months later, the body of Alice Haynes was found just across state lines from the site of Brenda Hagy (the first victim found in Bristol). It is known Alice Haynes was picked up in Silina, Kansas, and her body was dumped in Bristol, Tenn., nearly 1,016 miles away from where she was last seen alive.

Perhaps most disturbing was what Sean Patrick Goble did after the murders. The jewelry, shoes, and clothes he collected wasn't simply kept as mementos; it became part of an ongoing psychological ritual. He would gift these stolen pieces to family members and sexual partners, finding gratification in seeing others wear the jewelry of his victims. This behavior revealed the depth of his sexual fixation and his need for emotional reinforcement through the memories these objects represented.

The analysis painted a portrait of Sean Patrick Goble as an individual driven by a need for control and sexual gratification, someone who found comfort in low-risk situations and drew psychological satisfaction from the ritualized aspects of his crimes. His repeated behaviors demonstrated not just a pattern of violence, but a complex web of psychological needs that drove him to continue his deadly cycle.[11]

---

11 Roanoke Times 1995, published on Monday, June 19, 1995. Title: Serial Killer's Luck Ran Out In Unlikely Place.

The Virginian-Pilot. published on April 15, 1995. Neighbors Call Suspect Friendly, Scary Sean Patrick Goble Confessed to the Slaying of an Indiana Woman.

The Virginian-Pilot 1995, published on Saturday, June 17, 1995. Title: Detectives Credit Luck In Highway Killings Case.

The Virginian-Pilot. 1995, Published on April 18, 1995. Title: Trucker Admits 3rd Killing.

The Virginian-Pilot. 1995, Published on January 27, 1995. Title: I-81 SLAYING LINKED TO SERIAL KILLER.

The Virginian Pilot. 1995, Published on April 15, 1995. Title: NEIGHBORS CALL SUSPECT FRIENDLY, SCARY SEAN PATRICK GOBLE CONFESSED TO THE SLAYING OF AN INDIANAN WOMAN.

The Virginian-Pilot 1996, published on Tuesday, April 9, 1996. Title: Trucker Admits To Strangling Woman, Gets 14 Years More.

16:

HARRY EDWARD GREENWELL: CONFIRMED SERIAL KILLER

SUMMARY

Harry Edward Greenwell was born on December 9, 1944, in Louisville, Kentucky, to Dorothy Anne and Paul Bruce Greenwell. He passed away at the age of 68 in 2013 from cancer in Lansing, Iowa. Greenwell is a confirmed serial rapist and killer, with 3 confirmed kills and 5 confirmed sexual assault victims. Greenwell also had a vast criminal record and had assaulted at least one and possibly multiple of his wives. This case is historically significant because of the large geographic location in which his crimes took place, as Greenwell committed multiple crimes and felonies across many state borders, which I-65 intersected with.

Not much is known about his early life. The farthest back that was documented was in 1960. He was 15 when he was involved in a shooting teaming with 25-year-old Burns Arnold Stinson. In 1962, Greenwell escaped from a youth detention center, and one year later he was arrested for reasons unknown. In the same year, he was sentenced to two years in reformatory school with five years of probation. Two years later, he was charged with his first sodomy charge at 19.

Greenwell's crimes spanned between Iowa, Indiana, and Kentucky. His victims were typically women who worked at motels along I-65. Greenwell, as told by one of the survivors of his violent crimes, stated that he asked where he could get coffee and then later used the coffee as a weapon against the woman at the counter. This shows that Greenwell often used ruses to gain an advantage over victims. Greenwell often assaulted and shot his victims after robbing them of their money in an isolated space.

Greenwell was never arrested or tried for the I-65 corridor murders or related assaults, as he died in 2013 before being identified through forensic genealogy. During his lifetime he faced multiple arrests for other offenses, including escapes, restraining-order violations, and felony possession, but no homicide charges were ever brought against him.

Greenwell's identification in 2022 through forensic genealogy marked a major turning point in cold-case investigation, showing how modern DNA methods can resolve serial offender cases long after a suspect's death. His case continues to influence interagency cooperation and the use of advanced forensic technology in unsolved violent crimes.

VICTIMS

CONFIRMED

Vicki Heath

Vicki, 41, was working the overnight shift at the Super 8 Motel in Elizabethtown, Kentucky, when she was beaten, sexually assaulted, robbed, and shot twice in the head in the early morning hours of February 21, 1987. Her case remained unsolved for more than two decades until DNA recovered from her clothing and rape kit matched the unidentified offender responsible for the 1989 murders of Peggy Gill and Jeanne Gilbert, and the 1990 Columbus, Indiana, attack. In 2010, her homicide was officially linked to the I-65 Killer, establishing her as his earliest known victim.

Margaret "Peggy" Gill

Peggy, 24, was working the overnight shift at the Days Inn in Merrillville, Indiana, when she was sexually assaulted and shot to death in the early morning hours of March 3, 1989. Her body was found in a storage area near the motel's front desk. DNA evidence later confirmed that she was murdered by the same offender responsible for the killings of Jeanne Gilbert that same night and the earlier murder of Vicki Heath, identifying her as a confirmed victim of the I-65 Killer.

Jeanne Marie Gilbert

Jeanne, 34, was abducted from her overnight shift at the Remington Days Inn in the early morning hours of March 3, 1989. She was taken from the motel, sexually assaulted, and shot three times before her body was left in a rural ditch nearly 19 miles away near Brookston, Indiana. DNA and ballistic evidence later confirmed she was murdered by the same offender who killed Peggy Gill that same night and Vicki Heath two years earlier, identifying her as a confirmed victim of Greenwell.

Unnamed Survivor

On January 2, 1990, there was a 21-year-old night auditor working alone at the Days Inn in Columbus, Indiana, who was approached by a man posing as a trucker. After briefly leaving the lobby, he returned, threw hot coffee in her face, robbed her, sexually assaulted her, and forced her outside. She escaped after falling into an icy ditch and ran to a nearby trailer home for help. Her description and the DNA recovered from her assault later confirmed she was a surviving victim of Greenwell.

Unnamed Survivor

In 1991, an unnamed woman in Rochester, Minnesota, was robbed, sexually assaulted, and stabbed by an unidentified offender who matched the physical description later associated with Greenwell. DNA collected from her assault was entered into CODIS and, in 2013, matched the same unknown offender responsible for the murders of Vicki Heath, Peggy Gill, and Jeanne Gilbert, as well as the 1990 Columbus, Indiana, attack. This confirmed her as a surviving victim of Greenwell.

POSSIBLE

Terry Jo Greenwell

She was the first wife of Greenwell. She died in a house fire on April 28, 1978, from smoke inhalation and was found just inside the door of their home. This incident occurred in Genoa, Wisconsin. Both of their children, Tracey Jo and Jason Edward, survived the fire. Greenwell was suspected to be in the house at the time of the fire.

Victoria Harshman

She was working as the night auditor at the Holiday Inn in Lebanon, Indiana, a motel located directly off Interstate 65. She had only been in the position for about four months when she was attacked in the early morning hours of September 20, 1991. Her body was discovered around 3:30 a.m. inside the motel. An autopsy showed she had been stabbed between 15 and 20 times and also suffered severe blunt force trauma, including a blow with a golf club hard enough to crack her skull from ear to ear. The cause of death was listed as a combination of stab wounds and blunt force injuries.

Lois "Evelyn" Wright

She worked the overnight shift at the Colonial Inn in Rockford, Illinois, when she was found shot to death behind the front desk on the morning of December 18, 1988. Cash was missing from the register, and a bank bag was taken, suggesting a robbery. Her homicide remains unsolved, and while sometimes mentioned in discussions of interstate-corridor motel crimes, no confirmed connection to Greenwell has ever been established.

James Matthew Walton

He worked the overnight shift at the Envoy Inn in Florence, Kentucky, when he was shot multiple times and found in the motel's rear parking lot on the morning of December 31, 1988. The last register entry was a "NO SALE" at 6:24 a.m., and a single gunshot was fired inside the front office before Walton was attacked outside.

Shirley A. McNeal

At approximately 4:00 a.m. on Saturday, February 2, 2002, a man entered the residence located at 528 North 2nd Street with the intent to rob the occupants. It was well known in the area that the man who lived at the address kept large sums of money at home at that time. During the incident, the man's girlfriend, Shirley A. McNeal, was fatally shot before the armed robber fled the residence. Shirley A. McNeal was 51 years old at the time of her death. McNeal was found approximately 9 minutes away from I-65, where Greenwell killed.

Eva Sue Stroud

On Monday, November 19, 2001, patrol officers responded to a request to check on the welfare of an employee at the Phillips 66 service station located in Nashville, Tenn. When they arrived, they discovered Eva Sue Stroud lying on the floor deceased from a gunshot wound. Stroud had opened the service station at the usual time of 6:00 a.m., and it appeared that the shooting may have been part of an armed robbery. Eva Sue Stroud was 39 at the time of her death. Stroud was found approximately 11 minutes away from I-65, where Greenwell killed.

Jermaine L. Banks

On Saturday, October 3, 1998, Jermaine L. Banks reported to work at the Mapco Express located in Nashville, Tenn., where he was Assistant Manager and worked the night shift. Just before 6:00 a.m. on Sunday, October 4, 1998, the employee that was due to relieve Banks at the end of his shift arrived to find him lying dead on the floor. The Mapco had been robbed. According to the time Banks was last seen, it is believed he was fatally shot between 4:30 a.m. and 5:15 a.m. Jermaine L. Banks was 26 years old at the time of his death. Banks was found approximately 15 minutes away from I-65, where Greenwell killed.

TIMELINE

12/09/1944 Harry Edward Greenwell (HEG) was born in Louisville, Kentucky, to Paul Bruce Greenwell and Anna Dorothy Greenwell.

8/10/1960 15-year-old HEG was convicted with 25-year-old felon Burnes Arnold Stinson for a high-speed chase and shooting in Louisville, Kentucky.

10/01/1962 HEG escaped from Kentucky Village Youth Detention Center. The exact location is unknown.

1/17/1963 HEG was arrested for armed robbery in Louisville, Kentucky.

4/12/1963 HEG was sentenced to two years in the reformatory along with five years of probation in Louisville, Indiana.

2/23/1965 HEG was arrested in Jefferson County, Kentucky, for a sodomy charge on an unnamed victim.

3/01/1965 HEG escaped from a holdover cell at the Jefferson County Quarterly Court in Elizabethtown, Kentucky.

3/02/1965 HEG was apprehended at the Greyhound Bus Station in Elizabethtown, Kentucky. HEG plead guilty to robbery in Elizabethtown, Kentucky.

??/??/1969 HEG was granted parole in the Kentucky State Penitentiary.

1/29/1970 His mother, Dorothy Greenwell, died in Elizabethtown, Kentucky.

??/??/1970 He married Terry Jo Greenwell. The city and state unknown.

8/06/1977 Greenwell called the authorities and claimed he was robbed of $400 by five men in Louisville, Kentucky. We are un aware of the location of the incident.

4/28/1978 HEG's wife, Terry Jo Greenwell, died in a house fire in

Genoa, Wisconsin. HEG was not suspected of arson in the original investigation, although he should have been due to his criminal background.

8/21/1980 HEG remarried in Henry County, Kentucky, to Jennifer Thorud.

6/11/1982 HEG escaped prison multiple times and was caught twice in Waukon, Iowa. The reason for imprisonment is un known.

7/28/1982 HEG entered a Not Guilty Plea for the second escape charge in Waukon, Iowa.

8/10/1982 HEG was sentenced to Anamosa State Penitentiary in Iowa for two years for the escapes.

12/05/1983 HEG was released from prison. We do not know which prison he was released from.

??/??/1986 HEG divorced Jennifer Thorud due to domestic disputes. The whereabouts are unknown to us. We are also unaware of who filed for divorce.

2/21/1987 HEG murdered Vicki Heath in Elizabethtown, Kentucky. She was a clerk at the Super 8 Motel located in town.

3/03/1989 HEG murdered Margaret "Peggy" Gill in Merrillville, Indiana. Peggy was the hotel clerk of a Days Inn Hotel located in town.

3/03/1989 HEG committed a murder in Remington, Indiana. The victim was Jeanne Gilbert, who was the hotel clerk for the Days Inn Hotel located in Remington.

3/09/1989 HEG was arrested for a traffic violation in Minnesota.

3/24/1989 HEG was arrested for violation of a restraining order. This seems to have happened in Wisconsin.

3/23/1989 HEG committed a home invasion, dragged his ex-wife out of the home into the street, and choked and threatened her in Lacrosse, Wisconsin.

3/26/1989 HEG was arrested for violating the conditions of his bond and taken to jail in Wisconsin.

4/18/1989 HEG received a 15-month sentence for violating a restraining order in Lacrosse, Wisconsin. The person who sentenced HEG is unknown to us at this moment.

1/02/1990 HEG attempted murder on a motel clerk in Columbus, Indiana. We are not aware of the victim's name.

??/??/1991 HEG assaulted and stabbed a woman in Rochester, Minnesota. The victim survived. We do not know the name of the victim.

9/30/1993 Paul Bruce Greenwell (HEG's father) died in Louisville, Kentucky.

??/??/1994 HEG married Julie Jenkins in Minnesota.

10/11/1998 HEG was arrested in Iowa for felony possession.

10/12/1998 HEG was stabbed by Eva Smith in Waukon, Iowa.

11/13/1998 HEG was arrested for violation of his restraining order.

11/16/1998 The burglary case against HEG was dismissed in Iowa due to insufficient evidence (city unknown).

1/31/2013 HEG died of cancer in Lansing, Iowa.

2019–2021 Indiana State Police Cold Case Unit, with the FBI and Kentucky State Police, re-examined the I-65 Killer cases using forensic genealogy and advanced DNA technology.

??/??/2022 HEG was identified via DNA and forensic genealogy as the "I-65 Killer," responsible for murders in Kentucky and Indiana, and assaults in Indiana and Minnesota.

4/??/2022 Indiana State Police, with FBI, Kentucky State Police, and Minnesota BCA, publicly announced that HEG was identified via DNA as the "I-65 Killer," responsible for murders in Kentucky and Indiana, and assaults in Indiana and Minnesota.

MO

Harry Edward Greenwell's confirmed attacks occurred between 1987 and 1990, spanning a three-year period with one or two-year intervals between incidents. All attacks took place during nighttime to early morning hours, with the earliest occurring at 7:00 p.m. (Jennifer's strangulation) and the latest around 6:00 a.m. (Vicki Heath's body discovery at 6:38 a.m.).

Two of the three attacks occurred on weekdays: the strangulation of Jennifer on Thursday, March 23, 1989, and Vicki Heath's murder on Saturday, February 21, 1987. The Columbus assault deviated from this pattern, occurring on Tuesday, January 2, 1990. This demonstrates flexibility in day selection while maintaining strict adherence to nighttime timing.

All three incidents occurred during winter months when environmental conditions were dark, cold, and icy. The consistent seasonal timing suggests the offender exploited weather conditions that reduced visibility and limited potential witnesses outdoors. Greenwell's employment with Canadian Pacific Railroad in Public Safety from 1980–2010 provided a consistent work schedule that may have influenced attack timing. The pattern suggests an offender who planned around occupational obligations while capitalizing on low-visibility periods and reduced guardianship.

Greenwell's attacks occurred in semi-public locations including motels, residential areas, and streets within suburban to urban environments. Two incidents took place at Days Inn motels, public accommodations that provided 24-hour access without suspicion.

The geographic pattern shows clustering along Interstate 65 corridors, suggesting familiarity with transportation routes and selection of locations offering multiple escape options. Motel locations provided controlled indoor environments with limited witness potential and predictable staff presence.

Jennifer's strangulation occurred at a residential location where Greenwell violated a restraining order, representing a shift from stranger-focused attacks to domestic violence. Despite this variation, the location still provided relative isolation during nighttime hours.

Across incidents, locations offered vehicle access for approach and departure while limiting natural surveillance. The offender demonstrated ability to exploit both commercial and residential environments based on victim availability and situational opportunity.

Greenwell accessed victims through legitimate entry into public spaces (motels) and forced entry in domestic situations (Jennifer's residence). At Days Inn locations, he entered as a customer, using deception and normal business interactions to avoid suspicion before revealing criminal intent.

The offender employed disguise elements including beanies, beards, and casual clothing (jeans and plaid flannels) to alter appearance and reduce identification risk. Initial contact involved deceptive conversation before transitioning to force and intimidation.

Exit methods consistently involved vehicle departure, with evidence suggesting movement of victims toward parking areas before completion of attacks. In the Columbus case, the survivor reported being forced toward the parking lot, indicating a pattern of relocating victims to areas with vehicle access.

The domestic incident with Jennifer involved forced entry, physical assault, and subsequent transport to a hospital before departure, demonstrating adaptation of methods based on victim relationship and situational demands.

Greenwell demonstrated weapon versatility across incidents, using firearms (.38 handgun with Vicki Heath), improvised weapons (hands during Jennifer's strangulation), and everyday objects weaponized for control (hot coffee and knife in Columbus assault).

Planned attacks involved brought weapons, particularly firearms, for fatal assaults. The .38 handgun used in Vicki Heath's murder represents preparation and intent to kill. The Columbus assault involved multiple tools—hot coffee for initial control and a knife for continued intimidation.

Weapon selection appeared situational and related to intended outcome. Firearms were used when murder was the goal, while improvised methods occurred during impulsive actions. The hot coffee attack demonstrates tactical thinking in using unexpected weapons to gain rapid control. Overall, tool usage reflects adaptability and experience, with the offender comfortable employing various methods based on availability, planning time, and desired outcome.

Victim interaction varied based on relationship and attack type. With strangers (motel victims), interaction was initially deceptive, appearing as a normal customer before revealing criminal intent. The Columbus survivor reported Greenwell asking for restaurant recommendations before returning with hostile intent.

Verbal behavior included direct commands and threats, with the Columbus victim reporting statements like he "wouldn't hurt her if she kept her mouth shut and gave him the money." Control was established through intimidation and escalating demands for money, jewelry, and compliance with relocation. With Jennifer, interaction was prolonged due to their prior relationship and domestic context. The attack represented escalation from previous domestic abuse rather than stranger-focused predation.

Across incidents, the offender demonstrated ability to maintain control through verbal commands and physical intimidation without extended conversation. Interaction patterns suggest confidence in domination methods and understanding of victim psychology.

Greenwell consistently used vehicle transportation for departure, indicating pre-positioned transportation and planned escape routes. Highway access, particularly Interstate 65, provided rapid departure from crime scenes.

Escape behavior was generally calm and controlled rather than chaotic flight. In Jennifer's case, he transported her to a hospital before departing, suggesting confidence in avoiding immediate detection. The use of disguises supported escape by reducing identification accuracy.

The offender did not remain at scenes unnecessarily and avoided confrontation with potential witnesses or first responders. Consistent vehicle use suggests comfort with automotive escape and familiarity with local road networks through his railroad employment. Overall, escape methods reflect planning, environmental awareness, and experience in avoiding detection while maintaining operational security across multiple incidents.

SIGNATURE

Signature Statement

Harry Edward Greenwell demonstrates a repeated need for physical dominance and sexual control over female victims, shown through consistent patterns of sexual assault, manual strangulation, robbery, and disposal in public or semi-public locations. This suggests an individual who exhibits both organized and adaptable tendencies, operates with confidence in familiar environments, and derives emotional reinforcement from displaying power over vulnerable women and the excitement of operating in exposed locations.

Narrative

The offender Harry Edward Greenwell demonstrates a consistent pattern of behaviors that extend beyond what is required to commit the crimes themselves. Across multiple incidents spanning from 1987 to 1990, Greenwell repeatedly targets women in vulnerable positions at motels, employs manual force as his primary method of attack, robs the establishments, and consistently moves victims to public or outdoor locations. These behaviors occur regardless of his relationship to the victim, indicating they are ritualistic rather than situational. The consistency of sexual assault combined with robbery and public locations suggests that maintaining control and experiencing the excitement of risk are central to Greenwell's criminal behavior.

These repeated rituals appear to fulfill specific psychological and emotional needs. Greenwell's targeting of women working late-night shifts at motels points to a need for control over isolated, vulnerable victims while also providing robbery opportunities. The consistent sexual assault component indicates strong lust-driven motivations, while his method of manual strangulation suggests a desire for intimate physical dominance. The pattern of robbing motels demonstrates both practical and psychological motivations, while moving victims to public locations shows a need for the excitement that comes with potential discovery, indicating possible thrill-seeking behavior and confidence in his methods.

From these patterns, several probabilistic personality traits can be inferred. Greenwell appears highly organized, as shown by his methodical approach to targeting motel clerks during vulnerable late-night hours, robbing the establishments, and maintaining consistent escape routes through building rear exits. His adaptability is demonstrated through his use of different weapons and methods while maintaining core behavioral elements. The offender exhibits characteristics of a thrill killer, with the excitement of committing crimes in public settings being a consistent component. His willingness to commit crimes in exposed locations suggests both confidence and a desire for the adrenaline that comes with increased risk.

Environmental context further supports the development of this signature. Greenwell's crimes occurred in semi-urban motel settings that provided both victim access, robbery opportunities, and escape routes. His familiarity with these environments, particularly motels with rear exits and cash registers, enabled repeated successful attacks and robberies without immediate capture. The winter timing of several attacks suggests careful planning and comfort operating in challenging conditions. The availability of public locations near roadways and dumpsters allowed Greenwell to complete his criminal acts while maintaining mobility for escape.[12]

---

12 Allen, Jake. "What We Know About the 'I-65 Killer,' Also Known as the 'Days Inn Killer.'" *IndyStar*, 14 Apr. 2022. Accessed Dec. 2025.

Ancestry. "Harry Edward Greenwell Genealogical Records." *Ancestry.com*, publication date unknown. Accessed Dec. 2025.

Andone, Dakin, Amir Vera, and Abby Bustin. "Suspect in 'Days Inn' Cold Case Murders, Assault Identified." *Federal Bureau of Investigation*, 5 Apr. 2022. Accessed Dec. 2025.

Federal Bureau of Investigation. "Suspect in 'Days Inn' Cold Case Murders, Assault Identified." *FBI.gov*, 5 Apr. 2022.

Flynn, Sheila. "How One Serial Killer Evaded Capture for More Than Three Decades with a Quiet, Farmers-Market Life." *The Independent*, 6 Apr. 2022. Accessed Dec. 2025.

Fraga, Kaleena. "After a 30-Year Investigation, Police Just Identified the 'I-65 Killer' as Harry Edward Greenwell." *All That's Interesting*, 6 Apr. 2022, allthatsinteresting.com/harry-edward -greenwell-i-65-killer. Accessed 3 Mar. 2026.

"Harry Edward Greenwell." *Find a Grave*, memorial created by JD, 24 Oct. 2013, www.findagrave.com/memorial/119220962/harry_edward-greenwell. Accessed Dec. 2025.

"I-65 Killer Identified More Than 30 Years After Murder of Three Motel Clerks." *Sky News*, 5 Apr. 2022, news.sky.com/story/i-65-killer-identified-more-than-30-years-after-murder-of-three-motel-clerks-12583347. Accessed 3 Mar. 2026.

"I-65 Serial Killer Identified." *FOX 5 New York*, 5 Apr. 2022, www.fox5ny.com/news/interstate-65-serial-killer-harry-edward-greenwell. Accessed 3 Mar. 2026.

Jacobo, Julia. "'I-65 Killer' Who Murdered 3 Women in the 1980s Identified with DNA Evidence." *ABC News*, 5 Apr. 2022. Accessed Dec. 2025.

Johnson, Constance. "Police Say They've Solved Decades-Old Case of the 'I-65' Serial Killer." *Oxygen True Crime*, 6 Apr. 2022. Accessed Dec. 2025.

Johnson, Krista. "Police Say They've Identified the 'I-65 Killer.' Here's What We Know About His Victims." *The Courier-Journal*, 5 Apr. 2022. Accessed Dec. 2025.

Karpinski, Izzy, and Courtney Spinelli. "ISP, FBI Name So-Called 'I-65 Killer' Through Investigative Genealogy." *FOX59 News*, 5 Apr. 2022. Accessed Dec. 2025.

Moore, Damion. Personal interview. Zoom meeting, 9 Dec. 2025.

Moore, Damion. *The American Crime Journal*. Multiple articles.

Stacey, Madison. "I-65 Killer Harry Edward Greenwell Had a Lengthy Criminal History." *WTHR-13*, 5 Apr. 2022. Accessed Dec. 2025.

The Waukon Standard. "Investigative Genealogy Links Deceased Rural New Albin Resident to 'I-65 Murders.'" 13 Apr. 2022. Accessed Dec. 2025.

Vigdor, Neil. "I-65 Killer Who Terrorized Motel Clerks in the 1980s Is Identified." *The New York Times*, 5 Apr. 2022. Accessed Dec. 2025.

Whelan, Michael, producer. "Episode Title on Harry Edward Greenwell." *Unresolved Podcast*, 26 Jan. 2020. Accessed Dec. 2025.

17:

TRACY LEE HOUSEL: CONFIRMED SERIAL KILLER

SUMMARY

Tracy Lee Housel was born on May 7, 1958, in Bermuda to Clyde and JoAnn Housel. He was executed at the age of 43 on March 12, 2002, in Georgia after being convicted of murder. Housel is considered a serial killer and rapist, with three confirmed murders and multiple additional assaults connected to his 1985 crime spree. His victims included Troy Smith, Gary Lee Kennedy, and Carolyn Jean Dellinger Drew. This case is historically significant because Housel was born in Bermuda and therefore held British citizenship, which

created international attention during his death penalty appeals because the United Kingdom had abolished capital punishment.

Not much detailed information is publicly documented about Housel's early childhood, but records indicate that he was raised for a time in Rhode

Island after his family moved from Bermuda. In 1959, his family relocated again to North Carolina. Housel reportedly suffered from chronic headaches and illnesses growing up and experienced a difficult home life. At the age of 14 he ran away from home and later lived with a family friend. As a young adult he eventually moved to Iowa, where he married Robin Banks, though the marriage ended in divorce in October 1984.

Housel's crimes occurred during a short but extremely violent period between February and April of 1985. His confirmed attacks took place in multiple states, including Texas, Iowa, and Georgia. The victims included Troy Smith in Rose City, Texas; Gary Lee Kennedy in Urbandale, Iowa; and Carolyn Jean Dellinger Drew in Lawrenceville, Georgia. In these crimes, Housel used different forms of violence, including strangulation, stabbing, and severe physical assault. His attacks often involved robbery, sexual violence, and the theft of credit cards or personal property from victims.

Tracy Lee Housel was eventually identified and arrested after attempting to use stolen credit cards belonging to two of his victims. Investigators quickly connected him to several violent crimes committed across multiple states. Gary Lee Kennedy survived his attack and later testified in court, providing key evidence that helped secure Housel's conviction. As a result of the investigation and testimony presented at trial, Housel was found guilty and sentenced to death.

Housel was arrested on April 14, 1985, and faced charges including murder, rape, robbery, and credit card fraud. After his conviction, he was placed on death row in Georgia. During later interviews and statements, Housel confessed to the three known murders and claimed responsibility for as many as seventeen killings, although investigators were never able to verify those additional claims. His execution in 2002 ended the case, but his crimes remain an example of how a transient offender could commit multiple violent crimes across state lines in a short period of time.

VICTIMS

CONFIRMED

Troy Smith

South Dakota truck driver Troy Smith was the first confirmed murder victim in Housel's 1985 crime spree. The two men reportedly met in Texas and spent time drinking together before Housel attacked him. Smith was sexually assaulted and then beaten with a hammer inside his truck cab before being left to die. His body was later discovered in the sleeper compartment of his truck near Beaumont, Texas.

Gary Lee Kennedy

In March 1985, Housel encountered Gary Lee Kennedy at a truck stop in Council Bluffs, Iowa. Kennedy agreed to give Housel a ride along Interstate 80, but during the trip Housel suddenly pulled a knife, demanded his wallet, and repeatedly stabbed him. Housel pushed Kennedy into a roadside ravine and stole his car and credit cards before fleeing across several states. Kennedy survived the attack and later testified about the assault.

Carolyn Jean Dellinger Drew

Carolyn Jean Dellinger Drew, a 44-year-old woman from Georgia, was Housel's final confirmed victim and the murder for which he was executed. The two met at a truck stop in Lawrenceville, Georgia, in April 1985. After leaving together in Jean's car, they drove to a secluded area near Norcross where Housel violently beat and strangled her, then further assaulted her body with a stick. He stole her car and credit cards and was arrested several days later in Florida while attempting to use them.

Renee (Survivor)

A young woman identified in court records only as Renee survived an attack by Housel in Phillipsburg, New Jersey, in April 1985. After meeting her socially, Housel offered to walk her to her car late at night. Once inside the vehicle, he strangled her, sexually assaulted her, and robbed her before leaving her alive. She later testified about the assault and identified Housel as the attacker.

Suspected

No additional victims have been identified by law enforcement. However, Housel claimed before his execution that he had killed as many as 17 people, a statement investigators were never able to verify.

POSSIBLE

Michael James Morgan

On December 30, 1981, Morgan, the 31-year-old truck driver from Lakeside, Texas, was resting at a Travelodge in Tulare, Texas, when he answered a knock on his door and was fatally stabbed in the heart by an unknown assailant. Authorities at the time noted that this killing had similarities to that of Eligio Zamorano in the same town, but Housel was never officially connected to either killing.

Eligio "Eli" Zamorano

On October 31, 1983, the 29-year-old Eligio "Eli" Zamorano was murdered in Tulare, Texas. He was the head cook at the local Vejar's and was stabbed and beaten to death under unclear circumstances. Authorities at the time noted that both the killings of Zamorano and Morgan shared similarities with the later murder of Troy Smith, but Housel was never officially connected to either killing, both of which remain unsolved.

Nueces County John Doe

An unidentified male homicide victim found in Nueces County, Texas, on Oct. 29, 1984. The church had been burglarized. The victim was discovered with limited identifying evidence, suggesting he may have been a traveler or transient individual. The man appeared to be in his mid-20s, was white, and of a small build. A cause of death was not stated, but considering similarities between the circumstances of the crime along with timing and geography, Housel was considered a suspect.

TIMELINE

05/07/1958	Tracy Lee Housel was born to parents Bill Housel and Lula Housel in Paget, Bermuda.
??/??/1959	TLH and family moved to N.C., United States.
??/??/????	TLH and family moved to Columbia Heights, Rhode Island.
??/??/1960	TLH suffered from chronic headaches and illness and was abused at home throughout his childhood.
??/??/1972	TLH got "kicked out" and left his household, moved in with a family friend, and left for good 3 months later.
??/??/1980	TLH moved to Iowa and married Robin Banks.
1980–1984	Somewhere in between the years of 1980–1984, TLH took a job as a truck driver.

10/??/1984	TLH left Banks (his wife) in October due to him "being on the road all the time."
02/20/1985	TLH killed Troy Smith in Texas.
03/29/1985	TLH was found in possession of a gas receipt in Frankfort, KY.
03/30/1985	TLH stabbed and slit the throat of hitchhiker Gary Lee Kennedy in Urbandale, Iowa, took his credit card, his BRW Caprice, and left him for dead.
03/30/1985	TLH received gas tickets in Greeneville, IL; Carthage, IL; and Catlettsburg, KY.
03/31/1985	TLH was found in possession of a gas receipt in Henderson, KY.
04/01/1985	TLH was found in possession of a gas receipt in Phillipsburg, NJ.
04/03/1985	TLH committed sexual assault, robbery, and abandoned Kennedy's vehicle, as well as had gas tickets in Ashland, Va.
04/06/1985	TLH met Jean Dellinger Drew in Lawrenceville, GA, at a Unionville truck stop, murdered and raped her, then left her in her car.
04/13/1985	TLH is suspected in the murder of Jean Dellinger Drew. TLH was with Jean Dellinger Drew that night.

04/14/1985 TLH was arrested in Daytona Beach, FL, by the Daytona Beach Police Department for the suspected murder of Gary Lee Kennedy and Jean Dellinger Drew.

04/??/1985 TLH was tried and prosecuted by the judge and jury in Gwinnett County, GA.

03/12/2002 TLH was executed by lethal injection in Jackson, GA.

MO

Tracy Lee Housel's criminal behavior demonstrates methodical timing patterns that suggest strategic planning and risk awareness. His crimes consistently occurred during early morning hours, with two of three documented incidents taking place between midnight and 6 a.m. This temporal selection indicates understanding of reduced witness presence and diminished law enforcement activity during these periods.

The offender showed preference for weekend timing, with two of three crimes occurring on Saturday or Saturday nights. This pattern suggests either lifestyle flexibility that accommodated weekend criminal activity or deliberate exploitation of increased victim availability during these periods. The seasonal clustering is notable, with two murders occurring during spring months, and both the early spring and late winter incidents coinciding with daylight saving time transitions.

The regularity of these timing patterns demonstrates behavioral maturity in crime execution and suggests an offender capable of delayed action rather than impulsive behavior. The consistency indicates experience and learning capacity, with the offender appearing to balance opportunity recognition with risk mitigation strategies.

Housel's location selection reveals calculated risk assessment and environmental familiarity. He consistently utilized truck stops for initial victim contact in two of three documented cases, suggesting comfort with transient populations and understanding of these environments' operational patterns. This choice provided access to vulnerable victims while maintaining plausible explanations for his presence.

The geographic progression from public contact points to private execution locations demonstrates sophisticated planning and risk management. All crime locations maintained proximity to major roadways, revealing prioritization of escape route accessibility. The transition from suburban to rural settings for the actual murders indicates awareness of privacy requirements for crime completion.

The consistent selection of locations offering both victim availability and rapid departure options suggests experience navigating diverse geographic areas. This pattern demonstrates environmental awareness and ability to identify locations that serve multiple operational needs within his criminal methodology.

The offender's approach methods demonstrate procedural familiarity with victim manipulation and social engineering techniques. Housel consistently achieved non-forced access through deception rather than physical force, indicating preference for psychological control over physical dominance. His methods included climbing into victims' vehicles under pretense, presenting himself as a hitchhiker, and engaging in seemingly consensual sexual encounters.

This approach suggests experience with victim psychology and ability to project trustworthiness until strategic moments. The consistent use of deception across all incidents indicates a refined understanding of how to exploit victims' willingness to assist or engage with him. The efficiency of these methods demonstrates increasing competence and adaptation of successful techniques across multiple incidents. The uniform pattern of vehicle theft for escape shows systematic planning and understanding of mobility requirements for successful departure. This consistency reveals both practical thinking and experience with the logistics of crime scene departure.

Housel's weapon selection reveals adaptability and situational responsiveness rather than ritual attachment to specific tools. His weapons varied across incidents: an improvised hammer during a struggle with Troy, a premeditated knife for robbing Gary, and improvised beating and strangulation methods with Jean. This variation indicates flexible planning with ability to utilize available resources as situations developed.

The progression from improvised to brought weapons and back to improvised tools suggests learning and adaptation based on situational requirements rather than escalating violence patterns. The efficiency priorities appear focused on immediate control achievement rather than specific tool preferences. This pattern demonstrates comfort using various control methods and problem-solving ability when encountering unexpected resistance. The weapon choices consistently served functional rather than symbolic purposes, indicating a practical approach to victim control and crime completion.

Housel's victim interactions demonstrate practiced control methods with emphasis on efficiency over prolonged engagement. His interaction levels varied from minimal contact with Troy to extended travel periods with Gary to prolonged sexual interaction with Jean. Despite these variations, he maintained a consistent ability to project deceptive presentations until strategic revelation points.

The offender showed capability for behavioral control and planning, maintaining helpful or friendly demeanor until circumstances required revelation of criminal intent. With Troy, he initially provided assistance before robbing and killing him. With Gary, he posed as an innocent hitchhiker before using verbal threats to assert dominance. With Jean, he maintained cordial behavior until an argument triggered a violent response.

The escalation pattern correlating with interaction duration indicates potential trigger points requiring management but overall demonstrates experience with victim psychology and understanding of effective control mechanisms. The behavioral consistency across varied interaction types shows adaptability while maintaining operational effectiveness.

Housel's escape methods demonstrate high situational awareness and systematic approach to evidence management. He consistently executed smooth departures without confrontation or challenge, indicating experience avoiding detection and ability to maintain composure under pressure. His escape direction consistently led toward roadways, utilizing stolen vehicles for rapid departure.

The offender showed understanding of investigation procedures through consistent theft of victim identification materials, deliberately interfering with victim identification processes. He stole wallets and IDs to complicate law enforcement identification efforts and removed or disposed of victims' belongings as part of his departure routine.

The uniform approach across all incidents reveals learning capacity and refinement of successful techniques through repeated application. The systematic nature of these escapes, combined with their consistent success, indicates both planning ability and experience with the practical requirements of avoiding immediate detection and capture.

SIGNATURE

Signature Statement

The unsub demonstrates a repeated need for control and power, shown through consistent sexual advances toward victims and the maintenance of similar behavioral patterns across incidents. The ritualized repetition of these actions suggests an individual who values structure and predictability, and who likely prefers situations where dominance can be established and maintained. The lack of escalation indicates comfort with a familiar method rather than a desire for increasing risk. Overall, the behavior suggests someone who gains emotional reinforcement from exerting control and repeating actions that fulfill a psychological need for power and dominance.

Narrative

The systematic analysis of criminal behavior patterns reveals consistent ritualistic elements that extend beyond the practical requirements of offense commission. Through examination of three documented incidents, a clear behavioral signature emerges that demonstrates the intersection of psychological need fulfillment and environmental opportunity. Across all three documented cases, identical behavioral sequences occurred with remarkable consistency. Each incident involved attempted sexual advances toward victims while they remained alive, coupled with systematic theft of personal belongings. The only variation observed was in case #2GLK, where vehicle theft did not occur due to the absence of available transportation. This consistency suggests a structured approach to criminal activity, where specific actions serve purposes beyond mere opportunity or convenience.

The repetitive nature of these behaviors indicates habit formation and comfort with established patterns. The subject demonstrates repeated sequences that occur regardless of practical necessity, suggesting these actions fulfill deeper psychological requirements rather than situational demands. The persistence of sexual advances and item theft across varying circumstances indicates these behaviors form the core foundation of the offender's criminal signature.

The documented behaviors reveal consistent psychological needs being satisfied through criminal activity. Throughout all incidents, the subject exhibited a demonstrated need for power assertion combined with sexual intent. No escalation or evolution of these psychological drivers was observed across the timeline of documented crimes, suggesting stable underlying motivational factors.

The signature reflects psychological reinforcement through control and dominance over victims. The combination of sexual advances and theft of personal items suggests the subject gains emotional satisfaction through both physical dominance and symbolic possession of victim belongings. These behaviors serve to reinforce the perpetrator's sense of power and control, extending beyond the immediate criminal act to provide ongoing psychological gratification.

Environmental analysis reveals strategic location selection and timing preferences. All three incidents occurred during nighttime hours in winter months, with case #3JDD extending into early spring. Geographic settings varied between suburban and rural areas, but all locations shared proximity to roadways, suggesting accessibility and escape route considerations.

The consistent nighttime timing indicates comfort with low-visibility conditions and suggests planning around reduced witness presence. Road proximity across all incidents demonstrates strategic thinking regarding transportation access and potential escape routes. The progression from suburban to rural settings may indicate increasing confidence or evolving location preferences, though this pattern requires additional data for confirmation.

The environmental factors appear to support rather than limit the subject's ritualistic behaviors. Isolated nighttime locations provide the privacy necessary for extended victim interaction, allowing time for both sexual advances and systematic theft of belongings. This suggests the subject selects environments that facilitate complete expression of psychological needs rather than rushing through abbreviated criminal acts.

The documented behavioral patterns reveal a subject who demonstrates consistent need for psychological dominance expressed through sexual advances and symbolic possession of victim belongings. The ritualistic nature of these behaviors, combined with strategic environmental selection, suggests an individual who values control and systematic approach to criminal activity. The subject appears comfortable operating in varied geographic settings during consistent temporal windows, indicating adaptability within established behavioral parameters.

The evidence suggests emotional reinforcement is derived from the complete execution of both sexual dominance and theft rituals, with each element serving distinct but complementary psychological functions. The consistency of these patterns across multiple incidents, despite varying environmental contexts, indicates deeply ingrained behavioral drivers that transcend situational factors.[13]

---

13 "Housel, Tracy Lee." *Clark County Prosecutor*, www.clarkprosecutor.org/html/death/US/housel764.htm.

"Housel, Tracy Lee." *Murderpedia*, murderpedia.org/male.H/h1/housel-tracy-lee.htm.

Housel v. McDonough, 238 F.3d 1289 (11th Cir. 2001). *Justia Law*, law.justia.com/cases/federal/appellate-courts/F3/238/1289/515305/.

Housel v. State, 44110 (Ga. 1987). *Justia Law*, law.justia.com/cases/georgia/supreme-court/1987/44110-1.html.

"Information on the Execution of Tracy Lee Housel." *Georgia Department of Law*, 13 Mar. 2002, law.georgia.gov/press-releases/2002-03-13/information-execution-tracy-lee-housel.

Laccetti, Susan. "California Man Wanted in Four States Will Go on Trial in Gwinnett Slaying." *The Atlanta Journal-Constitution*, 27 Jan. 1986, via *Newspapers.com*.

"Man Executed Despite UK Mercy Plea." *CBS News*, 21 May 2002, www.cbsnews.com/news/man-executed-despite-uk-mercy-plea/.

"Nueces County John Doe (1984)." *Unidentified Awareness Wiki*, https://unidentified-awareness.fandom.com/wiki/Nueces_County_John_Doe_(1984).

Pendered, David. "Gwinnett Slaying Suspect Is Charged in Crime Spree." *The Atlanta Journal-Constitution*, 16 Apr. 1985, via *Newspapers.com*.

"Suspected Robber Is Arrested." *The Salinas Californian*, 16 Mar. 1984, via *Newspapers.com*.

"Tracy Housel." *Wikipedia*, en.wikipedia.org/wiki/Tracy_Housel.

"Tracy Lee Housel." *Amnesty International*, June 2021, www.amnesty.org/es/wp-content/uploads/2021/06/amr510432002en.pdf.

18:

JERRY LEON JOHNS: CONFIRMED KILLER, POSSIBLE SERIAL KILLER

SUMMARY

Jerry Leon Johns was born on November 16, 1948, in the United States and died in December 2015 while in prison. He was a confirmed serial offender responsible for the murders of at least one woman, he attempted murder of another, and investigators suspecting his involvement in several additional cases across Tennessee, Mississippi, Arkansas, and others. Since 2019 and his confirmation as the killer of Tina Farmer, Johns is often referred to as the "Bible Belt Strangler," and his case is historically significant for the methodical way he targeted vulnerable women along interstate highways, as well as for the decades-long investigation that ultimately used DNA evidence to identify him years after his death. His crimes and their resolution highlight the challenges law enforcement faced in tracking transient offenders across multiple jurisdictions during the 1980s.

Johns' early life was marked by family instability and criminal behavior. Born to Earl Leon Cogdill and Lucy Lee Nunley-Cogdill in Athens, Tennessee, his childhood was disrupted by his parents' divorce and his father's criminal activities. After his mother remarried Wilfred Johns in 1958, Jerry was legally adopted and took the Johns surname. School records from Homer L. Ferguson High School documented his tendency toward deception, noting he had "a habit of making untruthful statements with the intent of deceiving." His criminal behavior began in adolescence with vehicle theft charges, and he later enlisted in the Marine Corps but was dishonorably discharged after multiple incidents of going AWOL and vehicle theft.

Johns' confirmed murders occurred between late 1984 and early 1985 across Tennessee and surrounding states. His victims were primarily women involved in prostitution whom he encountered along major interstate highways. Johns employed a consistent method of ligature strangulation using improvised materials found at crime scenes. He targeted vulnerable women by posing as a police officer or potential customer, gaining their trust before attacking them in isolated rural locations. Law enforcement initially struggled to connect the cases across jurisdictions, but Johns was captured in March 1985 after attempting to murder Linda Schacke, who survived and provided crucial testimony. DNA evidence later confirmed his involvement in additional murders, though this identification occurred decades after the crimes.

Johns was arrested on March 6, 1985, following a high-speed chase after the attempted murder of Linda Schacke. He was charged with felonious assault with intent to commit murder, aggravated kidnapping, and various other offenses related to the Schacke case. In March 1987, Johns was convicted of felonious assault with intent to commit murder and sentenced to prison. He remained incarcerated until his death in December 2015. Notably, Johns was never formally charged with the murders later attributed to him through DNA evidence, as these connections were established after his death.

The Johns case significantly impacted law enforcement practices, particularly regarding interstate cooperation in serial murder investigations. The formation of the Redhead Murders Task Force in 1985, involving the Tennessee Bureau of Investigation, FBI, and multiple state agencies, demonstrated early efforts at multi-jurisdictional collaboration. The case also highlighted the importance of DNA evidence in cold case investigations, as Johns' connection to victim Tina Farmer was only established in 2019 through advanced forensic techniques. Additionally, the involvement of high school students in identifying Johns as the "Bible Belt Strangler" in 2018 showcased the potential for citizen participation in criminal investigations. The case remains significant as an example of how persistent investigation and evolving forensic science can solve decades-old crimes, providing closure to victims' families and contributing to the understanding of serial criminal behavior patterns.

VICTIMS

CONFIRMED

Tina Farmer

She was murdered in December of 1984 and found January 1, 1985, along Interstate 75 in Campbell County, Tennessee. She was strangled to death with a ligature Johns made from a pillow case used during the crime. He was identified as the killer of Tina Farmer in 2019 through DNA testing. He was not charged for her murder since he had died in prison four years prior in 2015.

Linda Schacke

She is the only survivor known for Jerry Johns. He had picked her up from Katch One in Knoxville, Tennessee where she worked and took her to a hotel pretending to be an officer. They had stayed there for a while until he had taken her back to meet with another girl called Shannon. That is when he bound and gagged her and decided he didn't want to wait for Shannon. He drove around acting like he was going to drop her off with another officer. He drove to Watts Road, where he ordered her out of the car and down to a culvert, and then he strangled her. After he believed she was dead, he left. However, she wasn't dead and was found near the interstate by passersby. The police were notified, and they caught him in her car pulling into the Holiday Inn.

SUSPECTED

Michelle Inman

She was murdered between October 1984–January 1985. Her skeletal remains were found in Cheatham County on the side of a highway near Nashville. She is suspected to be connected to Jerry John based on the method of killing, the location of the killing, and Johns' admission to police that he was in the area at the time of her murder.

POSSIBLE

Elizabeth Lamotte

She was killed in March 1985 in Greene County, Tennessee. She could possibly be linked to the Jerry Johns case because of the facts of her case. She was another reddish-haired young woman dumped on the side of a highway, similar to Johns' known victims. There was also a hotel matchbook that was found near her body. This hotel was on Loop Street in Houston, Texas. Jerry Johns was discovered with a receipt from a gas station that was also located on Loop Street in Houston, Texas, when he was arrested for the attempted murder of Linda Schacke. Although her body was found after Johns was arrested, her time of death makes it possible that he killed her shortly before his arrest.

Lorie Pennell

She was killed in January 1985 in Olive Branch, Mississippi. She was last seen at a truck stop in West Memphis, Arkansas, engaged in prostitution. She was a small, young, white, reddish-haired woman strangled with a ligature and dumped on the side of the highway, just like Johns' known victims. She also lived very close to Johns' sister, and he was known to live in the area for a while.

Lisa Nichols

She was a 28-year-old woman whose body was discovered on September 16, 1984, along Interstate 40 near West Memphis, Arkansas. Nichols had strawberry-blonde (reddish) hair and was found wearing only a sweater. She had been beaten and strangled with a ligature. She was engaged in prostitution at a truck stop in West Memphis, Arkansas. Johns also admitted he had been in the area where her body was found.

TIMELINE

6/14/1948	Earl Cogdill, Jerry Leon Johns' father, received a conditional pardon from the State Board of Pardons and Paroles, giving him a three year and one month credit on his five-year sentence in 1949.
11/16/1948	Jerry Leon Johns (JLJ) was born to Earl Leon Cogdill and Lucy Lee Nunley-Cogdill in Athens, Tenn.
6/??/1956	Lucy Lee and Earl Leon Cogdill divorced after Earl caused Loretta Lou Voy, a 17-year-old girl, to become pregnant.
6/23/1956	Earl Cogdill married Loretta Lou Voy, the 17-year-old he impregnated.

6/??/1958	Lucy Lee Cogdill married Wilfred Espin Johns II.
8/05/1960	Wilfred Johns legally adopted six Cogdill children (including JLJ) and changed their last names to Johns.
??/??/1963	Student progress report from Homer L. Ferguson High School recorded, "Jerry has a habit of making untruthful statements with the intent of deceiving."
12/??/1963	JLJ was charged with misappropriation of motor vehicle and placed on probation (given to Maryland Police).
11/03/1964	The McMinn County, Tenn., Courthouse burned, destroying birth certificate records for JLJ, later allowing the family to create a new certificate that listed Wilfred E. Johns as his father.
1/??/1964	JLJ was released from probation for motor vehicle misappropriation.
5/??/1965	JLJ completed 11th grade at Homer L. Ferguson High School in Newport News, Va., and did not return to high school.
11/16/1965	JLJ enlisted in the US Marine Corps (USMC). At some point in the USMC, he completes his GED.
4/28/1967	JLJ went AWOL from the USMC for 69 days.

11/16/1967	JLJ was charged with AWOL and auto theft out of Cumberland, Maryland, for stealing a 1966 Mustang and taking it to Miami, Florida.
1/18/1968	JLJ escaped the brig at Camp Pendleton, California, and traveled by airplane to Rockford, Illinois, and later stole an automobile.
2/29/1968	JLJ was arrested and charged with AWOL, auto theft, carrying a concealed weapon, and obstructing an officer in Rockford, IL. He was returned to USMC authorities. This is most likely when he was living in the attic of his parents' house and encountered Phyllis Cogdill.
4/01/1968	JLJ was released to Marines for four years of custody by the attorney general.
5/23/1968	JLJ reached Camp Pendleton, California, and escaped from an armed guard on the same day, stealing a 1967 Chevrolet on the base.
9/23/1968	JLJ was charged with interstate transfer of a stolen vehicle in El Reno, Oklahoma.
9/27/1968	JLJ's charges of AWOL and auto theft were dismissed in Baltimore, MD.
10/24/1968	A case worker report on Wilfred Johns' adoption noted that JLJ "was the only one (child) who did not favor adoption."

9/12/1969 JLJ was dishonorably discharged from the US Marine Corps.

4/16/1970 JLJ was sentenced to four years for interstate transfer of a stolen vehicle to serve 4 years in FCI Tallahassee, FL.

4/24/1970 JLJ was charged with arson in Pascagoula, MS.

1/10/1971 JLJ received 71 (or possibly 10) years in prison for arson in Pascagoula, MS.

5/18/1971 JLJ was declared a fugitive from the state of Virginia by the Public Safety Department in Miami, FL.

9/04/1971 JLJ was released to Virginia authorities by Public Safety Dept. of Miami, FL.

9/04/1971 JLJ was charged with failure to return a rented vehicle in Newport News, Va.

9/21/1971 JLJ was sentenced to 12 months at the Penal Farm/State Farm of Va.

11/??/1971 JLJ's 71-year sentence for arson in Pascagoula, MS, was revoked.

7/14/1971 JLJ was sentenced to complete his remaining 836 days by the Federal Correctional Institute of Tallahassee, FL.

10/??/1971 JLJ began living with Phyllis Cogdill.

1972	JLJ's parole was revoked for inability to abstain from further criminal behavior.
5/04/1972	JLJ was charged with a parole violation in Richmond, Va.
??/??/1972	JLJ claimed to have become a trucker this year, most likely for John Coach Trucking Co. in Houston, Texas (which is most likely a self-lease trucking company Jerry Johns started).
10/16/1973	JLJ escaped confinement and was later sentenced to 18 months by the Houston Treatment Center.
2/12/1975	JLJ was placed on restriction at Houston Treatment Center for lying to staff. Staff notes recorded, "Johns is a very immature, irresponsible, and hot tempered individual... He openly verbalizes anger and hostility toward authority figures."
5/26/1976	JLJ was charged with escape, NMUTA, and MRU in Oxford, WI, and sentenced to 447 days by the Federal Correction Institute.
11/01/1976	JLJ was released from Federal Correction Institute in Oxford, WI, after completing his sentence
1976–1985	No criminal activity was discovered under the name JLJ. However, he admitted to going by at least eight additional aliases, including Jerome Eric Starr. He had a social security card with that name when he was arrested on March 6, 1985. He also said that he was most likely in

	trouble with the IRS for not paying taxes, and his wife admitted that he stole several trucks around 1980 to start his own trucking company.
??/??/1978	JLJ began working as a trucker for Northern Star Plating in Loves Park, IL.
??/??/1979	JLJ stopped working at Northern Star Plating.
9/??/1979	JLJ married Phyllis Cogdill.
??/??/1980	JLJ claimed he began his own trucking company this year, mostly likely for Maggio Trucking Co. in Rockford, IL.
3/10/1980	Lee Espin Johns, Jerry and Phyllis Johns' youngest son, was born.
1/12/1982	Lee Espin Johns died.
??/??/1982	Lorie Ann Mealer Pennell went missing from a West Memphis, Arkansas, truck stop.
??/??/1982	Lorie Ann Mealer's biological father, Kenneth Mealer, attempted to file a missing persons report on Lorie at Weakley County Sheriff's Department, but he was rebuffed because she did not go missing from Weakley County.
??/??/1982	Lorie Ann Mealer's biological father, Kenneth Mealer, filed a missing persons report in West Memphis, Arkansas.

??/??/1983	JLJ and Phyllis Johns moved to Tennessee.
??/??/1984	JLJ left Maggio Trucking because he wanted to start his own trucking business.
??/??/1984	JLJ started his own trucking company with Earl Leon (AKA Rebel) Cogdill, his father-in-law and most likely birth father. He named the company Rebel Trucking to convince Earl to go into business with him. Also, he stole a truck for Earl to drive.
9/16/1984	Lisa Nichols' body was found in West Memphis, Arkansas. It was unidentified for several months.
9/20/1984	Tina McKenney married Richard L. Farmer, who provided her drugs and trafficked her at truck stops in the Indianapolis area.
11/22/1984	Elizabeth Lamotte (Greene County Jane Doe) disappeared from the Youth Development Center in Manchester, NH, after furlough to visit Gill Stadium for a high school f ootball game.
12/29/1984	Tina Farmer's likely date of death.
1/01/1985	Tina Marie McKinney-Farmer's unidentified body was found near the Stinking Creek exit of I-75 in Campbell County, Tenn.

1/24/1985	JLJ was charged with altering motor vehicle ID numbers and sale or receipt of stolen vehicles.
1/24/1985	Lorie Ann Mealer Pennel's body was found by a truck driver driving southbound on US Highway 78, a hundred feet east of Coldwater River Bridge at around 7:30 a.m. Her body was 20 feet south of the highway near Olive Branch, Desoto County, Mississippi. She was killed at approximately 1:30 a.m.
2/15/1985	A receipt from RACETRAC placed JLJ at 3059 S Loop East Houston, TX, the road near the motel on the business card that was found near Elizabeth Lamotte's body.
3/04/1985	At 2:36 p.m., JLJ was at McCoy Auto Parts in Cleveland, Tenn., only about an hour and 30 minutes away from Katch One Club where Jerry Johns picked up Linda Schacke. The way to get from Cleveland to Knoxville includes driving on I-75.
3/05/1985	
4:00 p.m.	Schacke arrived at Katch One.
7:00 p.m.	Jerry and Wayne Johns arrived at Katch One.
10:30 p.m.	JLJ returned to Katch One to meet Schacke.
11:00 p.m.	Schacke got dressed, and she and JLJ left Katch One.
11:30 p.m.	Schacke and JLJ arrived at Holiday Inn.
3/06/1985	
12:00 p.m.	Schacke told JLJ she needed to be home by 12:30, as her roommate was expecting her.

2:30 a.m.	Schacke and JLJ left the hotel room and went down to the parking lot and got into Linda's car and returned to the Katch One for Shannon. Schacke was bound and gagged.
1:00 a.m.	Around this time, JLJ did not want to wait on Shannon, so he left with Schacke and began to drive around acting like he was going to drop her off with another officer.
1:00–1:30 a.m.	Schacke and JLJ arrived at Watts Road, where he ordered her out of the car and down to a culvert, and then strangled her, leaving when he thought she was dead.
1:30–1:45 a.m.	Wayne Johns returned to Katch One, trying to get Shannon Anderson to leave with him. She told the bouncer to tell him to leave, which he did.
2:05 a.m.	Linda was discovered on the side of the interstate by a passersby, and police were notified.
2:30 a.m.	Linda Schacke arrived at Park West Hospital after attack.
3:00 a.m.	JLJ was spotted pulling into a Holiday Inn parking lot by police, and a chase ensued.
3:10 a.m.	JLJ was arrested in Schacke's blue Datsun 280Z.
3:25 a.m.	Linda Schacke was interviewed at Park West Hospital by David Davenport.
5:05 a.m.	JLJ signed the admonition and waiver at Knox County Sheriff's Department.
3/06/1985	Linda Schacke was almost murdered by JLJ with a capias issued or the arrest of charges stemming from Linda's assault. JLJ was arrested after a high-speed chase for being found driving Linda's stolen vehicle.
4/14/1985	Elizabeth Lamotte's nude body was discovered beside I-81 near the Jeroldstown Road exit.

4/24/1985 The Redhead Murders Task Force (TBI, law enforcement from five other states including PA, KY, MS, AR, and FBI) met at TBI headquarters in Nashville, Tenn., to compare notes on eight unsolved homicides–including three in Tennessee–with suspicious similarities to compare notes on, but they couldn't come to a conclusion if there was a serial killer operating in and around Tennessee. They asked the FBI to profile the killer of eight different murders. Knox County Chief of Detectives, John Maples, said that Jerry Johns is not considered a suspect.

4/25/1985 An *AP News* report by Marta Aldrich claimed that investigators had a fingerprint left at the crime scene of the Greene County Jane Doe (Elizabeth Lamotte).

6/??/1985 Lisa Nichols was identified.

6/30/1985 A *Memphis Commercial Appeal* newspaper article said that the person later identified as Tina Farmer was bound with strips of cloth from a pillowcase on her hands and feet, and she was strangled with the nylon band from the pillowcase.

7/15/1985 JLJ made bail for charges related to Linda Schacke's attempted murder. Linda Schacke attempted to leave the country but was talked out of it by Knox County Sheriff's Department Officer, Larry Johnson.

7/27/1985 Elizabeth Lamotte was officially discharged from the Manchester Youth Development Center as she turned 18 despite her not returning to the facility.

7/31/1985	True bill returned against JLJ for charges relating to Linda Schacke's incident.
8/06/1985	A truck was reported stolen in Pearland, TX. It was later found in possession of JLJ.
8/08/1985	JLJ was arrested near Springfield, IL, in a stolen truck from Pearland, TX.
9/03/1985	Charges were dismissed against JLJ for the stolen truck from Pearland, TX, by motion of the state.
9/31/1985	Charges in Springfield, IL, for driving stolen truck on 3/6/1985 were dismissed by a motion of the state.
11/??/1985	JLJ was indicted by a grand jury in Knox County, Tenn., for felonies related to the Linda Schacke incident.
??/??/1985	Research by the Knox County PD showed Jerry Johns' sister, Barbara Maxine Waters, living in Batesville, MS. (Ex-wife Phyllis confirmed he visited there several times per year).
2/19/1986	JLJ was formally indicted by a Knox County grand jury for felonious assault and aggravated kidnapping.
3/06/1986	JLJ and his brother, Wayne, were indicted by a federal grand jury for transporting a stolen vehicle across state lines. JLJ was also arraigned on state charges of kidnapping and felonious assault with intent to commit murder in regard to the Linda Schacke case.

5/06/1986 Attorney Charles Fels (JLJ's attorney) filed motions to sup press identification, compel discovery, suppress photographs, etc., to the Criminal Court of Knox County, Tenn., Division III in matters related to the Linda Schacke case.

5/27/1986 JLJ's trial began with suppression hearings on this date.

6/05/1986 Assistant District Attorney Robert Jolley Jr. submitted a court order notifying of additional witnesses to be added and notice of intent to seek enhanced punishment with Judge George Balisteros.

3/05/1987 JLJ was convicted of felonious assault with the intent to commit murder and various other charges relating to the Linda Schacke case.

4/01/1987 Linda Schacke was reinterviewed by Virginia Wolaver, a probation officer, to create an addendum to the victim statement. She said she would "die if he (Johns) ever gets out" and that she was afraid of Johns' brother, Wayne, and that he may seek revenge on her at a later date.

4/03/1987 Presentence report was filed for JLJ by Virginia Wolaver.

4/10/1987 This was the sentencing hearing date for conviction of charges relating to the Linda Schacke incident.

8/23/1989 Criminal Court of Knox County ordered the return of ring and pendant taken by JLJ to Linda Schacke.

??/??/1992 Tina Farmer's sister, Sandra Price, called Indianapolis Police to remind them Tina was missing and wanted answers.

12/??/2015 JLJ died in prison.

10/??/2017 Family and friends of Espy Pilgrim contacted Aaron Frederick of KSP to notify them that they thought the Knox County Jane Doe was their friend/relative.

5/15/2018 Elizabethton High School's (EHS) sociology class holds a press conference naming the heretofore unrecognized serial killer of redheaded women in and around Tennessee in and around the 1980s as the "Bible Belt Strangler."

??/??/2018 A woman who is a citizen sleuth listened to the *Out of the Shadows* podcast by Shane Waters about the Redhead Murders and found the Campbell County Jane Doe similar to a missing person on a website she had recently visited. She contacted Waters through an FBI messenger to inform him of her conclusions. Shane Waters submitted the tip to the TBI website tip page.

8/??/2018 Amy Emberton, TBI intelligence analyst, found fingerprints from Tina Farmer (the Campbell County Jane Doe) from a previous arrest.

8/??/2018 Detective Nick Hubbs of the Indianapolis Metropolitan Police Department collected DNA from Tina Farmer's family.

9/06/2018 It was announced that the Shelby County Sheriff's Office identified by fingerprint Tina Marie McKenney-Farmer of Indiana as the Campbell County Jane Doe that was found near the Stinking Creek exit.

10/01/2018 Espy Regina Black-Pilgrim was confirmed by KSP as the Knox County Jane Doe of 1985.

10/16/2018 EHS's sociology class presented findings to the Knoxville FBI field office. In attendance were four FBI behavioral analysts (three from Quantico and one from Chattanooga).

11/13/2018 Elizabeth Lamotte was identified as the Greene County Jane Doe.

12/19/2019 TBI announced that the deceased Jerry Johns is the killer of Tina McKenney-Farmer after finding his DNA on items left with her body.

8/30/2022 "Baby Girl" Jane Doe from Campbell County is identified as the 15-year-old Tracy Sue Walker of Lafayette, Indiana. The connection was made after Othram Laboratories located a possible family member in the Lafayette area, and TBI intelligence analysts located several relatives there, who confirmed they had a relative who disappeared in 1978.

2/09/2023 Linda Schacke, in an interview with Alex Campbell (editor of this book), said the police told her that the other women were strangled with a ligature that was not brought with the killer but made from items at the scene.

3/01/2024 It was announced that Lorie Ann Mealer Pennell had been identified as the DeSoto County Jane Doe by Othram Labs in Woodlands, TX.

MO

Jerry Johns' documented criminal activities occurred within a concentrated timeframe spanning from late 1984 through early 1985. The recorded incidents took place on March 5, 1985, during late night to early morning hours; December 29, 1984, during late night hours; and sometime between December 1984 and January 1985 with timing uncertain. All confirmed incidents occurred during late night hours when documented, with operations taking place during weekend to early week periods across winter and spring seasons. The timing pattern shows Johns operating during hours when potential witnesses would be minimal, particularly relevant given his targeting of women involved in prostitution who were active during these late hours. His occupation as a truck driver provided extended periods away from his home base, creating opportunities for criminal activity during these timeframes.

The Linda Shacke case provides the most detailed documentation of his operational timing, revealing he engaged in over an hour of conversation before attempting murder. The consistency in late night operations across documented cases demonstrates a pattern of utilizing specific time periods that aligned with both victim availability and reduced witness presence.

Johns selected locations exclusively along major interstate highways in rural settings for all documented incidents. The Linda Shacke case occurred on the side of Interstate 40, the Tina Farmer case on the side of Interstate 75, and the Michelle Inman case off Interstate 24 West. Each location was classified as public space in rural environments, providing isolation from populated areas while maintaining direct access to major transportation corridors. The geographic pattern shows Johns operating across multiple interstate systems, indicating familiarity with extensive road networks spanning different jurisdictions. Each selected location provided immediate escape route access through the interstate system while offering sufficient isolation to conduct criminal activities without immediate witness presence. The consistent selection of rural interstate locations demonstrates repeated use of similar environmental conditions across different geographic areas. The pattern shows Johns utilizing locations that balanced accessibility for both victim encounter and rapid departure.

Johns accessed all documented victims through their involvement in prostitution services, requiring no forced entry methods in any recorded case. The Linda Shacke case documents his use of deception, specifically posing as a police officer to gain victim compliance. Information regarding specific access methods for the Tina Farmer and Michelle Inman cases remains limited, though both victims were involved in prostitution and Michelle Inman may have also been hitchhiking. Exit methods consistently involved driving away from crime scenes, with all documented escapes utilizing highway access. The Linda Shacke case provides specific documentation of Johns initially using the victim's personal vehicle before transitioning to trying a highway departure. The pattern shows consistent use of vehicular transportation for escape across all cases where information is available. Johns demonstrated use of available transportation resources while maintaining consistent reliance on highway systems for departure from crime scenes.

Johns employed strangulation with ligature as the method in all three documented cases. The weapons used were classified as improvised rather than pre-selected tools, with the Linda Shacke case specifically documenting the use of clothing items as ligature material. The Tina Farmer and Michelle Inman cases also involved ligature strangulation, though specific materials used are not documented. The pattern shows absolute consistency in method selection across all cases, with Johns utilizing readily available materials rather than bringing pre-selected weapons. The use of improvised ligatures demonstrates adaptation to available materials at each crime scene while maintaining consistent technique application. The weapon selection pattern indicates reliance on materials that could be found at the scene rather than planned equipment procurement.

The Linda Shacke case provides the most comprehensive documentation of Johns' victim interaction patterns, revealing prolonged engagement with calm, conversational behavior. Linda Shacke reported that Johns was smooth and convincing in his approach, successfully maintaining his police officer deception throughout their interaction. He engaged in extended conversation for over an hour before attempting murder, demonstrating sustained behavioral control during victim contact. Limited information exists regarding victim interactions in the Tina Farmer and Michelle Inman cases, though documentation indicates Johns referred to prostitutes as "nuisances" across multiple incidents. The Linda Shacke case shows escalating threats over time within the single encounter, though Johns maintained controlled demeanor throughout the extended interaction period. The documented case reveals Johns' ability to sustain normal conversation while concealing criminal intent until the final moments of victim contact.

Documentation of escape methods remains limited across the three cases, with the most detailed information available from the Linda Shacke case where Johns initially moved toward Linda's personal vehicle before heading toward highway access. The Tina Farmer and Michelle Inman cases show escape direction toward highway systems, though specific transportation methods and concealment techniques are not documented for these incidents. The Linda Shacke case documents Johns' use of police officer disguise during the crime, which continued through the initial escape phase. All documented cases show movement toward interstate highway systems for departure from crime scenes. The pattern indicates consistent utilization of major roadways for escape routes, though specific vehicles and detailed escape procedures are only documented in the Linda Shacke case where Johns demonstrated adaptation by initially using available victim transportation before transitioning to highway departure.

SIGNATURE

Signature Statement

Jerry Johns demonstrates a repeated psychological need for control and ritual completion, evidenced by his consistent use of ligature strangulation and targeted selection of women involved in prostitution. This suggests an offender who values structured, repeatable methods and gains psychological reinforcement from symbolic acts of dominance and control rather than opportunistic violence.

Narrative

Jerry Johns demonstrated consistent ritualistic behaviors across all documented cases, establishing a clear pattern of repeated actions that extended beyond operational necessity. The Linda Schacke case documented strangulation with a ligature constructed from available materials, while the Tina Farmer case involved strangulation with a ligature following severe beating. The Michelle Inman case most likely involved strangulation, maintaining the consistent method across all incidents. The pattern reveals absolute consistency in the use of ligature strangulation as the primary killing method, with one notable variation in the Tina Farmer case where severe beating preceded the strangulation. Additionally, Johns placed a bag over Tina Farmer's head after death, representing a post-mortem ritual not documented in other cases. These repeated behaviors demonstrate habit formation that transcended practical considerations, suggesting psychological necessity rather than mere operational efficiency. The consistency indicates Johns would delay or modify circumstances to ensure he could perform these specific actions, even when simpler methods might have been available.

Johns' documented behavior patterns suggest consistent psychological reinforcement through his victim selection and treatment methods. The Linda Schacke case involved targeting a woman who fit specific physical characteristics that appeared to fulfill particular psychological needs. The Tina Farmer case continued this pattern, focusing on women involved in prostitution whom Johns appeared to view as having compromised moral standing. The Michelle Inman case maintained this victim selection criteria, suggesting ongoing psychological satisfaction derived from targeting women who represented specific symbolic meaning. The signature pattern reveals Johns' apparent need to repeatedly engage with victims who shared similar characteristics, particularly involvement in prostitution and specific physical appearances. The escalation observed across cases suggests intensifying psychological needs, with later victims bearing closer resemblance to whatever internal template drove his selection process. The ritualistic elements, particularly the consistent use of ligature strangulation and the post-mortem bag placement in one case, indicate symbolic behaviors that provided psychological reinforcement beyond the act of killing itself. These patterns suggest Johns gained control and reassurance from repeated actions that held specific symbolic meaning within his psychological framework.

Johns' documented behaviors suggest several probable personality characteristics based on observable patterns rather than speculation. His organized approach, particularly evident in the Linda Schacke case, demonstrates systematic planning and structured thinking. The extended interaction periods and successful deception indicate high levels of patience and self-control, allowing him to maintain false personas for extended periods without revealing criminal intent. The evidence suggests strong social confidence, demonstrated through Johns' ability to successfully impersonate law enforcement and maintain convincing conversations with victims. His apparent sense of superiority, evidenced by his references to victims as "nuisances" and his successful manipulation of vulnerable women, indicates an inflated self-image and comfort with social dominance. The ritualized behaviors and consistent methodology suggest someone who values control and structure, preferring predictable patterns over spontaneous actions. These traits collectively point to an individual comfortable with manipulation, patient in execution, and confident in social interactions while maintaining rigid internal requirements for how crimes must be conducted.

Johns consistently selected rural locations along major interstate highways for all documented crimes, creating environmental conditions that supported his ritualistic needs. The Linda Schacke case occurred in a rural setting at night during a weekend, the Tina Farmer case in a rural location during nighttime hours in early week, and the Michelle Inman case in a rural roadside location with uncertain timing. All locations shared the common characteristic of physical isolation combined with immediate access to major transportation corridors. The environmental pattern reveals how context supported Johns' ritual requirements by providing privacy for extended victim interaction and ritualistic killing methods while maintaining escape route access. The sparse population, limited surveillance, and reduced likelihood of witness presence in these rural interstate locations enabled Johns to perform his ritualistic behaviors without interruption. The consistent roadside locations suggest comfort and familiarity with highway environments, indicating these settings provided the psychological safety necessary for Johns to complete his ritualistic sequences. The timing patterns, when documented, show preference for periods with minimal witness potential, creating optimal conditions for ritual completion.

Jerry Johns demonstrates a repeated psychological need for control and symbolic completion of specific ritualistic sequences, evidenced through his consistent use of ligature strangulation and systematic targeting of women involved in prostitution who shared particular physical characteristics. His signature reveals an individual who requires specific environmental conditions and victim types to achieve psychological satisfaction, suggesting internal symbolic requirements that drive victim selection and killing methodology. The ritualistic elements, including the consistent strangulation method and occasional post-mortem behaviors, indicate emotional reinforcement derived from repeated symbolic acts rather than simple operational efficiency. Johns' signature pattern suggests comfort with rural interstate environments where he can perform extended ritualistic sequences without interruption. His need for control manifests through patient victim interaction, successful deception, and methodical execution of specific killing rituals. The consistency across cases spanning multiple years indicates deeply ingrained psychological requirements that supersede operational considerations, revealing an individual who gains emotional reinforcement from repeatedly engaging in symbolic acts that fulfill specific internal psychological needs through the targeting and ritualistic killing of women who represent particular symbolic significance within his psychological framework.[14]

14 DeSoto County Sheriff's Department. *[Investigation Report]*. 25 Apr. 1985.

"Jerry Johns Timeline Document." Campbell, Alex. "Sociology Class." *Elizabethton High School*, 2023–2024.

Jorge, Kaylin. "Tennessee Murder Victim ID'd 30 Years After Death Thanks to Missing Persons Blog."

Knox County Sheriff's Department. *Case Files for Jerry Leon Johns*. Case nos. 26668, 24893, and 24894.

National Institute of Justice, and National Forensic Science Technology Center. *NamUs: National Missing and Unidentified Persons System*. 2007, https://www.namus.gov. Accessed 3 Mar. 2026.

North, John, and Leslie Ackerson. "Appalachian Unsolved: The Trucker Who Liked Redheads." *WBIR*, 21 Feb. 2020, https://www.wbir.com. Accessed 3 Mar. 2026.

"Redhead Murders Cold Case Highway Killings." *Knox News*, 26 Oct. 2018.

Sullivan, Cole. "TBI Names Suspected Killer in 1985 'Redhead Murder' Case." *WBIR*, 19 Dec. 2019, https://www.wbir.com. Accessed 3 Mar. 2026.

"Suspect Named in 'Redhead Murders' Campbell County Cold Case." *Knox News*, 19 Dec. 2019.

"[Untitled Article]." *The Houston Post* [Houston, TX], 15 June 1948.

West Park Hospital. *Discharge Report of Linda Schacke*. 7 Mar. 1985.

"Young Man Found Guilty of Setting Fire." *The Mississippi Press*, 20 Jan. 1971.

19:

SAMUEL LITTLE: CONFIRMED SERIAL KILLER

SUMMARY

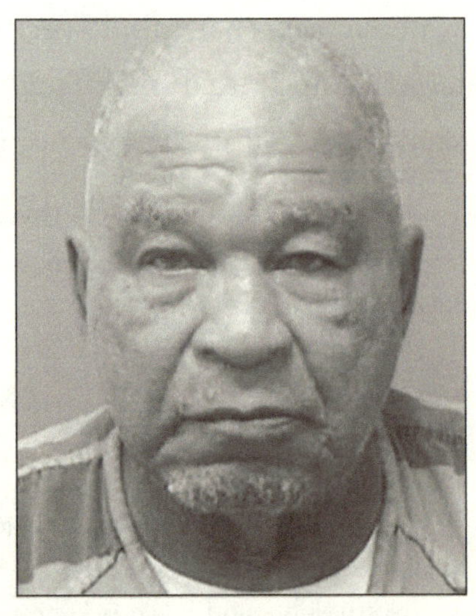

Samuel Little (June 7, 1940–December 30, 2020) was an American serial murderer active primarily between the early 1970s and the mid-2000s. He committed his crimes across the United States, making him one of the most geographically mobile serial offenders in American history. Little is confirmed to have murdered at least 60 women, though he confessed to killing as many as 93 victims, a figure supported in part by corroborating evidence and case matches. His case is historically significant due to both the extraordinary number of victims and the manner in which his crimes remained largely undetected for decades, exposing systemic failures in the investigation of crimes involving marginalized victims.

Little was born in Reynolds, Georgia, and experienced an unstable childhood marked by abandonment and inconsistent caregiving. His mother left him at a young age, after which he was raised primarily by his grandmother in Ohio. He had minimal formal education and became involved in criminal behavior early in life, including theft and burglary, leading to time in juvenile detention. During his youth, Little also began developing violent sexual fantasies, which investigators later cited as an early behavioral warning sign. As an adult, he worked intermittently as a laborer and truck driver, occupations that allowed him to travel frequently and maintain a flexible schedule. Psychological evaluations and investigative reports described him as socially confident and physically imposing, traits that enabled him to approach victims without immediate suspicion.

Little's crimes occurred between approximately 1970 and 2005 and spanned numerous states, including California, Florida, Texas, Louisiana, Mississippi, Georgia, and Ohio. His victims were overwhelmingly adult women, many of whom were vulnerable due to factors such as homelessness, substance use, or involvement in sex work. The crimes followed a consistent pattern: Little typically approached victims in public settings, gained their trust, isolated them, and killed them using manual strangulation. Bodies were often left in secluded or semi-secluded areas near roadways. For many years, law enforcement agencies failed to link these cases due to jurisdictional separation and the lack of forensic evidence. Little was ultimately identified through a combination of DNA evidence, investigative review of cold cases, and extensive confessions he gave while in custody.

Little was arrested on September 5, 2012, in California on narcotics-related charges. Subsequent DNA testing linked him to several unsolved homicides. In 2014, he was convicted of three murders in Los Angeles and sentenced to life imprisonment without the possibility of parole. Although he was never tried for the majority of the murders he confessed to, investigators from the FBI and multiple state agencies worked extensively to corroborate his statements. Over several years, Little provided detailed confessions and drawings of victims that helped identify previously unknown victims and close cold cases. He died in prison on December 30, 2020, while serving his sentence.

The impact of Samuel Little's crimes has been profound because he has been the most prolific serial killer in all of American history. His case highlighted longstanding issues in how law enforcement agencies investigate crimes involving marginalized populations, particularly women of color. The extensive review of his confessions led to renewed efforts to solve cold cases nationwide and emphasized the importance of victim-centered investigations. Samuel Little's case has influenced modern criminal profiling by exposing critical gaps in how law enforcement identifies serial offenders, investigative collaboration across jurisdictions, and public awareness regarding serial violence. Samuel Little's crimes continue to matter because they underscore how systemic neglect can allow extreme violence to persist undetected, and how accountability, even late in an offender's life, can still provide answers and recognition for victims and their families.

VICTIMS

CONFIRMED

- **Mary Jo Brosley** – A 33-year-old woman from Florida killed on New Year's Eve 1970 in Homestead
- **"Linda"** – Approximately 22 years old, disappeared in Miami, Florida, in 1971; identity remains unknown
- **"Marianne/Mary Ann"** – An 18-year-old in Miami during the early 1970s; real identity unverified
- **"Donna/Sarah"** – An 18 to 25-year-old woman sighted from the early 1970s in the Kendall, Florida, area; identity unknown
- **Prince George's County Jane Doe** – An unidentified white female

in her early 20s found in Maryland in 1972

- **Sarah Brown** – Approximately 39 years old; killed in New Orleans, Louisiana, in 1973
- **Agatha White** – 34-year-old from Omaha, Nebraska; killed in late 1973
- **"Kat"** – An unnamed woman aged about 22–23 in Savannah, Georgia, around 1974
- **Leola Etta Bryant** – 51-year-old from South Carolina, killed in 1974
- **Martha Cunningham** – 34-year-old victim killed in Tennessee on December 31, 1974
- **"Emily"** – An unnamed woman in her early 20s mentioned from mid-1970s Miami
- **Lee Ann Helms** – 21-year-old killed in Houston, Texas, in June 1977
- **Yvonne Pless** – 20-year-old from Macon, Georgia, killed in September 1977
- **Clara Birdlong** – 44-year-old victim in Mississippi in late 1977
- **Cleveland Jane Doe** – An unidentified female aged about 17–24 found in Cleveland, Ohio
- **Julia Critchfield** – 36-year-old killed in Harrison County, Mississippi, in January 1978
- **Evelyn Westson** – Approximately 19 years old, listed among victims in South Carolina
- **Brenda Alexander** – About 23, killed in Alabama in the early 1980s
- **Linda Sue Boards** – 23 years old, killed in Kentucky in May 1981
- **Patricia Parker** – In her late 20s, killed in Georgia in the early 1980s
- **New Orleans Jane Doe** – An unidentified woman from New Orleans; murder tied to confessions
- **Fredonia Smith** – About 18, listed from Macon, Georgia, in 1982
- **Rosie Hill** – 21-year-old from Marion County, Florida

- **Dorothy Richard** – Mid-50s, victim from Louisiana in 1982
- **Patricia Ann Mount** – About 26, killed in Florida in September 1982
- **Melinda Rose LaPree** – 22-year-old victim in Mississippi in 1982
- **San Bernardino Jane Doe** – An unnamed young woman in California
- **Auggie Gortz** – About 23, killed in 1984
- **"Granny"** – Approximately 50 years old from Los Angeles around 1987
- **Carol Ann Alford** – Victim from Ohio in the 1980s
- **Linda Bennett** – About 38, killed in Kentucky in the late 1980s
- **Guadalupe Apodaca** – 46-year-old victim in California in 1989
- **Alice Denise Duvall** – Aged around 40–45, listed from Los Angeles
- **Roberta Tandarich** – About 34, killed in Ohio
- **Alice Denise Taylor** – Listed jointly with another victim among records from Mississippi
- **Tracy Lynn Johnson** – 19-year-old from Mississippi
- **Las Vegas Jane Doe** – An unidentified woman from Nevada mentioned in the 1990s
- **Rubby (Ruby) Dean Lane** – About 19, victim from Florida in 1993
- **Jolanda Jones** – Around 26, listed from Arkansas
- **Melissa Thompson** – About 29, victim from Louisiana
- **Daisy McGuire** – 40-year-old victim from Louisiana
- **"T-Money"** – An unnamed young woman from Los Angeles in the mid-1990s
- **Los Angeles Jane Doe** – Another unidentified female from Los Angeles
- **Priscilla Baxter-Jones** – 36-year-old listed from Arkansas
- **Nancy Carol Stevens** – About 46, victim from the late confessions

SURVIVED

- **Pamela Kay Smith** – From Sunset Hills, Missouri; assaulted on September 11, 1976
- **Hilda Nelson** – From Pascagoula, Mississippi; assaulted on July 31, 1980
- **Leila Mae (McClain) Johnson** – From Pascagoula, Mississippi; assaulted on November 19, 1981
- **Laurie Kerridge (Barros)** – From San Diego, California; assaulted on September 17, 1984
- **Tonya Jackson** – From San Diego, California; assaulted on October 25, 1984

SUSPECTED

- **North Little Rock Jane Doe** – Her body was discovered in North Little Rock, Arkansas, on March 15, 1994.

POSSIBLE

- **Tuscaloosa Jane Doe** – Her body was discovered in Tuscaloosa, Alabama, on July 23, 1979, and her estimated time of death was four weeks prior.

TIMELINE

2/09/1921	Paul McDowell (later Samuel Little's father), was born in Reynolds, GA.
??/??/1923 or ??/??/1924	Bessie Mae Little (later Samuel Little's mother) was born.
6/07/1940	Samuel Little was born to Bessie Mae Little and Paul McDowell in Reynolds, GA.
??/??/1940 or ??/??/1941	Samuel's mother left him, and he moved in with his grand mother in Lorain, OH.
??/??/1945	Samuel Little started having sexual fantasies about strangling women.
2/??/1954	Samuel was sent to a Boys' Industrial School for stealing a bike at 13/14 in Lancaster, OH.
11/??/1956	He was convicted of breaking and entering in a property in Omaha, NE.
??/??/1956	He was held in an institution for juvenile defenders for breaking and entering. He then began a short-term professional boxing career in prison.
6–12/??/1960	Samuel moved in with his mother in Florida.
??/??/197?	Sometime in the 1970s, Samuel Little became a truck driver.

12/31/1970	He murdered Mary Jo Broseley (33) in a bar by strangulation. She disappeared in MA, and her skeletal remains were found in Miami, FL.
5/28/1971	Samuel Little was first arrested for robbery but was found not guilty.
??/??/1971	Little murdered "Linda" (22) by manual strangulation in Miami, FL.
??/??/1971 to ??/??/1972	Samuel Little murdered a black transgender woman. He claimed his victim's name was Marianne/Mary Ann (18). He killed her on a driveway, possibly near a sugarcane field in Miami, FL.
??/??/1971 to ??/??/1972	Little murdered "Donna/Sarah" (18–25) in Kendall, FL.
??/??/1972	Little murdered Prince George's County Jane Doe (20–25) in Prince George's County, MD.
??/??/1973	Little killed Sarah Brown (39) by strangulation in New Orleans, LA.
11/??/1973	Little strangled Agatha White Buffalo (34) in Omaha, NE.
??/??/1974	Little murdered "Kat" (22–23) by strangulation in Savannah, GA.
3/??/1974	Samuel Little murdered Leola Etta Bryant (51) by strangulation in North Charleston, SC.

12/31/1974	Samuel Little killed Martha Cunningham (34) by strangulation in Knox County, Tenn.
??/??/Mid-'70s	Little murdered "Emily" (23–24) by strangulation in Miami, FL.
9/11/1976	Samuel Little was arrested for rape, robbery, and the assault of Pamela K. Smith in Sunset Hills, MO. He was then sentenced to 3 months in county jail.
6/??/1977	Little murdered Lee Ann Helms (21) by strangulation in Houston, TX.
9/??/1977	Samuel Little killed Yvonne Pless (20) by strangulation in Malcom, GA.
12/??/1977	Samuel Little killed Clara Birdlong (44) by strangulation by hand in Pascagoula, MS.
??/??/1977 to 1978	Little murdered Cleavland Jane Doe (17–24) in Cleveland, OH.
1/??/1978	Samuel Little murdered Julia Critchfield (36) by strangulation in Harrison County, MS.
9/??/1978	Samuel Little murdered Evelyn Westson (19) by a gunshot to the head in Columbia, SC.
8/??/1979	Samuel Little killed Brenda Alexander (23) by strangulation by hand in Phoenix City, AL.

5/??/1981	Samuel Little kills Linda Sue Boards (23) by strangulation in Grove, KY.
9/??/1981	Little murdered Patricia Parker (25–30) by manual strangulation in Dade County, GA.
8–11/??/1981	Little murdered the New Orleans Jane Doe (30–40) in New Orleans, LA.
7/??/1982	Samuel Little murdered Fredonia Smith (18) by strangulation in Macon, GA.
9/??/1982	Samuel Little strangled Rosie Hill (20) and killed her in his Ford Pinto Station Wagon in the space between his front and back seat in Marion County, FL.
9/??/1982	Samuel Little murdered Dorothy Richard (56) by strangulation in Houma, LA.
9/??/1982	Little murdered Patricia Ann Mount (26) by strangulation inside of his Ford Pinto Station Wagon in Alachua County, FL.
10/??/1982	Little murdered Melinda Rose LaPree (22) by strangulation in Pascagoula, MS.
11/25/1982	He was arrested for shoplifting and suspicion of the murder of Melinda Rose LaPree but was not convicted.
??/??/1984	Little killed the San Bernardino Jane Doe (18–23) in San Bernardino, CA.

??/??/1984	Little strangled Auggie Gortz (23) to death in Savannah, GA.
2/01/1987	Samuel Little was released from prison, after serving less than the 3 years he was convicted of (served 19 months).
2/??/1987	He moved to Los Angeles, CA.
??/??/1987	Little killed "Granny" (50) by strangulation in Los Angeles, CA.
7/13/1987	Samuel Little murdered Carol Ann Alford by manual strangulation after beating her in Los Angeles, California. He then dumped her body in an alleyway in South Central Los Angeles, CA.
5/??/1988	Samuel Little murdered Linda Bennett (38) by strangulation from his hands in Owenton, KY.
9/03/1989	Little killed Guadalupe Apodaca by strangulation in Los Angeles, CA.
6/10 or 11/1991	Samuel Little killed Alice Denise Duvall (40–45) by strangulation, and her body was discovered by an industrial area on Long Beach, CA.
9/??/1991	Little strangled a mother of two, Roberta Tandarich (34), in Akron, OH.

12/??/1992 Little murdered Alice Denise Taylor (27) by manual strangulation in Gulfport, MS. Her body was under a pile of tires on the side of the road.

12/??/1992 Little manually strangled Tracy Lynn Johnson (19) by strangulation in Gulfport, MS. Her body was then later found on a dirt road.

??/??/1993 Samuel Little murdered the Las Vegas Jane Doe (40) in Las Vegas, NV.

5/??/1993 Rubby Dean Lane (19) was strangled by Little in Perry, FL.

2/??/1994 Little murdered Jolanda Jones (26) by strangulation in Pine Bluff, AR.

1/??/1996 Little murdered Melissa Thompson (29) by strangulation in Opelousas, LA. Her body was later found under a pecan tree in Little Zion Cemetery.

2/??/1996 Little killed Daisy McGuire (40) by beating her in the head with a jack iron in Houma, LA.

??/??/1996 Little murdered "T-Money" (23–24) by strangling her to death in the parking lot of a hamburger stand in Los Angeles, CA.

??/??/1996 Little killed the Los Angeles Jane Doe (23–25) in Los Angeles, CA.

??/??/1997 Little killed Priscilla Baxter-Jones (36) in West Memphis, AR.

8/??/2005 Little murdered Nancy Carol Stevens (46) by strangulation in Tupelo, MS.

9/05/2012 Little was arrested in Los Angeles, California, for three of his murders and was later found guilty for three dozen.

??/??/2018 Samuel Little confessed to killing 93 victims to James Holland and many FBI crime analysts.

12/30/2020 Samuel Little died in Los Angeles, California.

MO

Samuel Little's documented criminal activities spanned an extensive timeframe, with the three representative cases occurring on December 31, 1970; July 13, 1987; and in August 2005. The Mary Jo Brosely case occurred during late night to early morning hours on New Year's Eve in winter conditions. The Carol Ann Alford incident took place during late night to early morning hours on July 13, 1987, during summer. The Nancy Carol Stevens case occurred sometime in August 2005 during late summer to early fall, though specific timing within that period remains unknown.

The documented pattern shows Little consistently operating during late night to early morning hours when timing information is available. The cases span weekdays based on calendar dates, occurring across different seasons from winter through late summer. Little's criminal activity extended over a 35-year period with multiple murders documented annually, indicating sustained criminal behavior over decades. His occupation as a truck driver provided the flexible scheduling necessary to maintain this pattern of criminal activity across extensive geographic areas. The consistency in late night operations, when documented, demonstrates repeated utilization of time periods with minimal witness presence and reduced law enforcement patrol activity.

Little's location selection varied across the three documented cases, showing adaptation to different environmental conditions and geographic areas. The Mary Jo Brosely case occurred in a concentrated crime area within an urban, public setting. The Carol Ann Alford case showed crime location variation within an urban, public environment. The Nancy Carol Stevens case took place in an isolated location with unknown public or private classification in a rural setting.

The geographic pattern demonstrates Little's operations across multiple location types, from urban public areas to isolated rural locations. Documentation shows clustering of multiple victims within the same general geographic areas, indicating Little's tendency to operate within familiar territories before moving to new regions. His escape method consistently involved vehicular transportation, requiring locations with road access for departure. The variation in location types from concentrated urban areas to isolated rural settings shows adaptability to different environmental conditions while maintaining consistent access to transportation routes for escape purposes.

Little employed non-forced entry methods across all documented cases, utilizing his ability to gain victim compliance through social interaction rather than physical coercion. The Mary Jo Brosely case documents his use of alcohol as a luring mechanism, isolating the victim before employing strangulation. The Carol Ann Alford case shows brief interaction before fatal assault using blunt force and manual strangulation. The Nancy Carol Stevens case involved brief contact followed by blunt force and strangulation.

The pattern reveals consistent use of social approach methods rather than forced entry techniques. Little demonstrated procedural familiarity with victim access through established social patterns, particularly targeting women involved in prostitution who were accessible through normal social interaction. His exit methods consistently involved driving away from crime scenes using personal vehicles. The approach shows repeated utilization of similar access techniques across different time periods and geographic locations, indicating established methodology for victim approach and scene departure.

Little employed manual strangulation using his hands as the primary method across all three documented cases. The Mary Jo Brosely, Carol Ann Alford, and Nancy Carol Stevens cases all involved hands as the weapon, classified as improvised rather than brought to the scene. The Carol Ann Alford and Nancy Carol Stevens cases also documented the use of blunt force in combination with manual strangulation.

The weapon pattern shows absolute consistency in the use of hands for strangulation across all documented cases, with occasional incorporation of blunt force trauma. Little's approach utilized readily available body parts rather than external weapons or tools, eliminating the need for weapon procurement or transportation. The consistency in manual strangulation technique across cases spanning decades indicates established methodology and procedural familiarity with this particular method of victim control and killing. The pattern demonstrates reliance on physical capability rather than external tools or weapons.

Little's victim interaction patterns varied in duration but remained consistently brief overall. The Mary Jo Brosely case documented several hours of interaction, during which Little lured the victim with alcohol and referred to her as "easy prey." The Carol Ann Alford case involved brief and fatal interaction, with documentation that the victim asked why he touched her and questioned if he was a serial killer. The Nancy Carol Stevens case showed brief interaction with unknown verbal content.

The documented interactions reveal Little's ability to engage victims for varying time periods while maintaining control of the situation. The Mary Jo Brosely case shows his capability for extended victim engagement when circumstances allowed, while the other cases demonstrate rapid progression to fatal assault. Little's control methods included isolation techniques and physical restraint through strangulation across all cases. The pattern shows escalation in approach over time, with later cases involving more immediate fatal assault compared to the extended interaction documented in the earliest case.

Little's escape methodology remained consistent across all documented cases, utilizing personal vehicles for departure from crime scenes. The Mary Jo Brosely case documents his driving to a secluded area where he buried the victim before driving away. The Carol Ann Alford case shows escape in a blue Buick with wood trim. The Nancy Carol Stevens case involved departure in a recreational vehicle. None of the cases document the use of concealment or disguise during escape.

The escape pattern demonstrates smooth, planned departures rather than chaotic flight from crime scenes. Little consistently utilized large vehicles for transportation, providing both mobility and potential space for victim transport when necessary. His escape routes showed no documented anticipation of immediate law enforcement response, suggesting confidence in his ability to depart scenes without immediate pursuit. The pattern shows improvement and consistency over time, with Little maintaining similar escape methodology across the decades-long span of documented criminal activity. The use of different vehicle types indicates adaptation to available transportation while maintaining a consistent vehicular escape approach.

SIGNATURE

Signature Statement

The unsub demonstrates a repeated need for power and control, expressed through consistent methods of victim selection, killing technique, and body disposal. This pattern is reinforced through ritualized behaviors such as strangulation, targeting vulnerable women, and the repeated use of familiar environments. These behaviors suggest a mixed offender who gains emotional reinforcement from dominance and successful repetition rather than from the act of killing alone.

Narrative

The offender exhibits clear ritualized behaviors that occur across multiple incidents. Strangulation is the primary method of killing, appearing in the majority of known cases, while victims are most often adult women. Bodies are frequently left along roadways, indicating a recurring disposal pattern that is not strictly necessary to complete the crime. Although exceptions exist, such as occasional use of blunt force or variations in disposal, these deviations appear situational rather than indicative of a changing behavioral pattern.

These repeated actions suggest a structured but flexible approach. The offender follows the same general sequence unless environmental or situational factors interfere. The consistency of strangulation and victim type indicates comfort with physical control and close-contact violence, while repeated disposal near roadways suggests familiarity with the area and confidence in avoiding detection. The repetition of these behaviors over time reflects habit formation and psychological comfort with known routines.

The offender's signature reflects a consistent pattern of psychological reinforcement centered on power, control, and sexual gratification. Observable behaviors indicate that emotional satisfaction is derived from dominating vulnerable victims rather than from novelty or escalation. The repetitive nature of these crimes suggests that successful exertion of control reinforced the offender's behavior, motivating continued offending. The lack of significant escalation across incidents indicates that the offender's core psychological needs remained stable over time.

From these ritual and signature patterns, several probabilistic personality traits can be inferred. The offender appears to be a mixed type, displaying both organized and disorganized characteristics. Moving victims without bringing a weapon suggests planning and confidence, while reliance on opportunity indicates impulsivity. Victim selection appears opportunistic, yet time spent with victims before killing suggests patience and delayed gratification. Thrill-seeking tendencies are suggested by repeated sadistic behavior and continued offending despite risk. Repeated success without immediate detection may have contributed to increased social confidence and a sense of invulnerability.

Environmental context plays a significant role in reinforcing these behaviors. The offender appears most comfortable operating in familiar urban environments, where vulnerable populations are present and anonymity is easier to maintain. Familiarity with local geography likely allowed for repeated disposal behaviors without heightened anxiety. Environmental accessibility supported the offender's ability to repeat rituals consistently while adapting when obstacles arose. This interaction between environment and behavior further reinforced the offender's sense of control and confidence.[15]

---

15 Almasy, Steve, and Faith Karimi. "Samuel Little Confessed to 90 Murders, Making Him the Deadliest Serial Killer in US History." CNN, 28 Nov. 2018.

Andone, Dakin, et al. "Most Prolific Serial Killer in America Confesses to Murdering 5 More Women in Ohio." NPR, 7 June 2019. Accessed Mar. 2026.

Associated Press. "Serial Killer Samuel Little Linked to Dozens of Deaths Across the US" AP News, 2018.

"Behold the Monster by Jillian Lauren: Review." The Telegraph, publication date unknown.

Blinder, Alan. "He Handed Over a List of 90 Names. Now Investigators Are Trying to Find the Victims." The New York Times, 26 Nov. 2018.

Chuck, Elizabeth. "Suspected Serial Killer Samuel Little Connected to at Least 90 Murders." NBC News, 28 Nov. 2018.

Doe Network. "Case File 108UFAL." DoeNetwork.org, publication date unknown.

Federal Bureau of Investigation. "Samuel Little: Most Prolific Serial Killer in US History." FBI.gov, 6 Oct. 2019.

Ferrise, Adam. "Convicted Serial Killer Samuel Little Charged in the Slayings of Two Cincinnati Women." Cleveland.com, 7 June 2019.

Othram Inc. "Owen County Jane Doe 1988 Identified as Linda Bennett." DNA-Solves.com, publication date unknown.

10-Minute Murder. "Samuel Little: The Unmasking of America's Most Prolific Serial Killer." 10MinuteMurder.com, publication date unknown.

Texas Department of Public Safety. "New Details Released in Unsolved Samuel Little Murders." DPS.Texas.gov, 30 Nov. 2021. Accessed Mar. 2026.

The Fall Line. "Season 11: The Victims of Samuel Little." The Fall Line Podcast, publication date unknown.

The Washington Post. "Samuel Little: The Convicted Killer Linked to More Than 90 Murders." The Washington Post, 2020.

WAFF 48 News. "FBI Confirms Killer's Confession in Decatur Woman's Murder." WAFF.com, 8 Oct. 2019.

Roanoke Times 1995, published on Monday, June 19, 1995. Title: Serial Killer's Luck Ran Out In Unlikely Place.

The Virginian-Pilot. published on April 15, 1995. Neighbors Call Suspect Friendly, Scary Sean Patrick Goble Confessed to the Slaying of an Indiana Woman.

The Virginian-Pilot 1995, published on Saturday, June 17, 1995. Title: Detectives Credit Luck In Highway Killings Case.

The Virginian-Pilot.1995, Published on April 18, 1995. Title: Trucker Admits 3rd Killing.

The Virginian-Pilot. 1995, Published on January 27, 1995. Title: I-81 SLAYING LINKED TO SERIAL KILLER.

The Virginian Pilot. 1995, Published on April 15,1995. Title: NEIGHBORS CALL SUSPECT FRIENDLY, SCARY SEAN PATRICK GOBLE CONFESSED TO THE SLAYING OF AN INDIANAN WOMAN.

The Virginian-Pilot 1996, published on Tuesday, April 9, 1996. Title: Trucker Admits To Strangling Woman, Gets 14 Years More.

SECTION IV:

Student Biographies and Reflections

MYRA ALLMAN

My name is Myra Allman. I am a sophomore at Elizabethton High School. I am in their theater program, and I am also in the Betsy Color Guard. I never would have imagined doing anything dealing with the law because, when I was younger, I had a fear of the criminals they showed on the news channels. This opinion changed when I signed up for Mr. Campbell's sociology class. In the earlier weeks of his class, we had learned about Kitty Genovese Syndrome (often referred to as the Bystander Effect). Her case moved me in so many ways that my brain made a connection with my newly made love for law. It encouraged me to continue in the class and push harder to uncover the mysteries of the victims, both known and unknown.

When I was little, I had the undeniable urge to find my purpose. I felt as if I had no meaning. The cycle of continuous failure washed over me until I learned that there were such things as murder documentaries and that *people* actually helped solve 40-years-old unsolved cases to bring justice to the innocent. It intrigued me enough that I started researching and watching cases continuously to help me before I signed up for the class. It sparked something inside of me that made me want to continue learning and gradually have enough knowledge to put missing pieces together.

My group focused on a cold case in Texas that strongly resembled a solved case in Memphis, Tennessee, involving Suzanne Collins. Her name was Sherri Ann Jarvis. She was a 14-year-old girl who was brutally murdered in 1980. We suspect the murderer of Suzanne Collins, Sedley Alley.

One of the things I learned in Mr. Campbell's class is that when you're learning about victims, it does not matter what they did in their personal lives, such as their career choices, their lifestyles when they were alive, or anything else that was affected by their childhood or previous home lives. Instead, the focus should be on understanding the circumstances that led to them becoming victims and showing empathy for their experiences. By approaching each case without judgment, we are better able to see the bigger picture and recognize the importance of treating all victims with respect and dignity. This perspective has helped me become more open-minded and less likely to make assumptions about people based solely on their histories.

Before taking this class, I was never truly aware of how many people are driven to kill out of emotions like rage or powerful, uncontrollable desires. Learning about the different motives behind violent crimes opened my eyes to just how complex human behavior can be. It's surprising and unsettling to realize that ordinary people can be pushed to such extreme actions by their emotions, sometimes with little warning. Through our class discussions and case studies, I have seen how factors like jealousy, anger, or lust can completely override a person's judgment. This new understanding has made me more curious about what causes individuals to act in such destructive ways and has deepened my interest in exploring the darker sides of human nature. It has also reminded me that understanding these motives is important if we want to prevent such tragedies in the future.

As I reflect on everything I have learned, I am overwhelmed by a mix of emotions and deep reflection. I have discovered not only the complexities of crime and justice, but also my own capacity for empathy, resilience, and growth. The stories of victims and the failures of the justice system have moved me, sometimes making me feel angry, sometimes sad, but always more determined to understand and help. Even in the darkest circumstances, there are lessons in compassion, perseverance, and the importance of never giving up in seeking the truth. I carry these lessons with me, knowing they will shape how I see the world and how I choose to make a difference, no matter where life takes me next.

Because of Mr. Campbell's class, I have become much more aware that our justice system, while flawed, does serve an important role in society. Studying cases in which authorities made mistakes or were indifferent revealed that justice is not always served and that flaws can have serious consequences. However, I also learned about instances where the system worked as intended, protected the innocent, and held the guilty accountable. While it was frustrating to see people let down by those meant to protect them, learning about both the failures and successes has inspired me to think more critically about what true justice should be. Now, I try to stay informed and open-minded, realizing that understanding both the strengths and shortcomings of the system is the first step toward a fairer society.

ALIVIA ANDERSON

My name is Alivia Anderson. I am a junior at Elizabethton High School. I was born in Johnson City, Tennessee. My family has never liked law enforcement or anything to do with people in power. If my aunt wasn't yelling at the TV over politics, she was yelling about corrupt people in office. Somehow, that made me want to go into law enforcement. I've always had an interest in storytelling. I thought it was fascinating how lawyers could shape stories to fit their narrative. Once I realized how much paperwork was involved in being a prosecutor, I decided on policing instead. Chasing down the bad guys and helping the victims has always stuck with me through school. It helps me realize who I am. When I first learned about these victims, I wondered why their lives didn't matter. Was it just because someone's daughter wasn't special or powerful? I wanted to bring attention to people who society overlooks, because at the end of the day, that's someone's baby.

I grew up in a Southern Baptist family raised on the love of God. No matter what the world threw at us, we were in the church pews crying out for guidance. I've lost many people through death, mainly through old age or lung problems in their late seventies. Yet, the one that affected me most wasn't even family. A family friend named Victor was in my life for nearly five years. After losing all my grandparents in six years, I latched onto any older person I could find as a protector. After some issues, I didn't see him much anymore until I saw an article about a man who had gone missing. They searched for him for months before they found him. He was discovered abandoned in the mountains, after the man who killed him left his body there and drove away in Victor's car.

I never saw him, but the stories I heard from responding officers were that he was unrecognizable due to animals. The only way we could identify him was through dental records. I still go and sit in the woods where he was found and think about our times working on planes at the airport. I try to imagine that he's still in his hangar at the Elizabethton Airport, complaining about ordering parts. But then I remember he's not at the hangar; he's not sleeping at home. All I can picture is his body lying cold and lifeless in the forest. That's how I learned death can be both calming and devastating. No one cared about his case. Even when we begged for help, no one cared because he was just a Tennessee man who went missing. I begged for someone to care about my papaw. No one did. I will never forget how no one cared about the only man who was there for me and how the world took him from me without remorse.

When we were first introduced to these cases, I felt almost unbothered by them. I knew the world was cruel, and we are all promised one thing in life: death. As we slowly dug into them, I realized the patterns and lack of choices. Those women had no choices, even from birth. Life kept throwing things at them, and they were never able to stop and breathe. I remember thinking things like, "Why would they do that? I wouldn't get involved in prostitution." Then I remembered I was given a life of choices, something I take for granted too often. I had spoken to many kids who sounded like they wanted to be Batman or some kind of vigilante to help these women. All I wanted was for them to hear a voice that was silent for far too long. These were women who made poor choices, yes. But they were mothers, sisters, daughters of Christ. At one point in time, they had their first cries, not knowing that in the future those cries would be their last shout of hope. At the end of the day, we are all someone's baby—flesh and blood. We might not all be equal in the world, but there is a place where we all are.

In Sociology, there were many lessons that could not be found in the textbook; they were life lessons. These are things I want my great-grandchildren to know. If I could summarize the most important things I have learned into one word, it would be "humanizing." I've always been a "thriller" person. I was always watching horror movies and listening to murder podcasts, and I never noticed till now how desensitized I had become. I'm a teenage girl. I should be scared of blood and dark alleyways and scary men in cars, yet I wasn't. It was thrilling to me to hear about people's last moments, and I never stopped and thought about *who* I was hearing about. I never thought about how maybe, on a murdered woman's last night, she was going home to her kids or was going to see her grandmother. I thought about how I would have done things differently. I slowly idolized the story over the human. I had learned the world was incredibly good at blaming the person but never acknowledging the problem. Conveniently, it was always too late.

I never thought about the person until I had become filled with so much anger over no one knowing my grandfather. I heard people talking about it, because it was all over the news and on the local papers, and they would talk about how cool it was that his stuff was stolen, and no one noticed the killer had escaped for nearly 12 hours. All I ever heard was talk about the sheriff and people in office, and how it's their fault this man escaped, yet not a single person talked about Victor. They didn't have to drive past the airport and pray to see the hangar door open. They didn't stay up at night thinking of bugs eating the brain of the man who once loved me so dearly. I will never know how much anger and sadness those families felt of their little girls laying on the side of the road. I knew I couldn't breathe any time I imagined those things and the disgust I felt with people idolizing the man that ruined Victor's future. They never even made him human. He was just a story on a page. This project taught me compassion through comparison. Every victim is someone's little girl or little boy—someone who cried at night in their crib and screamed for their mother. Not just a story to listen to with your dinner.

These stories have taught me lessons that no textbook ever could. They have shown me the true meaning of compassion and empathy. Our generation has become increasingly desensitized through constant internet exposure. We witness terrible events without reaction, finding it somehow acceptable to watch others suffer or listen to someone's final moments with their loved ones. What connects our entire class is the experience of growing up. This course has shaped us into the kind of people the world desperately needs. We need individuals who can confront difficult topics while maintaining their humanity. In other classes, we read textbook accounts of war and tragedy that feel distant and impersonal. Those events happened long ago. What difference can we make now?

We see posts from families pleading for help. We witness their tears and desperate appeals. We learn about their childhoods, their roles as parents, their complete life stories, and we become emotionally invested. We pursue justice because we know it is achievable. This ignites a passion in young hearts, and I believe that once a young person develops the desire to serve others, that flame cannot be extinguished. This class is built on resilience. We have been challenged in ways many of us never experienced before. We have faced rejection through countless emails and phone calls, yet we persevered. Many students in my class who typically avoid conversation found the courage to speak up. While some might have participated solely for a grade, no student who truly listened to these stories could remain passive. This class taught me countless lessons that no dusty textbook ever could.

While I could say it has prepared me for adulthood, that would not be entirely accurate. Age does not matter when it comes to learning about humanity. This course taught me exactly how to be human.

AFTON BAILEY

I used to be scared of true crime, but here I am. My name is Afton Bailey, and I'm a junior. I spend most of my time listening to music or working, and depending on who you ask, I'm either really chill or just a funny guy. Going into this class, I thought it would be some boring sociology class; therefore, I didn't expect it to stand out much. Once we started working on Tennessee cold cases, especially ones that didn't get much attention, it became something a lot more real. Consequently, it stuck with me more than I thought it would.

I've grown up in a pretty stable environment, with good parents and solid people around me. As a result, I never really questioned how different life could be for others. One of the biggest shifts in my perspective came during the pandemic. That's when things started to feel real, when I became more aware and created memories that actually mattered. I also grew up watching horror movies from a young age, which sparked an early interest in slasher stories. However, true crime always scared me, because I knew it was real people. I remember watching a Ted Bundy documentary with my dad, and it genuinely terrified me. That fear eventually turned into curiosity, and now I have a way to engage with real cases and help bring attention to them.

Before this project, I thought of crime as something that happens, but not really something local or personally relevant; therefore, I never considered it in depth. That changed when we studied the Harry Edward Greenwell case. At first, it felt impossible to work on. There wasn't much information, and it stumped our group for a moment. As we dug deeper, we started uncovering details, and I realized how much work it takes to make things work. I also noticed that some cases received little attention, while others seemed to be prioritized. Furthermore, I became aware of the unequal ways society recognizes certain victims.

In class, we looked at how people react during emergencies, especially when others are present. I learned that hesitation and assumption are common, but studying these cases showed me the importance of taking responsibility. Now, I know I would step in to help someone in need rather than assume someone else will. I also gained insight into how social context, media attention, and how many systemic factors influence both victims and offenders.

At first, I wasn't sure I liked sociology. It didn't feel like a traditional class. However, I realized that I was learning more than I would have in a conventional classroom. I developed stronger research skills, critical thinking, and an ability to connect concepts to real situations. Moreover, I feel more prepared to understand complex social issues. This project taught me that knowledge isn't just tests. Knowledge truly contains hard work and reflection.

Overall, this experience has changed how I think in ways I didn't expect. I pay attention to stories that most may overlook. I see victims as humans rather than statistics, and I question assumptions I used to take for granted. I've grown in empathy and understanding, and I recognize that fairness is often inconsistent. Some things receive attention, while others do not, depending on circumstances beyond control. This class showed me that there is always more going on behind the scenes, and therefore I look at society, justice, and humanity through a much more thoughtful lens.

MADISON BARNETT

My name is Madison Barnett, and I'm a sophomore at Elizabethton High School. I play on the school's basketball team, and I'm currently pursuing the Pre-Law program. I've always been drawn to understanding how our country works, especially through the lens of US history and law. I never expected a sociology class to change the way I see justice, but it did. When I first learned about cases like Kitty Genovese and the Tennessee cold cases, I realized how much the stories of victims reveal about the society around them and how often those stories are ignored.

Growing up, I never imagined myself being interested in anything related to crime. I loved history, learning about laws, and understanding how our government was built, but crime didn't seem like a possibility. That changed during my freshman year when I chose Pre-Law and began learning about how the American justice system fails people over and over again. I started to see that justice isn't just a set of rules, it's a responsibility.

My older brother, Andrew, played a big role in shaping my interest. He took Mr. Campbell's class his senior year, and we talked about it. He told me that the class involved a lot of hard work, but not the kind you forget after turning it in. He said it was work that could change your life and possibly someone else's. So, I decided to take the class.

One of the first things we learned was about Kitty Genovese and the Bystander Effect. The idea that people are less likely to help when others are around made me question how I would react in a moment like that. It made me realize that even if something "isn't your business," it becomes your responsibility when someone can't help themselves. That idea followed me into our cold case research, where I saw just how many victims were overlooked because society didn't see them as worth saving. This idea connected directly to the cold cases we studied. So many victims weren't helped, not because no one cared, but because society had already labeled them as "less important." Learning about social norms, deviance, and inequality helped me understand how these labels form and how dangerous they can be.

As we researched victims and offenders, I started to see patterns. Many victims tried to get help but were ignored due to their backgrounds, lifestyles, or circumstances. They weren't targeted because of what they did, they were targeted because of vulnerabilities society refused to acknowledge. Studying these cases made me realize how media influence, stereotypes, and systemic failures shape the way victims are remembered or forgotten.

Researching Clark Perry Baldwin was one of the most impactful parts of this class. Not because of the details of his crimes, but because of what I learned about the victims connected to him. Sharing what I learned about Baldwin wasn't just about explaining a case; it was about making sure the victims weren't forgotten. I hope that by informing others about him and the women he targeted, I helped bring awareness to the patterns of neglect and vulnerability that allowed these crimes to go unnoticed for so long.

While researching Clark Perry Baldwin, one of the stories that impacted me the most was that of Mary Ann Newton, his first known victim who survived. Learning about her experience changed the way I understood the entire case. She was the one who managed to escape him, but she was also terrified so terrified that when it came time to appear in court, she couldn't bring herself to face him again. Because of that, the case was dismissed. What struck me wasn't that she didn't show up, but why she couldn't. She was young, scared, and completely alone in a system that didn't protect her or make her feel safe enough to testify. It made me think about how different things might have been if she had been supported, not because she was responsible for stopping him but because the system failed to give her the strength and safety she needed. Understanding her story taught me how fear, trauma, and lack of support can silence victims, and how those silences can have consequences far beyond one person. It made me recognize how important it is for victims to have people who stand with them and not judge them.

Before this class, I didn't realize how often victims were blamed for their own circumstances. I used to think their choices put them in danger, but now I understand that the real issue is the way society treats people who don't fit its expectations. This project helped me see victims as full human beings with families, dreams, and lives—not just as names in a case file.

Looking back on everything I've learned, I can see how much this class has changed and taught me. This class has encouraged me to approach discussions of crime with greater empathy and respect for the individuals whose stories deserve to be remembered with dignity. This class also connected deeply to my faith. I've always believed that every person is created with purpose and worth, and most importantly that no one's background or lifestyle makes them less deserving of justice. As I learned about these victims, I kept thinking about how easily the world judges people based on their circumstances. My faith reminds me that God doesn't see people that way. To him, every life matters. The class didn't just teach me about crime; it taught me compassion, responsibility, and the kind of person I want to be.

KEIRA BLACKSTON

I'm Keira Blackston, a sophomore at Elizabethton High School, where I've maintained a 4.3 GPA while staying active in travel volleyball and Key Club. When I'm not studying or playing sports, you'll find me exploring back roads on drives, shopping with friends, hitting the gym, discovering new coffee shops, or spending quality time with my family. My faith and love for Jesus is central to everything I do and guides my decisions daily. After graduation, I plan to pursue a master's degree in early childhood education with a possible minor in psychology. My fascination with true crime and unsolved mysteries runs deep, and it's what initially drew me to this class and shaped my current path. As I delved into Tennessee's cold cases, I found myself asking a haunting question: why haven't I heard these victims' names or learned about the killers who terrorized our state? The silence surrounding these stories troubled me deeply. That realization sparked something within me, and I decided that my mission for this school year would be to honor these forgotten victims and give a voice to their stories in whatever way I could.

Growing up in a loving household, I spent countless evenings curled up on the couch with my parents, captivated by *Dateline* episodes that flickered across our television screen. Those hours of watching real stories unfold planted the first seeds of my fascination with true crime, though I didn't realize it at the time. As I matured, this interest deepened, and I found myself diving into popular cases, analyzing evidence, and reading countless opinions from amateur detectives online. This passion naturally led me to enroll in this class, eager to explore the darker corners of human behavior.

Walking into this course, I carried assumptions shaped by my privileged upbringing and limited life experience. I believed that victims somehow placed themselves in dangerous situations through poor choices or lack of awareness about their surroundings. I grew up in a stable, supportive family and naively assumed everyone else had similar foundations and opportunities. However, as I began studying Tennessee's cold cases, my perspective underwent a profound transformation. The more I researched these forgotten women, the more I realized how wrong my initial judgments had been. These weren't women who chose dangerous paths out of recklessness, but rather individuals forced into impossible circumstances by poverty, addiction, and systemic failures. Many had turned to prostitution not by choice, but out of desperation to survive, making them vulnerable to predators who exploited their circumstances. This realization shattered my preconceived notions and taught me the invaluable lessons of empathy and understanding, showing me how easily society overlooks those who need protection the most.

Throughout this sociology class, I've had to confront some uncomfortable truths about my own assumptions and the society I live in. Learning about concepts like media influence, social norms, and systemic inequality wasn't just academic for me; it became deeply personal as I realized how these forces had shaped my own worldview without me even knowing it. I found myself questioning why I had heard about certain high-profile cases but never about the women whose stories we were studying. The media's tendency to sensationalize some crimes while completely ignoring others hit me hard when I realized I had unconsciously absorbed these biases. I began to see how my own middle-class background had shielded me from understanding how poverty, addiction, and desperation could trap people in dangerous situations. This wasn't just about learning sociology concepts anymore; it was about examining my own privilege and the blind spots it had created in my understanding of justice and human worth.

The moment that changed everything for me was when I dove deep into Lorie Pennell's case, and we had the chance to speak with her brother. Hearing his voice break as he talked about his sister, seeing the decades of pain still raw in his words, made this intensely personal for me. I found myself lying awake at night thinking about Lorie, imagining what her life was like, what her dreams were, and how her family has carried this burden for so long. Her brother's simple plea to know who hurt his sister shattered any remaining distance I had from these cases. I realized that my fascination with true crime had often been detached and almost entertainment focused, but now I felt a genuine responsibility to these victims. Working in different research groups opened my eyes to patterns I couldn't see before about how these offenders specifically chose women they thought society wouldn't miss. But sitting in our classroom, collaborating with my classmates, and seeing how much we all came to care about these forgotten women, I knew the killers were wrong. We proved that these lives matter, and that realization has fundamentally changed how I see my role in seeking justice for the voiceless.

After immersing myself in these cold cases, I find myself constantly wondering how many other people are still waiting for justice, still deserving of someone to care about their story. This awareness has made me hypervigilant about issues in my own community, scanning news stories and local events with new eyes, recognizing patterns I never would have noticed before. The empathy I've developed through this experience has become a cornerstone of who I want to be in my future career as an early childhood educator. I now understand that I'll likely encounter students who are living in circumstances similar to these victims' backgrounds, facing poverty, instability, or neglect that could put them on dangerous paths.

This knowledge has equipped me with the sensitivity to recognize warning signs and the compassion to approach struggling students with understanding rather than judgment. Most importantly, this project has fundamentally changed how I process the world around me. Instead of making snap judgments about people's choices or circumstances, I now pause to consider the complex web of factors that might have led them to where they are. I've learned to think before I react, to ask myself what someone might be going through that I can't see on the surface. This shift in perspective extends far beyond my future classroom; it has changed how I interact with everyone I meet, from the cashier having a rough day to the classmate who seems withdrawn. I've realized that behind every person is a story I don't know, and that understanding has made me more patient, more curious, and more committed to seeing the humanity in everyone, especially those who society tends to overlook or dismiss.

KAILEY FURCHES

My name is Kailey Furches, and I'm 18 years old. I was born in Elizabethton, Tenn., and have always attended Elizabethton City Schools. Ever since I was little, I've enjoyed art, crafting, and helping others around me. When I first heard about my school's sociology class, I was excited to have the opportunity to help others and their families, so I joined. I knew I would be getting into social situations, which I hated—and still do, to be honest.

Ever since I was little, I had a knack for helping anyone and anything. When I was in fifth grade in 2018–2019, at the age of 10 years old, I donated $147 that I had saved up on my own. I saved up ice cream money and allowance, then later donated that money to the Carter County Animal Shelter. It's one of my biggest accomplishments that I don't talk about. And now, having the chance to look back and see how it shaped me as a person makes me happy to have the chance to put it out there.

The topic of sociology grabbed my attention because of that knack I have for helping. I saw the victims and their families, and I wanted to help—not just to try and get the victims the attention they deserve, but to give the families the closure they need. While I looked at the cases from the class, I got a deeper look at some of the things I had already understood. I was previously aware of the judgment that someone in a bad place may go through, but seeing what they went through in detail helped me really grasp the understanding. It helped me actually see what it was like for them and know how it must have felt.

The biggest example that gave me the best insight was Kitty Genovese. Seeing the details of her case and how others reacted while it happened was a shock. When I had first read how the people in the apartments around the area where she was murdered were ignoring her cries for help, yelling at the killer and never going out to check on her, or making the excuse of being tired or it being too cold outside, it completely shocked me that people could do something like that. I knew about the Bystander Effect, but seeing how it played out in the real world, in writing, in full detail, was like the insight I knew I needed but hadn't gotten. When we looked at her case, I then understood the true depth of how it was—how victims, bystanders, and criminals all play a part.

I've always known about this thing called "the perfect victim complex," and I've always hated it, because while it technically could happen, it's not necessarily true for many cases. The perfect victim complex is where a victim of a crime is completely innocent or out of blame, often portrayed as weak or vulnerable. Many of the victims we looked at either had done drugs, were involved in prostitution, hitchhiked, or had a criminal record. When people have a perfect victim complex in mind, they tend to blame the victim if they have a past of crimes or anything that would cause them to be in a more vulnerable state. This is victim blaming.

I've learned of something called victim precipitation. Victim precipitation is where a victim does something that would put them in a more vulnerable state, but it's not their fault. There are people who may look at a victim and their past and say it's completely their fault, but it's not. When a victim is hooked on drugs and put in a situation where they leave, they will get sick and die due to withdrawal. It's not their fault, is it? While these victims have done these things, and while they also are wrong, that leads me to the patterns. Each thing they may have done that made them more vulnerable has a reason as to *why* they did it. The victims may have lived a life of abuse, were told to steal as a child, hung around the wrong crowd, were pushed towards drugs, or even worse. Everything that I have mentioned is a real reason why victims may have been led to do the things they did. Everything has a reason and a pattern.

Because of this sociology class, I've changed. I understand things I've always known in a deeper way that, without this class, would not be possible. I've grown to be bolder, if need be, to put more of my ideas or possible solutions out there. While I'm still not a social person, I would like to do what I can to teach others what I've been taught and give them the skills I now have.

In the future, I do believe my skills will help me see things much more clearly and not have a mess of thoughts when trying to understand something confusing or intense. I've already mentioned her, but the case that impacted me the most was Kitty Genovese. Looking at her case, what she said, and the circumstances of her death moved me. It deeply saddened me to see the lack of people willing to help, either because they were "too tired" or it was "too cold." But as much as it saddened me, I believe it is the reason I understand everything the way I do now. That is why I love this class; it really helped me learn and work on a case to understand what it's like. I deeply appreciate having the opportunity to take my teacher's sociology class, and if I could, I would do it again.

But most importantly, the biggest thing I learned in the class was *not to be a bystander*. When Lorie Pennell was with the wrong crowd, not going to school, and getting hooked on drugs, what she needed was help. Instead, she was sent to a youth correction facility. While working on Warren Luther Alexander, I saw how if his victims had gotten the help they needed, they wouldn't have been in danger. If they had gotten the help they needed, they would've had a nicer life and could've stayed out of the situations they ended up being in. What I've learned is not to be a bystander. If I see something bad happening, despite how young, short, or weak I may be in comparison, I will say something and I will do something. I refuse to be a bystander.

BAYLEE HAMM

My name is Baylee Hamm, and I am a sophomore at Elizabethton High School. I am actively involved in a variety of activities, including Betsy Band, Betsy Winterguard, Key Club, the Criminal Justice program, chorus, and sociology. When our class began and Mr. Campbell introduced the number of serial killers active in Tennessee during the 1980s, I was surprised. Out of the nine individuals he mentioned, I recognized only one name. This realization led me to reflect on the victims who received little to no justice, which ultimately inspired my interest in writing this book.

I started school at Hunter Elementary wanting to become a professional singer and teacher. As I've gotten older, my goals have obviously changed, and I now want to pursue a career in law enforcement. Because of that, I moved in sixth grade to T.A. Dugger Middle School, where I had access to more opportunities, including both the arts and a strong criminal justice program. I was raised as an only child, so I have always looked up to my parents in the same way some people look up to their siblings. My mom works in accounting, and my dad works in law enforcement, and their careers have strongly influenced my interest in criminal justice as well as my curiosity about how people think. When I got to high school and learned that Elizabethton offered a sociology class, I was interested, even though I wasn't completely sure what it would involve at first. After talking to previous students, I realized it was something I would truly enjoy.

The first victim I researched was Tina Marie Farmer. She was a young woman who was murdered and dumped just north of Knoxville, Tennessee, and left on the side of a highway. Out of every group in our class, hers was the only case that had been solved. Jerry Johns murdered her in 1984 and was later caught while attempting another crime. It made me wonder how many other victims he may have whose cases remain unsolved.

At the beginning of this project, I believed these cases went unsolved mainly because resources were limited, and that law enforcement and communities were doing the best they could. However, as I continued my research, I began to understand how social constructs influenced the amount of effort put into solving these cases. Many of the victims were involved in prostitution, were runaways, or struggled with addiction. It was heartbreaking to realize that they often did not receive the attention they deserved because of these circumstances, especially considering that everyone makes mistakes. This realization is what truly strengthened my desire to bring attention to more unsolved cases.

Our next case was the biggest project. My group focused on a cold case in Texas that strongly resembled a solved case in Memphis, Tennessee. Her name was Sherri Ann Jarvis. She was a 14-year-old girl who was brutally murdered in 1980. The fact that she was so young and never got to live the life she deserved really opened my eyes to how short life can be. Through this case, we learned about several sociology concepts, including inequality, justice systems, and media influence. Inequality played a major role because she was young, a runaway, and hitchhiking at the time of her death. She never received justice for her murder, but I am hopeful that with more attention, her case may eventually be looked at more thoroughly.

Before this class, I believed the justice system was fair, but now I see that I was mistaken. Sociology has taught me that victim blaming is real and that different levels of effort are often put into different cases. I hope that one day this will change and that the world will see all victims for what they are: innocent people in need of help. Since completing this class, I view the world differently and with more awareness. It has definitely strengthened my desire to pursue a career in law enforcement, so that when my time comes to speak for victims, I will make their voices heard loud and clear.

RILEY HART

I am Riley Hart. I was born in Johnson City, but I was raised and have always lived here in Elizabethton. I have two siblings, a brother and a baby sister. I've always been interested in the way people act and the way society itself works. I never knew how much a few 40-year-old cold cases could reveal about how some people in law enforcement work and how much they care.

I've been curious about the way society and people work without any real outside influence. It's always been intriguing to me how people would act if they had been raised even a little differently, or if they and their siblings were treated just a tiny bit differently and see how they would each act in the real world. Even just one tiny change could easily make someone a completely different person than who they are today. I've always assumed that all my friends have had the same good family as me, but now I realize that even the tiny differences in growing up separate huge differences in who we are now.

I chose this class because I thought it would let me learn about those differences in growing up that change people. I had assumed that all the victims had made most of their own choices (like becoming involved in prostitution), but for most of them it was the last option, and by that time, it didn't even seem like much of a choice at all. None of them chose to go that way; it was the only thing they had left. The victims grew up with abusive, drug-addicted, and alcoholic parents, leading them to also be affected by some of those same problems. These differences led them to make completely different choices than someone like me would. Some never really had a choice; they were forced into those situations. I used to believe that if I and one of these victims were presented with the same choice, I would be able to choose differently, but now I am not so sure.

One of, if not the most influential, lessons of this class was Kitty Genovese and Genovese Syndrome. Genovese Syndrome is where people refuse to act and remain a bystander out of fear. Kitty Genovese was a girl who was killed out on the streets, where several people saw her. Despite all the people who saw her get attacked and killed, only one person decided to yell at the attacker.

I want to avoid being a bystander because of Genovese Syndrome, so something like that won't happen again. Even if I'm just a teenager with no high school diploma or anything fancy, I can still stop something like that if I decide to step out and avoid being a bystander. So, it doesn't matter if you're just a normal person, or someone special. If you see someone suffering, you should step out and stop it no matter what kind of person you are. I want to make sure people know and are aware of Genovese Syndrome so they can do something if they see someone and not be scared to help them just because other people aren't doing anything about it.

After going through this class, I've grown to not be too quick to judge someone based on their position in life. Just because someone is in a bad position doesn't mean that they are a bad person. All of these victims were also victims of circumstance with them being forced into prostitution. I've become more compassionate and understanding because of these victims. Now, I see these tragic results as less of the victims' fault and more the fault of circumstances.

MAGGIE JAMES

My name is Maggie James, and I'm a 10th grader at Elizabethton High School. I'm originally from Philadelphia, Pennsylvania, but I've lived in Tennessee for most of my life, so I really consider it home. I've always been fascinated by true crime stories, but I never realized how deeply they could connect to the places around me. I began to see how these stories weren't just random mysteries; they were part of my own community's history and showed broader societal issues that often go unnoticed.

My dad always watched horror movies and true crime documentaries when I was little. He loved them, and I remember sitting beside him, half-curious and half-nervous, as we watched stories about mysterious disappearances or unsolved murders. At the time, I didn't fully understand what I was seeing, but those moments sparked my curiosity about why people commit crimes and how investigations work when answers aren't clear. As I got older, I began to see those stories not just as entertainment, but as windows into real lives and communities marked by loss and unanswered questions.

When I joined our sociology class, that early curiosity turned into something more meaningful. The idea that some families wait decades for closure really struck me. I realized these cases weren't just about evidence or mystery, but about people who had been forgotten. Hearing from people who came to talk to our class like Lorie Pennell's brother, Darrell, who talked about his sister's life, is a moment I remember constantly. Hearing him speak about how much he loved and misses Lorie, and how he felt that her killer had never been found and justice had not been served to the perpetrator.

Studying these cases made me reflect on how society values certain lives over others, often based on race, class, or where someone comes from. I was surprised to see how many victims were overlooked simply because they didn't fit the image of the "ideal" victim. It made me more aware of the inequalities built into our justice system and how easily some stories fade from public view while others dominate the headlines. This experience has changed how I think about fairness and made me want to help bring more awareness to those whose voices were never fully heard.

I started to see how cold cases connected to bigger concepts like social norms, deviance, and inequality. We talked about how society often labels certain people as "outsiders" or "less deserving," which can affect how seriously their cases are investigated or remembered. The idea of social disparity really stood out to me, not just in terms of criminal behavior, but also in how victims who don't fit social expectations get ignored. It showed me that crime and justice aren't just personal issues, but reflections of society's biases.

Researching both victims and offenders changed how I view crime altogether. I realized that while some offenders were shaped by personal choices, others were also influenced by social environments, poverty, trauma, or lack of community support. The victims' stories reminded me that behind every statistic is a human being, and behind every case is a social story about how our systems work or fail. Sociology helped me look beyond shock or mystery and start asking why these things happen and what we as a society can do differently.

Working on this project completely shifted how I see justice and the people behind headlines. I used to think of crime as individual choices, one person doing harm to another, but now I realize how deeply social factors shape every story. I've started noticing patterns in news reports and in my own community, like which cases get attention and which don't, and I find myself asking why. Studying sociology has helped me see that true justice isn't just about punishment; it's about fairness, equality, and remembering everyone who might otherwise be forgotten.

This project has not only made me more empathetic but also more determined to keep telling the stories that might otherwise fade away. Learning about victims whose cases went cold for decades showed me that awareness is a form of justice, too. Every time we remember a name, we honor those who were forgotten. I've learned that caring isn't passive; it's action. Through sociology, I've realized that change begins when we choose to see the humanity behind every case, and I want to be part of that change by continuing to speak up for fairness, equality, and memory.

ISABELLA MCMULLEN

My name is Isabella McMullen, and I am a sophomore at Elizabethton High School. I am originally from Michigan, but I moved to Tennessee when I was 11 months old. Now I visit Michigan occasionally during summer break. I have eight siblings in total: seven brothers and one sister, and I love all of them dearly. I have five older siblings and three younger brothers. Two of my younger brothers still live in Michigan. I have always felt a strong connection to crime shows and anything related to crime, but I never realized how much the stories of victims along Tennessee highways in the 1980s could reveal about society until I took Sociology.

I was surprised to see how many victims were overlooked because of how I was raised as a kid. My family always tried to keep me from knowing all the bad stuff in the world, which I think made me want to learn about it even more, because I am a pretty curious kid who wants to know everything that goes on. They would change the channel when the news came on or stop talking when I walked into the room if they were discussing something serious. I could tell they were trying to protect me, but it just made me more interested in finding out what they didn't want me to know. I would sneak and watch the news sometimes or look things up online when they weren't around. This class finally gave me the chance to learn about all the real problems that exist in the world that my parents had been shielding me from. It was eye-opening to discover how much suffering and injustice happens that I never knew about before.

I grew up with a great family, and I thought everyone else did too until I took Mr. Campbell's class. This class completely changed how I look at people around me. Before, I used to make quick judgments about classmates who seemed different or acted out. Now I realize there might be serious problems at home that I never considered. When I see someone who looks tired or upset, instead of thinking they're just being dramatic, I wonder what they might be going through. I've become much more aware of my surroundings and the signs that someone might be struggling. The class taught me to be more empathetic instead of being judgmental. I've learned to listen more and assume less about people's situations. This new perspective has made me a better friend and a more understanding person overall. I now try to be kinder to everyone, because I never know what battles they might be fighting at home.

Studying the lives of the victims showed me how society can make people feel invisible when they're ignored. I've never had to worry about whether I'll have dinner or if my mom will be home when I get there. I don't have to be scared of getting hurt or attacked. I've never thought about missing school or not being able to join clubs and play sports. Learning about their experiences really changed how I see my own life. I started to realize how lucky I am to have a safe place to live. Being able to go to school without being afraid is something a lot of people don't get to experience. While I'm thinking about college and my future, other people are just trying to make it through each day.

This whole experience has made me see the world differently. I now understand that not everyone has the same opportunities I do. Comparing my life to what these victims went through made me more thankful for what I have. It also made me more aware of all the problems and unfairness that exist in our world today.

ADDISON MERRYMAN

My name is Addison Merryman, and I am a sophomore at Elizabethton High School. I am actively involved in track and field, Key Club, Student Government, and advanced choir. I find enjoyment in outdoor activities, reading, singing, and spending quality time with my family. My family has always been my strongest support system. Unlike many of these victims, I've never had to worry where I'll be sleeping or if I'll have food to eat. Until recently, I didn't realize how lucky I was to have a nurturing family and the opportunity to go to high school and have an education as well as a social life.

Following graduation, I plan to pursue a degree in criminal justice at Appalachian State University, which is driven by my fascination with understanding the criminal mind and the psychological factors that influence destructive behavior. I've always been captivated by the darker corners of human psychology. What drives someone to commit these terrible acts? What secrets lie in the criminal mind, and how can I understand it? Although I was fascinated, I soon realized that these criminals had taken away someone's mother, sister, daughter, and even someone's friend. I knew that something needed to be done, and that realization inspired me to join this class and research the Tennessee cold cases.

I grew up in a great family and always assumed everyone else did too, which shaped how I originally viewed the world and issues of crime and justice. My early experiences made me believe that people generally had support systems and that justice worked fairly for everyone. However, working on this project challenged those assumptions and made me more curious about the realities others face. This topic grabbed my attention because it showed how many cases remain unsolved and how some victims don't receive the same level of attention or effort. I was surprised to see how many victims were overlooked because of factors like their background or economic status.

I had specifically studied Michelle Lavonne Inman's murder case. She was a young woman who became involved with prostitution mostly through her association with other people close to her involved in criminal activity (including her husband). She had a rough upbringing and a tough family situation, which was the reason she was involved in those crimes. Her case made me realize that inequality plays a huge role in the justice system, and not everyone is treated fairly. Because she had a criminal record, people could easily dismiss her murder as her own fault. Studying these cases opened my eyes to patterns in society, especially how certain groups are more vulnerable and less likely to receive justice. Overall, this project helped me see that while I was fortunate in my upbringing, many people experience a very different reality, and it made me think more critically about fairness, empathy, and responsibility in our society.

This class transformed my perspective on justice, empathy, and personal capability. I discovered that many people turn to destructive paths due to trauma, and that understanding victims requires looking beyond surface judgments. The experience taught me resilience when facing rejection and dismissal while seeking information. I learned that law enforcement can be unreliable, with some officers genuinely trying to help while others dismiss cases as worthless. Through public records requests, I accessed previously unavailable documents including coroner's reports and newspaper clippings. Our research proved that dedicated students can uncover information that police missed on cold cases. The class revealed how prejudice affects investigations and that everyone deserves justice regardless of background. I developed awareness of the systemic failures in our society that allow violence against vulnerable victims. Most importantly, I realized that teenagers can create meaningful change and that adults do recognize our capabilities when we demonstrate commitment.

At the beginning of this project, I viewed these cases as just another assignment, something to complete for a grade. Over time, that perspective completely changed. I began to see the victims as real people with stories that deserved to be told and remembered. This shift forced me to rethink my understanding of justice and society. Now I pay more attention to systemic inequalities and how they affect people's lives, especially those who are often overlooked or dismissed. I realized that victims are frequently targeted because of societal vulnerabilities, not because of their own choices. This project has inspired me to be more aware of stories that are hidden or ignored and to question how institutions, like law enforcement and the media, decide which cases receive attention. It also showed me that human behavior is deeply influenced by trauma and circumstance, which has made me more empathetic and less quick to judge others.

Personally, this experience helped me grow in ways I did not expect. I became more patient and resilient, especially when facing challenges like rejection or difficulty accessing information. I also developed stronger communication and problem-solving skills, and I gained confidence in speaking up about issues that matter. This project has changed how I see social issues in my community and the world; I no longer ignore them or assume someone else will take action. Instead, I feel a responsibility to be aware and involved. Looking ahead, what I've learned will continue to shape my actions and possibly my future career interests. I want to help change how victims are perceived, particularly those who are unfairly judged, and advocate for more equal attention in criminal cases regardless of social status.

Ultimately, this experience has shown me that even as a teenager, I can contribute to meaningful change by raising awareness, challenging perspectives, and refusing to be a bystander. There aren't enough words to describe how this class has shaped me and my future, and I am beyond thankful for everything I have learned and experienced.

MORGAN MIEARS

My name is Morgan Miears (pronounced like Myers), and I am in my sophomore year of high school at Elizabethton High School. My hometown is Elizabethton, and I have two cats that I love a lot. When I started this class, I really only thought about how it would help my career in the future; however, when I got invested in these women's stories, I realized that this was never about myself.

My mom has always wanted to be an officer; she wanted to bring justice to those who were wronged. When my mom finished her police training and got into the policing system, she soon went back to her old job, working in the blood lab at Ballad Health in Johnson City. Even though she quit, she still volunteered there as often as she could. Before working for the police, she volunteered at a local fire department. My mom always wanted to help people, and I guess that rubbed off on me.

I started wanting to become a forensic scientist about two years ago, and by reading about these cases, I've only become even more interested in that field of work. "I want to help people, and if I can do so by bringing awareness to the situation through this class, then I will do all I can." That was my thought process throughout this project, and it helped me believe in myself and the others in this class to help bring these victims' families a sense of closure. When I took this class, I already knew there was a lot of corruption in society, with the most notable being the corruption in police forces. That being said, when I took this class, we saw corruption somewhere else that is almost more important than in police: writers. Writing articles and newspapers help get things out there to people, so when I saw that there were barely any articles on these victims, I was flabbergasted. In hindsight, however, I can see now that the lack of information on these victims is the reason why I've never heard of any of these murderers before.

The lack of media influence on these victims has helped lead to unsympathetic people on the internet. When murders are not published or looked into, it leads to those in society to think they live in a safe environment, and this assumption brings malice to those who are harmed. When you feel safe, you find that you can say anything and not feel bad about it, so when people on the internet slander the victims who were killed due to their circumstances, they feel confident that what happened to those women could never happen to them. Along with that, there is bias. Many of the victims in these cases were involved in prostitution, and lots of people definitely looked down on them because of that. All of these things combined can be brought into a class, and they can bring harm to students. It's good to strike at a problem when children are still young so that they don't become biased and unsympathetic, like many who look at these cases are.

When I look at these victims, I don't see prostitutes, nor do I see troublemakers. Instead, I see young people who were killed by people who thought they were smart enough to not get caught. I was one of the people that worked on the Harry Edward Greenwell section of this book, and when I say I was disgusted by what he did to those poor women, it's an understatement. I was utterly confused why I had never heard of this man until my group and I dug deeper. There was barely anything on these women and what was done to them; almost all of the information came from one site, called the *American Crime Journal*, due to the others lacking much of the information listed. We would've gotten anywhere if it weren't for Damion Moore and *American Crime Journal*, as we couldn't even find some of the newspaper clips listed on the website. When I look at the other murderers, I see this pattern as well. The killers find people who they perceive as "weak" or "deserving" and use them for pleasure. This fact sickens me, and I cannot wait to get this out to the world so we can show those who like to stay ignorant how horrible this world can be.

During the start of this class, I knew that some people were bad, but I believe that I underestimated what people out there can do. Now that I know, I know to be more careful. When I think of these cases, I like to think that our justice system has improved in the way of holding people accountable for their actions, even if in some cases that isn't true. In the end, I still want to become a forensic scientist, even more so than before, because I now have a larger want to help those who are harmed.

BREANNA MILLER

My name is Breanna Miller, and I am currently a junior at Elizabethton High School. I was born in Ogden, Utah, but now live in Piney Flats, Tennessee. I am a member of the high school soccer team, and I'm currently enrolled in the pre-law program. Outside of school, I love to spend time with my friends and family. When I first began researching cold cases in this sociology class, I never realized just how many people have been forgotten over time. Learning about these cases has really opened my eyes to the importance of remembering those who have been overlooked and wanting to help give closure to their families and communities.

At the beginning of this class, I questioned whether it was really the right fit for me, but as time went on, I realized it was exactly where I belonged. Ever since I was young, I've always been very interested in learning about what's going on in the world, especially the different stories and cases in the places I've lived. Growing up, my family has lived in four different states (Utah, Idaho, Minnesota, and Tennessee), which are all in different areas of the United States. I've seen many different environments and crimes based on the areas

I've lived in. For instance, the crimes that happened in my small town in Idaho were very different from those in Johnson City, or other places throughout Tennessee. While population size played a huge role, since more people can often mean more crime, the situations were also different just because of the different culture and communities. Seeing all these varying scenarios really started to make me wonder why things happen the way they do, and I wanted to learn more about the different crimes in different areas in the United States.

Another thing that really caught my attention was when my mom started to tell me about the cold cases from her hometown in Northern California. The specific case was closely related to my mom and had to do with her teachers from high school. This is when I really became more interested in things like this. Hearing about this case made me realize how much more there was to learn, especially since it seemed like no one had put enough effort into solving the cases. Over time, as I learned about more cases from different states, I began to see a pattern, which is that many of them did not receive the attention they deserved, especially with older cases. The victims were often overlooked and forgotten.

This surprised me because, as an empathetic person, I feel strongly about helping others, and it is difficult to understand how law enforcement could overlook certain cases and victims. In many of the cases we researched, the women were in vulnerable situations, whether it was at home or while they were alone. Their cases were often treated differently compared to other people based on who they were. Each of these women and victims had families and people who were left wondering what happened to them, and I believe these cases deserve more attention so that their stories are not forgotten.

Being in sociology this year really changed my perspective on things. The cases we focused on this year all were very similar. Every case was related in the way that the victims were targeted at truck stops, and all the women were involved in prostitution. At first, I really didn't understand why someone would put themselves in that situation, since it puts them at a much higher risk compared to someone who stays at home. But as I started to look deeper into their stories, it made me realize that they didn't want to choose the lifestyle they lived. Many of them had to escape their toxic home environments and were so desperate for money that they did the only thing they could think of. Learning about this made me realize how unfairly certain people are treated and judged based on their circumstances.

One concept that we learned towards the beginning of the year that really stuck with me was the Kitty Genovese Bystander Effect. This is a proven theory that explains how people may choose not to help someone in an emergency, even if they are able to, often because they assume someone else will step in. Kitty Genovese was a bartender that was on her way home from work that was stabbed to death outside her apartments on March 13, 1964. After the incident, it was shown that there were many witnesses to this crime, and maybe if someone had tried to help, there might have been a possibility that she could've lived. Many of those people had reasons for not getting involved, or they believed someone else would act instead. Learning about this really just made me realize how little people care about each other.

Key concepts like this have inspired me to be more aware of my surroundings and not be afraid to act. For example, if I were ever in a situation where someone needed help, and it did not put me in direct danger, I would step in right away because there is always a chance that no one else will. At the same time, I understand that not every situation is safe to get directly involved in, so if I couldn't step in myself, I would make sure to call someone who could help. Overall, this class has taught me that I can make an impact in people's lives. Never would I have thought that I could be doing the work that we do in this class. Even though the cases we've been studying may never be fully solved, bringing attention back to these forgotten victims still matters, especially to their families. I know that if something happened to someone important in my life and no one paid attention to it, it would deeply affect me. Being able to help find information and raise awareness about what happened to these people may not fix everything, but it can bring some comfort to the families and remind them that their loved ones are not forgotten.

COLIN MILLER

Crime has always interested me, but this class has turned it into an obsession. My name is Colin Miller, and I am a sophomore at Elizabethton High School. Outside of class, I enjoy participating in track and staying active. I have always been fascinated by why people do the things they do, especially when it comes to concepts like justice and fairness. I took this sociology class because I wanted to learn more about these topics. One of the most interesting things we have done in this class so far has been reading about cold cases in Tennessee and cases like the Kitty Genovese murder. I didn't know you could actually learn so much about society from cases like these and how you can make a real difference in the world.

I live in Elizabethton, Tennessee, which is a great place to live with wonderful people. Having always been around these wonderful people, it is hard to assume that people could be suffering so much or be so evil. After researching Jerry Johns, I can't look at everyone the same way knowing that there is evil lying in many people all across the state and country. I also learned that I can't judge based on what I think. Victims like Linda Schacke had been through so much and yet were still looked down upon for their pasts. This made me realize that others could be in the same situation she was, and that I shouldn't just assume things. I have always felt that I have a supportive family and community behind me. I always assumed that everyone has someone in their corner, but as I began reading about some of these Tennessee cold cases, I discovered that not everyone has someone to stand up for them. This really made me think deeply about these issues. I began to consider the concept of being seen versus unseen, something I think about often when I consider becoming a lawyer.

The more I read about these cases, the more I see how patterns exist in how social systems function and how they can fail. The victims were often from disadvantaged groups, and inequality was one of the largest factors in determining who received help and who did not. This makes me think about how justice is not always equal for everyone. I had not considered these issues until taking this class, but now I see how they play a role in criminal cases. It's not just about one person doing something wrong; it's about society as a whole and how it allows things to happen. One of the most important things I have learned from this class is how deviance, justice, and social norms are all interconnected. The Kitty Genovese case, which taught us about the Bystander Effect, was particularly eye-opening for me. It made me think about what I would do if I were in that situation and helped me realize that even a teenager can make an impact on an entire situation. One small act can make all the difference, which is something I learned from class. The class discussions also opened my eyes to how powerful youth can be when we care enough to try.

This class has changed the way I view the world. I have learned that you must never give up—not only on the track field, but in life as well. I have learned that you must never forget those who have been taken from us, because remembering them is a way of fighting for justice. I have learned to recognize patterns of inequality in my life and to listen to untold stories. Although I still want to be a lawyer, I have learned there is more to justice than just the courtroom. Through studying sociology, I have learned the impact of being aware and empathetic. I have learned that even though my voice is young, it can make a big difference.

CALLIE MOSLEY

My name is Callie Lynn Mosley. I am a junior at Elizabethton High School, where I have attended city schools my entire life. I was born in September of 2008 in my hometown of Elizabethton. I have a big family I am very close with. I am lucky enough to have both sets of my grandparents, who I am *very* close with: my Grammie, PopPop, NayNay, Poppi, and Pappy. I have been super close with many of my cousins since I was younger.

I also have two of the best friends in the entire world, Kate and Ava Jane. My sister Millie and I have known them since we were born. I spend a lot of time with them, and I wouldn't change it for the world. I started playing golf when I was eight years old and never stopped until I got hurt and had major surgery my junior year. Golf has always been a part of me, and it forever will be. I have also been in choir since I was around 10. I've always loved music, and it's probably the biggest part of my life. I was in band, I play multiple instruments, and I have sung in many choirs throughout my years of performing. Anyone who knows me knows that my love for Harry Styles speaks for itself, and I wouldn't have it any other way.

After I graduate high school, I plan to attend college out of state and experience the world. I dream of attending New York University and studying cybersecurity to eventually become an employee of The Internet Crimes Against Children Task Force Program group. I have always had a passion for helping children, and throughout high school I have found a sense of purpose in preventing children from being sexually exploited online. I spend time volunteering at Isaiah 117 House, which is a non-profit organization that provides a safe, loving environment and a place to stay for children recently removed from their homes due to neglect or abuse.

Throughout my life, I had heard of true crime stories, but I never had imagined that I would get to be a part of one. Not a victim, an officer, or a government official, but just a high school girl who is spending her fourth-period elective researching killers from 40 years ago. Growing up in a small town, you always hear people talk. The next-door neighbor had an affair, the cousin is now on drugs... Whatever the talk may be, it always exists. You hear stories about women involved in prostitution and automatically assume, "Oh, what a piece of trash!" and "They must be a terrible person!"

But that is just the surface diagnosis. The eye cannot see things that are internal. You never know the internal battles the women who chose to sell their bodies were facing, and we never truly know the first-hand accounts of the women who were murdered by these men or their life situations that led them there. This topic grabbed my attention because of my passion to work with abuse victims. While studying the more victimology side of things, I realized that most of these women did not grow up in a stable household or live a stable life. For example, Espy Pilgrim, who I got the chance to study at the beginning of the school year, grew up in a household with a mentally unstable mother and a father who was working much of the time. She grew up to be a mother and suffered from the same mental effects passed on from her own mother. She eventually ran away, got involved in drugs and prostitution, and was murdered by an unknown suspect back in 1985. She was not defined by her actions. She was a wife, a mother, and so much more than what the world will ever know. She deserved the same chance at life that everyone reading this today has been given.

In some ways, I feel that social injustice has progressively gotten worse throughout history. You see stories of millionaires committing these heinous crimes, and the punishment received is not nearly as bad as what some others face. I noticed in the media, it is always urgent for someone with money, fame, or power to get justice for an action committed against them. These women were poor, and they needed help. It's been 40 years, and they have never received it. They may have committed crimes and gotten involved in awful things, but they did not deserve to die. I feel so deeply for these women and how they may never get the justice they deserve, and I hope throughout reading this book, someone may be able to feel the same.

While approaching the end of the semester, I wake up every day with a sense of urgency to look at things a little bit deeper than how I did before. Throughout my life, I have been very privileged to not have to suffer in ways that these women did. I never truly understood the depth of the struggles faced by so many people, but now I am able to at least try to understand. I am forever grateful for the day I wrote down sociology for my fourth-period class on the registration paper, for it has taught me so many different things. I have never forgotten one specific day in class where we got to talk to one of the victims' family members. He told our class that he would always be grateful for the work we were doing and that he was given hope by the work our class and previous classes had done for these women.

With my dream being to work in the childcare system, I hope to be able to help some of the children of the future to not be affected by some of the same issues that I have learned so much about. I hope that in future generations, this book will truly inspire other kids our age to understand that their actions and time are so much more valuable than what society may make them out to be. You truly can change something if you put your mind to it. I also want to make sure that Mr. Campbell is proud of the work that we have done. I am inspired by all the work Mr. Campbell has done throughout his career, and I really want to push myself to the limit just like he has done. He goes above and beyond for people he doesn't even personally know, and I hope that I and other people are able to be the same way.

It may have been 40 years ago when these women were killed, but 40 years can mean nothing to someone who truly wants to change something, and with this book, hopefully someone is inspired to do the same thing my class has worked so hard for.

BRENDON ORELLANA

My name is Brendon Orellana. I am a sophomore at Elizabethton High School. I was born and raised in Elizabethton, Tennessee. I play football, and I love weightlifting. I am interested in business and like learning new things about the economy. I never realized how much forgotten victims could reveal about society until I began learning about cold cases, especially those along Tennessee highways in the 1980s. It shocked me that so many lives were lost and slowly forgotten, with cases left unresolved over time. This made me question why some victims didn't receive the attention or justice they deserved. The more I looked into these cases, the more I felt a need to bring awareness back to them, because every victim's story matters and should never be overlooked.

Growing up, I was surrounded by law enforcement, where conversations about justice, responsibility, and protecting others were part of everyday life. Being around officers gave me a firsthand look into how the system worked, but it also made me question what happened when things didn't go as they should. I began to wonder about the cases that didn't get solved, the ones that didn't receive attention, and the people who were left without answers. That curiosity deepened as I learned about cold cases, which stood out to me because they represented real victims whose stories were slowly forgotten. It didn't sit right with me that some investigations were simply set aside over time, and I strongly believed that law enforcement agencies should not dismiss or overlook these cases, no matter how much time has passed.

As I explored more, I realized that while many officers genuinely care and work hard to protect their communities, the system itself hasn't always been consistent. Looking back at cases from the 1980s, it became clear that not every victim received the same level of urgency or attention, leaving families without closure. This shaped my perspective on society. I still believe law enforcement can be strong and committed, but I also recognize that there were times when the system didn't care as much as it should have, which is why it's so important to continue bringing light to these forgotten cases.

Studying sociology through the lens of 1980s cold cases has significantly changed the way I understand justice, society, and human behavior. What once seemed like straightforward cases now feels much more complex when you consider the social conditions surrounding them, things like economic status, race, neighborhood, and how much attention a victim receives from the public or law enforcement. It made me realize that justice is not always equal, and sometimes people are judged or overlooked based on their social class or background rather than the facts of the case. This project helped me see how society can unintentionally influence which cases get solved faster and which ones are forgotten, and it challenged my earlier belief that the system always treats everyone the same.

On a personal level, this experience helped me grow by making me more aware of social issues that exist in everyday life, not just in history. It changed how I see people and situations, especially the importance of not making assumptions based on appearance, income, or where someone comes from. Looking forward, what I've learned from this project is likely to guide my decisions and interests, especially in my potential future career in law enforcement. I want to be someone who helps make justice fairer and more consistent, and who pays attention to cases that others might overlook. This project has motivated me to contribute to a system where every person is treated with equal importance, and where fairness is not influenced by social status but by truth and accountability.

Studying Samuel Little was especially impactful because it revealed both the scale of his crimes and how social inequality can influence the way victims are treated and remembered. Samuel Little was later confirmed as the most prolific serial killer in US history, with over 90 confessions linked to him, many of which went unnoticed for years because many of his victims came from marginalized backgrounds. One victim who stood out to me was a woman experiencing homelessness whose disappearance did not receive immediate attention or urgency, which made me realize how easily people can become invisible in society when they lack stable housing or strong support systems.

Her story showed me that it is not only the crime itself that matters, but also how differently society responds depending on who the victim is. From a sociology perspective, this case connects to concepts like social stratification, labeling theory, and inequality, showing how people in lower socioeconomic groups may receive less attention from institutions and the justice system. It also highlights how society shapes outcomes through structures and perceptions, not just individual actions. This case helped me understand that justice is deeply influenced by broader social conditions that determine who is seen, prioritized, or overlooked, and it reinforced the importance of recognizing these patterns in order to build a more fair and equal system.

SHAIN PIERCE

My name is Shain, and I'm in my junior year of high school. I'm from Cleveland, Ohio. I'm an amateur game designer, and I cook and draw in my free time. My work on the Redhead Murders and other true crime cases in and around the state of Tennessee have shown me a few nasty truths about the world we all share. I've been shown how unforgiving society is to people involved in sex work and other people who are deemed as "undesirables." However, through all the bad I was shown, I also saw some good. When I dug through old newspaper clippings and websites that haven't been updated since before my birth, I found quotes from close friends and families of these victims. The quotes I found really started to humanize the murder victims who had previously been reduced to just prostitutes. It showed me that regardless of how quickly society had forgotten these people, their families still cared about them and remembered the good rather than the bad.

I actually ended up taking this class by complete accident. I have zero interest in criminal justice or law, but I enjoy some hobbies that almost relate to them. Auto-mechanic work, although seemingly completely unrelated, has us diagnose a car and figure out how, and why, it broke. This skill translates pretty well to detective work, letting me reason through every step of the murders and the circumstances surrounding them. I've been able to use my outside view on criminology to keep our research accessible. I don't know what many of the words we throw around actually mean in this context, so I like to make sure that the surrounding language is enough for others like me to easily understand.

I've really been shown a lot about the inequalities of society through all this. Earlier, I mentioned how no name sex workers are quickly forgotten when killed. I think a great example of the opposite public reaction would be JonBenét Ramsey. At the time of her murder, her father owned a subsidiary company of Lockheed Martin and was absolutely loaded. As such a wealthy and powerful family, JonBenét's death was researched and investigated and talked about for years. Regardless of what you think about the case, it's a clear example of someone rich getting much more research and investigation done on their case, while lesser-known people are completely forgotten. I was already aware of how big the disparity between rich and poor people was, but studying real life examples of it puts it into perspective. Sort of like how you think you can imagine a million of something, but when you actually see how massive that number really is, it is more than you could have ever imagined.

I think it's easy to degrade people in prostitution. When you do this, you remove all of their personality, their memories, and their humanity. You just see them as if their entire personhood is embodied by that one act, and don't really think about their hobbies, family, friends, hopes, and dreams. That's the main reason why the cases of murdered sex workers are so commonly abandoned. A lot of cops don't view these people as important or worth their time, just because of a small fraction of the person's identity. No one would care about this missing person, so why should I even bother investigating? I guess what I am trying to say is, I learned that "prostitute" is a verb, not a noun.

In the groups I've been in, and the people we've researched, I noticed a lot of killers thought in similar ways to this. Jerry Johns thought he was doing the world a favor and cleaning up the highways. Samuel Little thought that the homeless people and drug addicts would be completely unnoticed if they went missing. Even all the way back to Jack the Ripper; he killed poor drinkers and lesser-known people. Throughout history, killers have loved to target completely unknown people because they know the world will never miss them.

I've started to look for more obscure details in the cases we studied and haven't been overlooking things that I otherwise would have. Even when I was wrong about things, I ended up learning something new because of my research. I discovered that John Chapman's second victim, a nun named Vickie Metzger, had a heavier right lung that was outside of a normal weight difference. I looked into it, found some stuff about alcohol or drug overdose messing with lung size, then found that the left lung was just smaller because of the space your heart takes up. Even when I put together a wrong theory, I still learned from it.

The process of writing this book has taught me many new skills that I can use in my life to better others. By calling attention to these unknown victims and doing our own research, I hope that I can encourage others to do the same. Maybe a cop reads this and decides to reopen a case. Maybe someone with free time investigates a niche murder only they know about. Whatever the case may be, if I can get even one hidden case reopened or researched, I think my time this year will have been well spent.

AVA SHEETS

My name is Ava Sheets, and I am a sophomore at Elizabethton High School. I live in Johnson City, Tennessee. I used to play basketball and was involved in it for nine years, which made it a big part of my life and taught me a lot about teamwork and dedication. At home, my mom and I take care of chickens, ducks, and cats, which keeps us busy but is also something I enjoy. In my free time, I love spending time with my friends and being around the people who make me happy. Before taking this class, I never realized how much the stories of victims along Tennessee highways in the 1980s could reveal about society and the way people are treated.

When I was younger, my granny used to watch true crime shows all the time, and that's what first sparked my interest in true crime. I remember being curious about the stories and always wondering what really happened in those situations. That curiosity is what made this class stand out to me, because I wanted to learn more about real-life cases and understand what people go through. I also wanted to see if other people's lives were similar to mine or completely different.

Throughout this class, I've learned that many victims come from very difficult backgrounds, and those experiences can lead them down hard paths in life. At first, I didn't fully understand why people made certain choices, but as we learned more, I realized that many of them didn't have the same opportunities or support systems. It made me recognize that my life is not as bad as I once thought, because some people are put in situations where they have to do whatever they can just to survive. This class has really opened my eyes to how unfair life can be for some people.

Overall, this class has changed the way I see others and how I treat them. It has taught me to be more understanding and less judgmental, because you never truly know what someone is going through. I've learned the importance of showing kindness and respect to everyone, no matter their situation. This experience has not only helped me learn about true crime, but also it has helped me grow as a person and become more aware of the world around me.

BROOK SPARKS

My name is Brook Sparks, and I am a sophomore at Elizabethton High School. I am a student athlete who plays softball and aspires to play the sport I love at the collegiate level. In my spare time, I enjoy reading, drawing, and spending time with my friends and family. Before I moved to Elizabethton High School, I lived in Western North Carolina. I moved to Elizabethton prior to starting high school. Writing this book and putting in the constant amount of work and dedication has made me question why I even wanted to pursue this career and success in this classroom. I have always been a straight-A student, and the pressure of maintaining my GPA has often caused me to wonder why I push myself to the level that I do. This reflection has caused me to rediscover the reasons why I push myself so hard, especially for this class.

During my life, I have always had an interest in criminal psychology and crime. If I had to answer the question as to what drew me to be interested in crime and psychology, I would have to say the trait was inherited from my mother's side. I remember during my early childhood always watching crime drama shows like *NCIS*, *Blue Bloods*, and *CSI* with my mom and grandma. I will never forget my young, childlike mind thinking, "Why would someone want to hurt someone else?" I guess that thought just never went away, even as I got older.

When I was required to take Mr. Campbell's World History class freshman year of high school, I already had an interest in the work that his yearly Sociology class had been partaking in. From seeing the film crew roam the halls of Elizabethton High School and documenting alumni of this class to the infamous "murder board" that decorated Mr. Campbell's classroom, I knew for a fact that I wanted to register for this class the upcoming year. Looking back at my naivety, I realize I underestimated the amount of work that it would take in order to succeed like my predecessors. Although this class requires a tremendous amount of hard work and discipline, what I learned from this experience has forever changed me as a person, and I am extremely thankful for what I have learned.

When working on this project, I was extremely surprised at what I have been shown about society. When we started learning about the psychology of the Bystander Effect and the Kitty Genovese case, I strictly remember the emotions I was feeling while reading about the case. The idea that nobody decided to aid this poor woman while she was fighting for her life only because bystanders believed that they were not fit to help will always surprise me. The ignorance of her community will forever stick in my head. This case started my realization of what society does to those who are on the bottom; society has the power to sweep an innocent life under the rug. When we began our investigation into our serial offenders and their victims, that was what made me realize that justice for victims does not always happen, and that even in the worst cases, society does not remember these victims. They are swept away underneath the rest of the unsolved case files in the world.

To say that working on these cold cases and serial offenders was difficult would be an understatement. Before we were even able to open our files on our designated offenders, Mr. Campbell would have to educate us on our understanding of criminal psychology and victimology. He taught us that every detail matters when investigating a victim. Not only did he teach us that, but he gave us the opportunity to speak with other experts in this field. We talked to state, local, and federal agents for tips on investigating, and how to study victims and offenders. We were also taught about serial offender profiling, and how to create a general picture of an offender based off the facts from the case.

That was just the beginning of our journey as a class. Even after we had been taught numerous topics, we had to use these resources on our own. We were assigned into groups to work on our offenders, and we had to learn how to improvise, adapt, and overcome challenges we would encounter during this project. The adversity we had to have as a group is something I am extremely grateful for, as that is a skill which will stick with me after I graduate.

In this project, the serial offender assigned to my group was Harry Edward Greenwell. I remember the first time that I started researching his name. The first thing that I found was his obituary for his death. I learned that he lived a long, fulfilling life and died of cancer in 2013. In fact, only after his death was he found to be a serial rapist and murderer. This shocked me! I could not grasp the idea that this man had snuffed out and destroyed so many lives and had been able to live a long life, dying surrounded by people who adored him. This sick, twisted, harsh fact stirred an anger inside of me. It made me wonder who else this man could have hurt and how many of his crimes are still unnoticed. This also made me wonder what other serial killers could have lived their life without the consequences for their actions. It makes me want to provide justice for their victims and their families.

After being in this class, I feel like I have been educated on topics that I never thought I would learn in a public high school. If I was to tell my past self that my new school would offer a class on psychopathy, sociopathy, inequality, injustice, and societal structures in the world, my younger self would be in awe. This class and our work have shown me that we, as teenagers, have the potential to change the world regardless of our age. This class has also shown me that yes, we have the potential to change the world, but the victims that we studied never had the opportunity to create change or grow old to see change in their world. I will always be thankful for the opportunity to be in this class and the experience of hopefully changing the world in the process.

CHLOE STATHAM

My name is Chloe Statham, and I am a junior at Elizabethton High School. Some things I enjoy doing are reading, writing, baking, and gardening.

Mr. Campbell gave us a choice at the start of the year. Do we want to learn out of the book, or open the files he had? He made it known we couldn't turn back from our choice. These files changed my life as he had promised, although it wasn't in the way I thought. This led to our class working together on these cold cases around Tennessee from the 1980s.

Ever since I was young, I wanted to help people. My mom worked to help elderly perform basic daily tasks, and my aunt is a traveling certified nursing assistant. Having people in my family that help others further solidified my path into helping whoever with whatever I could. So, when I heard about this class through a friend that was taking it, I knew I had to join. I heard about how they had helped bring light to these cold cases and how they wanted to increase awareness of cases like these. Even though I was not fully sure if we would continue the great work they put so much time into, I just knew this sociology class would teach me more about helping others.

These cases are quite interesting to me. We started off continuing previous work on the Redhead Murders. There were nine women killed and dumped beside highways around Tennessee. They were involved in prostitution, whether or not it was voluntary, or they were a runaway. This was a big factor in why they did not get the justice they deserved; although, there were other factors like costs and lack of information to connect the cases. So, when I first started on these cases, I believed it was just a corrupt and judgmental system that decided these women were not worth their time. Then, I learned about all the problems and struggles that the police had to deal with during those times. It is sad and upsetting that their families don't have answers to what happened to their daughter, sister, or mother.

Starting the cases in class, I had first questioned how going over these cold cases would teach me anything about sociology. Turns out, it was one of the best ways to learn about society. Before we really got into these cases, we did learn about something pretty interesting. It is named "Genovese Syndrome" or the "Bystander Effect." It is described as "the psychological phenomenon where individuals are less likely to offer help in an emergency when other people are present." Mr. Campbell also showed us videos where that was the case. In every case, there were so many people around, but nobody helped the person in trouble. That is what happened with Kitty Genovese. People heard and saw it happen, but nobody did anything about it, except for one person that only yelled at the attacker and then went back inside. Seeing this through videos and realizing just how much this happens shows a lot about societal psychology and how people react around others during an emergency situation.

Then, there are the cases. We researched many different victims and killers around Tennessee. Many of these victims were vulnerable women alongside roads, and many of the killers were mobile men using their job to prey on them. What I learned from the victims is that we need to be more aware and do more for cases like theirs. These women were horribly taken advantage of, and because of their upbringing or situations, they were pushed off or seen as unimportant. From the offenders, I learned that people can be vile and made into how they are. They used their "power" and took away the lives these women had ahead of them. What I learned from both victims and offenders is that your childhood and what you learn really affect you. When growing up, the people around you, how you are raised, how you are treated, and the experiences you have shapes you into the person you are, or could be.

This class has taught me a lot. It has even changed my views on some things. I always knew that human behavior is an interesting topic, but it really adds to the concept of good and bad. I think about how everyone has their own lives they live and how everyone has a different outcome. Also, just because you may have had a bad upbringing doesn't mean you have to grow into a horrible person. On the other side of that, just because you had a great childhood doesn't mean you are going to be a good person. We also talked with many people in class or by video conference, and they have brought tremendous insights to me. The one that really affected me was a brother of one of the victims. When he talked to us, he was very interested in our work, but also grateful that people were still looking into his sister's death. He said he was happy that people actually care about his sister, and all he wanted was answers. It was really emotional and made it clear that the families of these victims just want answers about their family members.

I want to take what I have learned and use it to make me better at communication and problem solving. I hope to help people and use my knowledge later in my career in healthcare. I hope to be a nurse or forensic scientist so I can help people physically or create vaccines, medicines, or anything that could help the human population against sicknesses. I feel this class has overall helped me learn more about being empathetic or to think of myself in someone else's shoes to better understand them.

One thing I do want to add is a quote my classmate, Alivia Anderson, said: "I have realized how murder podcasts are a form of entertainment, but they are the last moments those people had." This is a wakeup call to how desensitized society is to murder cases like these. Cold cases deserve to be more recognized and brought to light so their families can get answers. I hope that through this book, we can inspire people to be curious and to do more when it comes to unsolved cases.

LOUIS TRIVETTE

My name is Louis Trivette. I am a sophomore at Elizabethton High School, and I enjoy hiking and swimming. When Mr. Campbell put us on these serial killer cases, I was surprised that I had never heard of them or their victims.

This piqued my interest for this class because these people should be heard of. I wanted to learn more about these cases and why they haven't been brought into the public eye.

Since I was young, I have always been curious about why some people act the way they do. As a child, I would always listen in on conversations around me and wonder, "Why would they do something like that?" I joined Sociology to get the answers to that question. The topic of the cold cases we researched grabbed my attention for multiple reasons. One of the major reasons was that I had never heard of any of these. As a class, we studied nine different serial killers that were active in or around Tennessee, yet we had never heard of any of them before this. I assumed that the victims somewhat deserved what happened to them, due to the position they were in; however, that isn't the case. Victims are merely prey of their circumstances.

So many law enforcement professionals gave their time generously to help us develop our skills. We were also taught by professionals such as Scott Barker, a retired FBI profiler; Jim Clemente, a retired FBI supervisory special agent and former profiler; JD Anderson, the head of our local FBI office; and Mike Little, the investigator for our local district attorney's office. Later in the semester, our work was checked by 10 law enforcement officers from several agencies around our region. Each one spurred us to keep searching.

Initially, I believed that the social system wasn't right. The media focused more on events surrounding government officials or upper-class people, often brushing off cases that were about the common person. Throughout these cases, I noticed that multiple victims of these killers were women involved in prostitution. This further confirmed that the media and potentially even the police brushed off cases about people who are struggling to get by in life.

Throughout this class, I have learned multiple valuable skills and lessons. I have learned that just because we aren't adults doesn't mean we aren't capable of doing good work. I developed advanced skills to better look at the depth of situations. This class taught me to be resilient in difficult tasks, as well as learning that victims don't choose to be put in their situations. They are put there by circumstance. One topic that we learnt about that sent chills down my spine was the Genovese Syndrome (more commonly known as the Bystander Effect). Genovese Syndrome is an effect where people are less likely to help if there are more people around the area. This is because people believe that there is someone better suited than themselves to help out.

At the start of this school year, I originally didn't think much of these cases. I saw them as assignments to get another 100. However, as this class progressed, I saw these cases less as projects, and it became more about the victims that were murdered or attacked. I have become a better communicator, and I am now more capable of expressing my thought process or ideas to others.

I hope to change how the media and police view murder cases. Oftentimes in the media, more attention is brought to the murders of important people, such as doctors or government officials. However, I want there to be equal attention amongst all murders. Otherwise, cases are forgotten or not even heard of, and families of the victims don't get the answers they deserve. Over the course of this class, my perspective on human behavior has changed wildly. I have developed a pessimistic view towards how society looks at victims and cases and have slowly become more infuriated by our mindsets. However, my curiosity for why we act the way we do has flourished more than ever before.

This project changed my view on things wildly. Before I started this project, when I heard about cases, my mind would immediately go to blaming the victim, thinking along the lines of, "That's stupid; they should know hitchhiking is a terrible idea." However, now my view has changed towards what puts the victim in that situation, like their home life.

The knowledge this class has taught me has inspired me to be a kinder person in the future. It has helped me understand more about how the media works. It has also changed the way that I hope to do things in life. I want to be able to help people as much as possible and not be a bystander when it really matters.

TEE VAUGHN

My name is Tee Vaughn, and I'm a junior who has lived in Elizabethton my whole life. I really like sports, and I spend a lot of my time watching or playing them. I also really like true crime podcasts. My favorite is *Murder 101*, and I think it's really cool, because it was recorded in my town and is about my teacher and students from my school. That made it feel more real to me. I've always thought sociology was interesting, and I like this class because it helps me understand how people think, act, and live in society.

I grew up with my mom, dad, and my brother, and we are a close family. Because of that, I always thought most people had a good home life like me. I didn't really think about how different other people's lives could be. This project helped me see that not everyone grows up the same way. Some people go through really hard things, and that can affect their whole life. I've always liked learning about crime, so learning about real cases made it even more interesting to me. It made me think more about why people do what they do and how their life can lead them to certain choices.

The cold cases project really got my attention, because I wanted to know why some cases never get solved. I was surprised to see how many victims didn't get much attention or were ignored. That didn't seem right to me. It made me think about how society works and how some people don't get treated the same as others. I started to notice that things like where someone is from, how much money they have, or their background can affect how much people care about their cases. That is not fair at all, and it made me feel bad for the families who never get answers.

In this class, I learned about things like deviance, social norms, and how people react to crime. These ideas helped me understand the cold cases better. I started to see patterns in the cases we looked at. For example, sometimes the media only focuses on certain victims, and others don't get talked about.

Studying the victims taught me that some people are basically overlooked, which is messed up and sad. It showed me that not everyone gets the same attention, even when something really bad happens to them.

Researching the offenders helped me understand how social and mental factors connect to crime. Like with Clark Perry Baldwin, it showed me that things happen for a reason. There are warning signs or patterns, but people don't always notice or take them seriously. It made me realize how important it is for people to pay attention and speak up if something seems wrong. If people ignore signs, things can get worse.

Working in class and talking with other students helped me a lot, too. We talked about different cases and shared ideas, and that helped me understand things better. We noticed that a lot of cases are similar in that they don't get enough attention or take a really long time to solve. It made me realize that it's not just about the criminal, but also about how society and the system handle the case. If people don't care or don't act fast, cases can stay unsolved for years.

This project changed how I think about justice and society. Before, I thought most cases got solved and everything was fair, but now I see that's not true. Some people don't get as much attention, and their cases can be forgotten. Now I pay more attention to how unfair things can be and how it affects people in real life. It made me think more about how important it is for everyone to be treated the same.

This project also made me realize there are a lot of stories that people don't talk about. It makes me want to pay more attention instead of just ignoring it. I think more people should care about these cases and the victims. It also got me more interested in crime and how the justice system works. This could even affect what I want to do in the future, like maybe working in a job where I can help people or learn more about crime and society. Overall, this project has changed me and how I look at the world.

ABOUT THE TEACHER

Alex Campbell is a high school teacher who lives in Elizabethton, Tennessee, with his lovely wife and two amazing sons. His classroom has become an unlikely force in real-world criminal investigation. A two-time Teacher of the Year, author, and nationally recognized speaker, Campbell is known for transforming students into investigators, journalists, and advocates through authentic, real-world projects.

His students' work has reached far beyond the classroom through projects such as reexamining cold cases like the Redhead Murders, contributing to efforts to free the wrongfully convicted, and even collaborating with law enforcement, including work with the Tennessee Bureau of Investigation on the Tracy Walker case. Their efforts have also supported justice-impacted individuals, including advocacy connected to cases like Suzanne Johnson's imprisonment and early release.

Campbell's work is featured on the chart-topping *Murder 101* podcast, which reached #1 in several countries and is the subject of an upcoming documentary of the same name. His classroom productions have earned national recognition, including honors in the PBS NewsHour Student Reporting Labs Student Journalism Challenge and NPR Student Podcast Challenge, highlighting his students' ability to produce professional-level investigative journalism.

He is also the author of *Ten Lessons That Will Get You Fired: But You Must Teach Immediately*, and is a frequent presenter at major education conferences such as ISTE, SXSW EDU, and Aurora Institute (formerly iNACOL), where he shares his approach to project-based learning, student agency, and authentic assessment.

At the core of his work is a belief that students learn best when their work matters. By connecting education to real people, real problems, and real outcomes, Campbell empowers students to see themselves not just as learners, but as changemakers.

ACKNOWLEDGEMENTS

When we began to reflect on all the people who made a project like this possible, the list quickly grew very long. Most days were spent working quietly inside a small room with no windows, but this work was never done alone. The support behind it stretches back decades and carried all the way through to the final pages.

When a class sets out to study real-life cold cases, it naturally raises some eyebrows. School administrators have every reason to ask hard questions. Is it safe, is it appropriate, are students ready to face material like this? We are grateful that, over the years, those concerns were met with trust. The administrators who supported this work gave students the opportunity to learn in a way that goes far beyond a traditional classroom. These students are still young, but they are growing into the next generation of leaders, voters, parents, and citizens. Sometimes that growth requires facing difficult truths. Not every lesson can come from a textbook or a worksheet. Some lessons ask more of us.

The support from families has meant just as much. One of the most common questions is how parents feel about a class like this. The answer has been clear. There has been curiosity, thoughtful questions, and honest conversations, but never rejection. That kind of trust is not taken lightly. It reflects a shared belief that students should learn to think carefully, to withhold judgment, and to understand that the world can be both good and deeply flawed. Many families want their children to learn how to stand with others, especially those who have no voice. That support has made this work possible.

We also want to recognize the families for helping to raise some amazing young people. These students consistently challenge the stereotypes often placed on their generation. They approach this work with empathy, curiosity, and a strong sense of responsibility. When they encounter these cases, they do not see headlines; they see people. They look for understanding instead of judgment, and they work to speak for those who no longer can. Those qualities were not taught in a single classroom. They were shaped long before, in homes and communities. However those families are formed, they have sent in young people who are ready to take this work seriously, and that is something worth recognizing.

This work is not easy, and it quickly moves beyond what any one classroom can handle alone. Over the years, many professionals have stepped in to guide and support it. Members of law enforcement at the local, state, and federal levels have given their time and expertise. Publishers, media specialists, victim advocates, attorneys, and many others have invested in this process. They taught skills, asked hard questions, reviewed work, and encouraged growth. They returned again and again, not out of obligation, but because they believe in what these students are doing. Their presence has shown what professionalism and service can look like at their best.

There have also been challenges, including learning about times when systems failed victims and their families. But alongside those lessons, students have been able to meet individuals who represent the very best of those same systems. Those examples matter. They show what it means to do the job the right way, and they set a standard to aim for.

Projects like this also require resources. Printing and distribution come with real costs, and those costs went far beyond what could be covered in a typical classroom. Support came from people across the country. Some gave a little, others gave more, but every contribution reflected belief in this work. Many supporters had never met these students, yet they chose to invest in them anyway. That kind of faith leaves a lasting impression.

Finally, we want to thank our publisher. Jan-Carol Publishing may be local, but it is a respected and established company with a wide reach. Their support was not automatic. It was earned. Once they saw the work, they chose to stand behind it. They gave their time, adjusted to a school schedule, and helped guide this process from start to finish. Whether or not this project brings them any financial return, they committed themselves fully. This book exists because of that partnership, and we are proud of what was created together.

In the end, this project is a reminder that work like this is never done alone. It takes a classroom of amazing students, but it also takes families, professionals, supporters, and a community willing to invest in something different. Every page reflects more than just student effort. It reflects the time, trust, and care of many people coming together for a shared purpose. That is what truly brought this work to life, and this is what makes the work that much more satisfying.

This is a work produced by an entire community regardless of social standing, age, or ability coming together and trying to right a wrong and bring justice to the victims and closure to the families of some of these still forgotten victims. This is exactly what should have happened four decades ago, but for various reasons it did not. But now, because of the people who supported this work, these young people can see that this is how a society is supposed to function. This is how a community is supposed to care for every member, even the most vulnerable and downtrodden. And this is how students can bring about the world they want to see when they are in charge.

THANK YOU TO OUR GENEROUS SPONSORS!

YOUR SUPPORT MADE THIS POSSIBLE!

To a truly inspiring teacher—

and the students who bring that inspiration to life—

the lessons you create together
go far beyond any classroom.

You push one another to think bigger, dig deeper,

---

and to see the world not just as it is, but as it could be.

The impact of that work reaches well beyond your walls.

From two people your work has inspired,

Stacey & William

www.ingramcontent.com/pod-product-compliance
Lightning Source LLC
LaVergne TN
LVHW091116080826
845145LV00008B/1944

* 9 7 8 1 9 7 0 4 7 1 3 2 8 *